Feminist Activism
in Academia

Feminist Activism in Academia

Essays on Personal, Political and Professional Change

Edited by
Ellen C. Mayock *and*
Domnica Radulescu

McFarland & Company, Inc., Publishers
Jefferson, North Carolina, and London

LIBRARY OF CONGRESS CATALOGUING-IN-PUBLICATION DATA

Feminist activism in academia : essays on personal, political and
   professional change / edited by Ellen C. Mayock and Domnica
   Radulescu.
        p.   cm.
   Includes bibliographical references and index.

   ISBN 978-0-7864-4568-4
   softcover : 50# alkaline paper ∞

   1. Feminism and higher education.   2. Feminism and
education.   3. Women — Education (Higher) — Political aspects.
4. Women educators.   I. Mayock, Ellen C. (Ellen Cecilia), 1965–
II. Radulescu, Domnica, 1961–
LC197.F4715   2010
378.0082 — dc22   2010020399

British Library cataloguing data are available

Cover images ©2010 Shutterstock

Manufactured in the United States of America

McFarland & Company, Inc., Publishers
   Box 611, Jefferson, North Carolina 28640
   www.mcfarlandpub.com

To Patrick, Charlie, and Susanne
and to Alexander and Nicholas

Acknowledgments

The authors gratefully acknowledge Erika Vaughn for her careful, steadfast contributions to this volume and Shirley Richardson for the many ways in which she facilitated this work. We also thank Washington and Lee University for research support through Glenn and Lenfest research grants. Finally, we give a powerful nod to all those feminists in the world who continue to think, write, protest, labor, and transform our world.

Table of Contents

Introduction

Ellen Mayock and
Domnica Radulescu

> Feminist education — the feminist classroom — is and should be a place where there is a sense of struggle, where there is visible acknowledgment of the union of theory and practice, where we work together as teachers and students to overcome the estrangement and alienation that have become so much the norm in the contemporary university.
> — bell hooks (*Talking Back*)

The Academy, with its capital "A," ivory towers, tall columns, and aged codes of honor and civility, is both a real place and a metaphorical space that sends explicit and implicit signals about the tradition of white male privilege and of hierarchy. In a sense, the Academy's existence in and of itself creates an ironic *de facto* need for feminist activism. Its lofty rhetoric about global citizenship, inclusiveness, and critical thinking confronts the everyday campus realities of sexual assault, disparities in work assignments and pay and in hiring, training, and promotion, gender stereotyping, and hate speech that violates Title VII mandates. Internationally recognized activist and scholar Charlotte Bunch describes her own "tendency to be radical but still to interact with mainstream institutions" (Brooks and Hodgson 63). This is precisely the balance that many feminist activists in higher education must strike in order to be true to themselves and to be effective laborers in the academic workplace. Bunch says, "I'm also an activist by temperament because when I see something amiss, my first reaction is, 'Well, what can we do about it?'" (61). In their work "What Counts as Activism?" Martin, Hanson, and Fontaine examine the role that individuals play as precursors to collective social action. The term they use is "individuals embedded in communities" (78), which aptly describes the position of feminist activists as individuals with particular agendas who are an integral part of their academic workplace.

This recognition of "something amiss," coupled with an immediate response towards action, characterizes many of the activists who have contributed essays to this volume.

The classroom brings together professors' nuanced notions of what is important in their individual fields and in the world around them and students' sometimes fresher thought processes and challenges to professors' authority. In *Teaching to Transgress*, bell hooks underscores the importance of making the classroom a crucible of feminist theory and practice. hooks states:

> Reflecting on my own work in feminist theory, I find writing — theoretical talk — to be most meaningful when it invites readers to engage in critical reflection and to engage in the practice of feminism. To me, this theory emerges from the concrete, from my efforts to make sense of everyday life experiences, from my efforts to intervene critically in my life and the lives of others. This to me is what makes feminist transformation possible. Personal testimony, personal experience, is such fertile ground for the production of liberatory feminist theory because it usually forms the base of our theory making [70].

In this volume, several essays highlight how feminist pedagogies — methodologies that take into account hooks' idea that theory emerges from the concrete — are their own form of activism.

All of the essays treat to some extent the ways in which feminists confront traditional power structures within the high walls or ivory towers of the Academy. At the root of this examination are the very basic, gendered assumptions about women and the inscription of women's bodies in the space of higher education. After all, many professors admit to "being a ham" and thus understand and embrace the performative aspect of teaching. Teaching happens at every moment of our academic lives — in the classroom, in our offices, in meetings, on the playing field, in the theater itself— and we bring to these pedagogical interactions our full minds and bodies, not to be ignored, not to be circumscribed by the A of the Academy. As Elin Diamond puts it, "Rather than being an object *of*, the body anchors us *to* consciousness, and it is that particular embodied relation that brings to light the essence of the play's action and characters" (394). The analogous relationship here is classroom as stage full of actors and shared lesson as play. Body, text, and semiotics all matter.

At what moment does a person in the Academy recognize herself or himself as a feminist, identify as an activist, seek out other women and men who find themselves similarly situated? Does feminism imply activism? Which are the circumstances that most define us as feminist activists? What does it mean to identify as two different "-ists" at the same time? What are the goals and methods of feminist activists? And, what are the perils and successes of feminist activism on today's college and university campuses? These are some of the broader questions that shape this book. They are questions that point to rupture and resistance — a violent intellectual and emotional rupture with idealistic expectations sowed in one's academic formation and career or a melancholy rupture of self as it confronts the often conflicting ideals of the Academy and finds itself molded and changed during its tenure there. Ruptured selves give rise to resisting bodies, as individuals recognize their own oppositional politics, find strength in intellectual debate and in real action, and collaborate with others who seek similar change. The move from rupture to resistance and from self to collective body is the essence of feminist activism as explored in this volume.

This collection examines the intersections among the personal, political, and professional realms and the ways in which feminist activists come to life in the Academy. It provides a forum for scholars to identify and define problems in their work lives or examine their own brand of activism as it pertains to their professional day-to-day lives and their careers as a whole, or both. The larger arch under which we conceptualize this volume is bell hooks' notion that "the classroom remains the most radical space of possibility in the academy" (*Teaching to Transgress* 12), the place where activism starts with the essential movement against and beyond boundaries. We explore the interconnections between feminist pedagogies and activism and between the status of feminist scholars and teachers in the Academy and institutionalized politics of exclusion or marginalization that adversely affect the overall status of women in the academic professions. The focus of the essays included is the Academy in the United States, although several of the contributors write from a perspective of international experiences and areas of expertise.

We have structured this volume in two parts: Feminist Pedagogies and Mentorship and Negotiating the Academy. These are clearly overlapping categories and, as such, essays in the collection are very much connected and bound by the overarching concepts of rupture, resistance, and feminist activism. This collection only scratches the surface of the multitudinous themes surrounding feminist activism, and we therefore anticipate that the book will encourage broader inquiry into concepts introduced or continued here.

The book begins with Beverly Yuen Thompson's discussion of her feminist video ethnography. Thompson compares and contrasts the parallels between national abortion rights issues and an ethnographic study based upon a South Florida grassroots clinic defense action. It covers historic abortion restrictions and contemporary political debates on abortion access. The ethnographic research was conducted at a women's health clinic named A Choice for Women, and the author employed visual anthropological/sociological methods incorporating film and photography. A short documentary movie was produced that chronicled six months of clinic defense participation. The author incorporates student participation in the clinic defense as part of the reflexive-educational process of combining academic and activist processes in a women's studies classroom. The conclusion stresses the importance of civic participation for students as part of their ethnographic learning process.

In "Get Out of My Uterus! A Manifesto Against Reproductive Politics in the Academic World and in the World at Large" Domnica Radulescu makes the radical suggestion that institutions refrain from discussing and dissecting women's bodies in their formal and informal discourses. She denounces the liberal fallacy of "hearing the two sides of the debate," arguing that the religious anti-choice position is untenable and, just like any other basic civil liberties we have learned to take for granted and no longer debate, so is reproductive freedom to be taken for granted while the "other side" is not worthy of being considered at the level of policymaking in a true democracy.

Robin M. LeBlanc achieves an unflinching examination of authority and position for women in male-dominated or male-privileged work environments. In "Teaching to Spite Your Body," LeBlanc questions how much to surrender to colloquial essentialization of female body parts in order not to point explicitly to the ways in which such language use asserts male dominance and undermines a female teacher's authority in her own classroom. LeBlanc ultimately asks readers to question masculinist standards for teaching, pedagogy, and overall presence in both the classroom and the field.

Norma Bowles, founder and artistic director of Fringe Benefits Theatre, shares stories about and questions raised by four theater for social justice workshops, residencies, and projects addressing sexism and discrimination based on actual or perceived gender in the Academy. Bowles' vast experience in the trenches of activist theater affords a revealing view of student culture and numerous concrete examples of theater strategies to raise consciousness and work towards real change in the Academy.

Next, Jennifer A. Boisvert explores feminist mentorship in the Academy. Boisvert writes from the perspective of clinical psychology and compares the degree of success women enjoy with female mentors versus without. She provides a literature review on feminist mentorship, explores the relevance of feminist mentorship and feminist activism in her life, and raises significant issues of diversity and values and how they influence women's leadership capabilities in the Academy.

Jeanine Silveira Stewart examines feminist mentorship through the lens of the "maternal wall." She defines key terms and explores how influential issues such as motherhood and benevolent sexism affect women at work. Stewart suggests ways in which women academics and administrators can learn from the literature and from each other's experiences in order to create an academic work environment that is more attuned to remedying gender inequities.

Part II begins with Kathleen Juhl's essay on the post-tenure period and subversion of institutional norms. Juhl recounts the experience of working towards tenure and framing her own identity, from feminine lesbian who could pass for straight to "fabulous femme lesbian" who could succeed in being herself, subverting institutional traditions, and translating the experiences into her art and teaching. Juhl addresses the ways in which feminist and queer ideas about gender can be circulated in the playfulness of classroom work and rehearsals, thus raising students' consciousness and encouraging discussions about the political and cultural issues that surround gender.

Ellen Mayock's essay examines the phenomenon of "mothering language" in the Academy, comments on how widespread this type of language has become in the popular press and the workplace, and then makes suggestions about how an organization can think more critically about its professional language and move more deliberately towards creating an environment that welcomes all employees, and especially women. Mayock links the concepts of body and self through the actual manifestation of the pregnant body in the workplace and its metaphorical ramifications. In the end, she argues that further understanding about sexist language in the workplace will serve as its own form of ongoing feminist activism.

In "On the Front Lines," Cate Siejk and Jane A. Rinehart explore what has happened in their university, where an anti-women's studies contingent has positioned itself as unwilling to accommodate any disagreements or deviations from authoritative pronouncements and to engage with those opposed to their views. Siejk and Rinehart present a case study of some contests around feminism at a Catholic university and propose that the construction of such disputes in terms of a defense of sacred traditions against the erosions of secularism and feminism ignores a crucial dimension that has important theoretical and practical implications.

Karin E. Peterson and Alice A. Weldon assert that flexibility and control of one's time are perceived benefits of working in a liberal arts university environment. Their essay explores the costs of flexibility and control as they play out in the lives of women faculty at a southeastern public institution. They argue that the hidden nature of these costs contributes to many of the strains they experience in academic work. They also specify how the strains vary by motherhood status (women with children and women with no children) and are complicated further according to faculty rank (lecturer and tenure-track women). They conclude by describing the need for collective support among faculty and institutional changes that recognize these costs and their impacts on work load, reward structures, and job security.

Sara Warner is the author of the final essay, on negotiating the academy. Warner examines the issues of effective labor and feminism in the Academy. Using the term "tender track," Warner explores how attitudes about gender and class have influenced her approaches to teaching, scholarship, and academic service as she navigates the tenure process at her institution. In the end, Warner laments the dissonance between the notions of higher education institutions as businesses and the work of the professor as true vocation.

The collection as a whole reflects the anxiety of ruptured selves in the academy and the strength of resisting bodies, the difficulty of being externally defined as a certain type of person and the rich diversity that emerges from those boxed-in definitions, the frustration with the academy's narrow definitions of women professors and the liberation in rejecting or revamping those definitions.

As readers are getting ready to grapple with the many questions raised by this collection, they might be inspired and emboldened by having a glimpse into a historical perspective of women's rights and proto-feminist activism. In 1791, the French feminist, revolutionary, activist and writer Olympe de Gouges wrote the *Declaration of the Rights of Woman and the Female Citizen* to complement the *Declaration of the Rights of Man and of the Citizen* that came out of the French Revolution and was approved by the National Assembly of France in August 1789. In Article IV of her Declaration, de Gouges states:

> The law must be the expression of the general will; all female and male citizens must contribute either personally or through their representatives to its formation; it must be the same for all: male and female citizens, being equal in the eyes of the law, must be equally admitted to all honors, positions, and public employment according to their capacity and without other distinctions besides those of their virtues and talents.

If governments, legislatures, nations, societies, communities, universities, institutions of all kinds had followed this very simple and firmly stated rule, feminism would be obsolete, as would women's and genders studies programs, as would this very collection, as would activism that engages in furthering women's causes. "Capacity," "virtues," "talents" are, according to this courageous revolutionary, who in 1793 paid with her own head for her boldness, what should constitute the positioning of women and men in society. Not bodies, not sexuality, not biology. Yet the bodies of women have been under attack for millennia. Our bodies have been a reason for inequality, target for violence, and our biology a justification to deny us access to "all honors, positions, and public employment" for millennia, since the all-too-revered Greek "democracy" to this very moment when this book is being composed and published.[1]

The authors in this collection, capture the wrenching paradox that women in the academic world and then in the larger professional world have to wrestle with on a daily basis: how to work, act, talk, and succeed in conditions where body or biology are actually placed on the same string as capacity, virtue and talents. This incongruity — if placed in an activity book with groups of words out of which a six-year-old would have to pick out the words that do *not* match — would be immediately noticed by such an intuitive youngster. A normal six-year-old would pick out "body" as the word that does not match in the string that also contains "capacity, virtue, talents."

In its various approaches, targets, stories of oppression and activism, this book is balanced on the paradox born out of this painful incongruity for women: How do we both make ourselves listened to, respected, rewarded, treated equally, as if our bodies or biology did not matter? Also, since our bodies and biology have been in every century, in every part of the world, at one point or another or at all times, reasons for exclusion, violence and inequity, how do we manage to be relentlessly *in* our bodies, *in* our voices, to put our bodies forth as weapons of resistance while also not being judged in the classroom or at faculty meetings for our bodies? And really how can we work and live happily in our minds and bodies without at some point or another having to play one against the other? How can we both be invisible as bodies and visible as professionals, experts, scholars, teachers, and administrators while also bringing these same bodies forth into public spaces, classrooms, meetings halls and representing ourselves *with* our own bodies and *with* our own voices? How can we, every day of our workdays, be as much of a generic human being as men have been for millennia while also demanding and expecting that our women's bodies, whose marginalization, inflicted violence, neglect, and oppression have ruptured our selves, fill those spaces?

Because the academy is the space where people forge themselves for a life in the public spaces of countries, states, communities, because it is the space from which women have been excluded until only decades ago, because women's education is more directly linked to issues of reproductive freedom and the construction of gender, and because American universities are places where selves can be either ruptured or made whole, these questions are both more pertinent and more painful when addressed in the context of the academic world. That women started to be accepted in universities at various points during the last century is certainly a big step in progress towards equal rights. But until the women who enter universities are being educated in ways that make them cope with and change a world still largely based on structures, legislation, customs, traditions, and discourses devised by men and for men, so that Olympe de Gouges' demand of more than 200 years ago become a reality, until that day we will have to continue to struggle with this mind-bending paradox. And for that day to be possible, the women who work, educate, administer, produce and impart knowledge in the academic institutions of our nations need to keep putting forth their resisting bodies, just as they equally need to be supported by processes, legislation, structures, discourses which judge them on the basis of their "capacity, virtues, talents." We need all this so that we don't have to be teaching "despite our bodies," as LeBlanc's essay argues, so that every time we walk down our campuses or enter our classrooms, we are not treated with some unconditional expectation of maternity, maternalism, nurturing, as Mayock's essay points out, so that we don't keep being startled and threatened by anti-woman, anti-choice pseudo-feminists trying to convince us or our students to give up our reproductive freedom, so that if we are of a different sexual orientation than the traditionally accepted heterosexual one, we don't have to splinter our selves into a painful theatrical game of personas and femininities as Kathleen Juhl describes.

Our dream is that this activism may take us a few steps closer to the day when we can actually be carefree on university campuses to fully and harmoniously live, work, create as much as physical people as thinking individuals, with no rupture between our selves and our bodies, not despite our bodies, but *with* and *in* our bodies. This is the book of a common dream that we teachers, scholars, and administrators may keep body and soul together throughout our workday as much as in our personal lives. It is a book created in the hope that maybe our grandchildren will pick it up from a university library shelf, leaf through it, and marvel at our struggles, saying, for instance: "I can't believe what our grandmothers had to go through.

Aren't we lucky?" Until that day we still need to tell our stories, heal our ruptured selves, and push forth our resisting bodies.

Notes

1. See the works of Sarah Pomeroy, Martha Nussbaum, and Froma Zeitlin on the position of women in society and their representations in art during the Attic period.

Works Cited

Brooks, Ethel and Dorothy L. Hodgson. "'An Activist Temperament': An Interview with Charlotte Bunch." *Women's Studies Quarterly* 35:3–4 (Fall/Winter 2007): 60–74.

Diamond, Elin. "The Violence of 'We': Politicizing Identification." In *Critical Theory and Performance*. Eds. Janelle G. Reinelt and Joseph R. Roach. Ann Arbor: University of Michigan Press, 1992. pp. 390–98.

De Gouges, Olympe. *Declaration of the Rights of Woman and the Female Citizen, 1791*. In *Women in Revolutionary Paris, 1791*. Eds. Darline Gay Levy, Harriet Branson Applewhite, and Mary Durham Johnson. Urbana: University of Illinois Press, 1980.

hooks, bell. *Talking Back: Thinking Feminist, Thinking Black*. Cambridge, MA: South End, 1989.

_____. *Teaching to Transgress*. New York: Routledge, 1994.

Martin, Deborah G., Susan Hanson, and Danielle Fontaine. "What Counts as Activism? The Role of Individuals in Creating Change." *Women's Studies Quarterly* 35:3–4 (Fall/Winter 2007): 78–94.

Nussbaum, Martha. *Sex and Social Justice*. Oxford: Oxford University Press, 2000.

_____. *Women and Human Development*. Cambridge: Cambridge University Press, 2001.

Pomeroy, Sarah. *Goddesses, Whores, Wives and Slaves: Women in Classical Antiquity*. New York: Schocken, 1995.

Zeitlin, Froma. *Playing the Other: Gender and Society in Classical Greek Literature*. Chicago: University of Chicago Press, 1995.

Defending a Choice for Women

A Feminist Video Ethnography

BEVERLY YUEN THOMPSON

Introduction

From nearly two blocks away I could see the crowd gathered. They were holding signs with full-color images, and their chanting broke through the endless white noise of traffic from the busy boulevard and nearby express-way. There were two police cars — one parked on the sidewalk, with the engine running for the air conditioner, the other sitting in the middle of the street between lanes, lights flashing. It created a spectacle, like a car accident that people were powerless to ignore. It provoked one window-tinted car to slow down, the driver showing a thumbs-up to those in the prayer circle, and this inflamed the crowd. I continued to walk closer, and suddenly, I could make out the images on the signs: bloody fetuses, slogans projecting god's judgment, and signs designating this business a Nazi death camp. The chanting and praying became hypnotic as it looped between Spanish and English, louder as I passed. There were about thirty-five pro-life activists by 7 A.M., by my estimation. I walked more quickly as I approached the driveway — the dividing line between their side and the clinic defenders that were holding the blue rounds stating simply and uniformly: "keep abortion legal." Once I made it across this divide I was greeted by friends, handed a sign, and assigned my task — sitting in a lawn chair and holding one end of a banner. This became our Saturday morning ritual. From my vantage point in a lawn-chair, I recorded the spectacle through video, photography, notes, interviews, and endless, politically heated banter.

This ongoing protest episode was located in South Florida and spanned a year and a half (continuing through this writing) — through humid summers and hurricane seasons — even the extremes of nature could not suppress those devoted to ideology and its practice.

This Saturday morning battle to defend A Choice for Women — a clinic that provided reproductive health care and abortion — provided a microcosmic reflection of the national abortion debates: binary ideologies, personal choices, and a multi-generational perspective informed by those who remembered pre–*Roe* days, and those just learning what *Roe* meant. This essay explores the parallels between the pro-choice movement, the abortion debates, and local activism. Some framing questions include: what is the status of the grassroots pro-choice movement and the defense of women's reproductive rights? How is the current political context shaping abortion laws and real access? Are younger generations equipped with the historic lessons necessary to inspire the committed defense for their *own* rights? The essay also explores the ethnographic research conducted in South Florida within the context of visual anthropology/sociology. While traditional ethnographic studies are ultimately boiled down to an essential written text, visual anthropologists and sociologists argue for visual technology (photography/video/film) to be included in the information gathering and disseminating process. By utilizing photography and video to capture the experience of the clinic defense action, a short documentary video was produced for public forums, film festivals, classroom presentations, and recruitment processes.

Historic Abortion Restrictions

The beginning of legal regulations of abortion in the United States is tied to the institutionalization of the medical community and the transition away from female dominated midwifery practices. The American Medical Association (AMA), established in the mid–1800s, lobbied for a ban on abortions that were provided by nonphysicians, as they considered it a dangerous, unregulated practice in society (Blanchard 12). Their campaign also had a moral element, as it encouraged chastity in women. The AMA had been established to create standards for medical education and practice, as well as to safeguard public health. It also embodied the struggle between female-based midwifery and the rise of the male-dominated professionalization of the medical industry, with restrictions on female education and advancement.

Therefore, abortion, along with other midwifery practices, was taken out of the hands of women and soon legislated by the patriarchal medical institution and the state.

Newly developed abortion restrictions were based upon precedence in British common law, which banned abortion only after quickening (Staggenborg 3). The first abortion law that passed in the United States was in 1821 in Connecticut, criminalizing abortion after quickening (Blanchard 12; Ginsburg 24; Deflem 787). Within decades, laws restricting abortion grew exponentially, between 1860 and 1880 forty anti-abortion statutes had passed; by 1890, every state had legal restrictions (Ginsburg 25; Blanchard 15). Abortion access was only half of the story when it came to legal control of women's bodies and reproductive functions. At the same time that abortion was being regulated and criminalized, other women, often poor women of color, suffered from mandatory sterilizations, especially those of African American and Native American descent. Between 1900 and 1960, approximately 45,000 to 60,000 women had been sterilized; furthermore, the state of California accounted for one third of the total (Saletan 199; Blanchard 13). *Buck v. Bell* was the Supreme Court decision that upheld the "constitutionality of a Virginia involuntary sterilization law" in 1927 (Roberts 144). Eugenics laws were also passed in twenty-one states; thus the United States "became the first nation in the world to permit mass sterilization as part of an effort to 'purify the race'" (Ross 170). Margaret Sanger's Birth Control Federation was even responsible for what they called "the Negro Project" in 1939, which promoted eugenics practices (Ross 171). Other birth control clinics established in the south had similar aims of lowering the black birthrate (Roberts 172). The racism of the birth control movement contributed to distrust and opposition between the black community and the women's movement (Ross 172; Roberts 132). Uncovered through a court case in 1974, "a federal district court found that an estimated 100,000 to 150,000 poor women had been sterilized annually under federally funded programs" (Roberts 132). It was not until 1979 when California finally rescinded its law authorizing involuntary sterilization (Saletan 200).

In 1960, the FDA approved the birth control pill, though its use was still limited. In 1965, the case of *Griswold v. Connecticut* was decided in favor of married couples obtaining access to birth control pills. In 1973, the same privacy argument legalized abortion through *Roe v. Wade*. Briefly, there was some reprieve in the abortion wars: President Johnson approved $20 million for use in contraceptive programs in 1967 (Ginsburg 38). And "between 1973 and 1977 the federal government paid for about one-third of all abortions:

294,600 in 1977" (Fried 213). This reprieve did not last long. Within months of *Roe* passing, a religious-based pro-life movement began to organize against abortion and birth control access. Following the historic *Roe* decision, "hundreds of bills to restrict abortion, most written in consultation with church leadership, were introduced into municipal councils and state legislatures across the country" (Baird-Windle and Bader 40). One of the blows included the Hyde Amendment, denying the use of federal Medicaid funds for abortion. After Hyde passed in 1977, "fewer than 2,500 abortions were covered" by the government (Deflem 792). Hyde applied not only to low-income women, it also applied to "federal workers, military personnel and their dependents, women living on Native American reservations, and women in federal prisons" (Fried 213).

Contemporary Abortion Issues

Today, abortion is legal, though regulated by state and federal restrictions that include denial of Medicaid coverage, time limits, waiting periods, parental notification, consent laws, and a significant decrease in the number of providers. Abortion procedures are only taught in approximately 12 percent of ob/gyn medical programs, and the access to this medical knowledge continues to shrink. Abortion services have moved from hospitals to private clinics, where the vast majority of procedures are performed by "two percent of the country's obstetrician-gynecologists, two-thirds of whom are sixty-five years of age or older — the country is facing a critical shortage of providers" (Baird-Windle and Bader 3). Because of political pressure, lack of medical education, and fiscal liability, abortion providers are becoming scarcer; this specialization often requires a commitment that extends beyond professional career interests, and borders on activism.

The pro-life movement has gained momentum during the decades since abortion has been legalized; and from lobbying to street level "sidewalk counselors," the movement aims to restrict access to abortion. At A Choice for Women in South Florida, the pro-life protesters "have stated openly that their objective is to close this clinic down" (Dawson). This clinic provides services to patients traveling from as far as the Caribbean Islands, some of which face more restrictive abortion laws that the U.S. (Pheterson and Azize 44). However, even in the United States, 84 percent of counties do not have *a single* abortion provider. Therefore, abortion is *actually* available in only 16 percent of counties. Major cities become hubs to which rural women must travel great distances. Compound that with 24-hour waiting periods and parental consent restrictions, and the process could require time off work, transportation, food, and lodging costs, creating a significant financial barrier.

The pro-life picketers do have an impact upon the patients entering the clinic. Eileen Diamond, the director of A Choice for Women, described her patients' reaction to pro-life protesters outside of their facility:

> Sometimes they say that they are just fools. How could they be so judgmental without knowing what their particular situation is? Many times they are doing it out of necessity, out of financial hardship, they just cannot afford one more child. There's young people who are on the springboard of their education, they're going from high school to college, or they're in college and they fought very hard to get in and to pay for it and they just can't take on the responsibility of a child. And I think our patients feel very frustrated that someone with a sign can look over the hedge and make a judgment on them.

Academic research on the after-effects of abortion, included studies by the American Psychological Association, has concluded that

> the time of greatest stress is before the abortion.... Access to legal abortion to terminate an unwanted pregnancy is vital to safeguard both the physical and mental health of women [quoted in Page 13].

The most prominent emotion following abortion is relief, whereas stress levels are highest during an unwanted pregnancy (Gold-Steinberg & Stewart 358; Paige). Therefore, while the patients are in the midst of a potentially high stress time period, they may be faced with unwanted interactions with pro-life protesters, graphic images, and violent verbal condemnations. Today, approximately one-third of all known pregnancies are terminated through abortions (Blanchard 31). The estimated number of annual abortions is approximately 1.5 million, and has remained fairly constant since legalization — and presumably, it would have been fairly consistent before 1973. And with the high rates of harassment reported by clinics (Ginsburg 50), this distressing encounter with clinic protesters is one which many women could face.

Defending a Choice for Women: A Feminist Video Ethnography

In 1998, Fay Ginsburg published an ethnographic study based upon the clinic defense efforts surrounding the first and only women's abortion clinic in Fargo, North Dakota. Her aim was:

to chart its historically changing contours over the years from both the local and national perspectives; to understand the sources of violence that periodically erupt; and to give more visibility to those aspects of the movement that are least well known [xxviii].

Her methodology included collecting life stories from activists on both side of the debate, as well as to gather video footage for a professional production. She was interested in capturing narratives as the rich sociological text that could provide for theoretical interpretations (Ginsburg; Burowoy). With her interest not only in capturing a traditional, *written* ethnography (Van Maanen 1), but also in producing a visual record, Ginsburg provides a model for conducting visual ethnographic research on clinic defense.

Nearly a decade later, I set out to document the activities of an ongoing clinic defense transpiring in a very different location of the country, comprised of a diverse demographic. Miami Clinic Access Project (MCAP) was

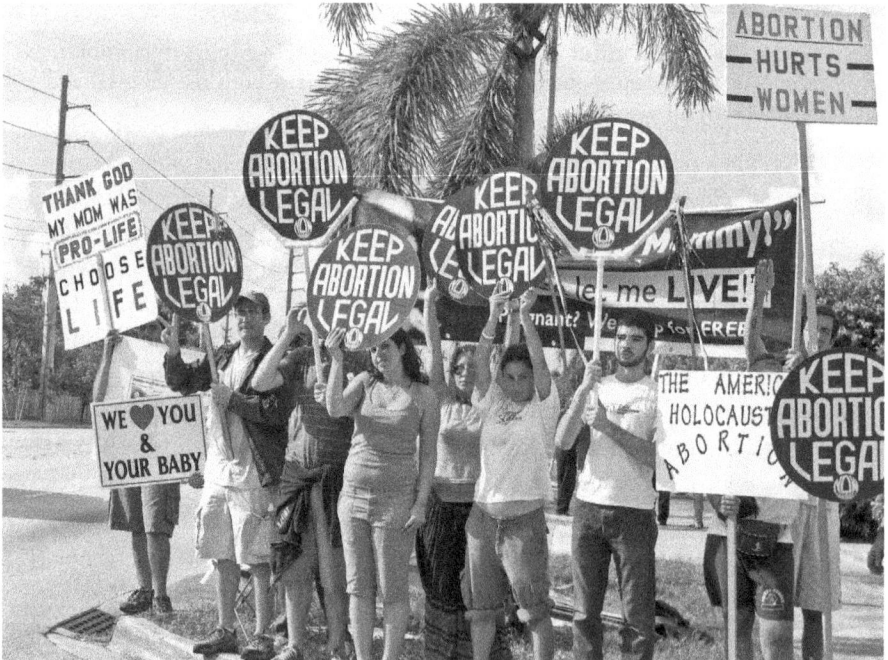

Since May 2006, pro-life protesters have besieged A Choice for Women, a women's health clinic in Miami, Florida. In this 2006 picture, pro-life and pro-choice protesters jockey for a position on the grassy yard facing the main street on which the clinic sits. Pro-life protesters would attempt to block or photograph people entering the clinic as clinic defenders attempted to block the photo, taking as well the other targeted harassment (photograph by Beverly Yuen Thompson).

a loose affiliation of activists committed to defending women's health clinics that come under attack by local Catholic pro-life organizations. Julia Dawson, the founder, had been active in the pro-choice movement locally in the 1980s, and in more recent years, as the occasion arose. In May 2006, the director of A Choice for Women clinic, Eileen Diamond, approached Julia Dawson and asked for assistance with clinic defense. The clinic was experiencing Saturday morning protests at which pro-life activists would approach and harass clinic patients as they entered the property. Dawson was able to organize a group of committed local activists to defend the clinic each Saturday morning. MCAP members would remain at the clinic until all patients had left the premises, usually leaving before the pro-life prayer circle had ended.

I began attending the clinic defense episodes in August of 2006 and continued each week for six months. Heeding John Van Maanen's call for researchers to "share firsthand the environment, problems, background, language, rituals, and social relations of a more-or-less bounded and specified group of people" (3), I set out to capture the on-going protest. This South Florida activism provides a window into the world of clinic defense, an important part of defending women's reproductive rights in the current political climate. President Bush damaged the global family planning infrastructure by attaching a global gag rule to U.S. funds — organizations receiving dollars cannot mention contraception or abortion. Under Bush, further abortion restrictions, such as the ban on late-term abortions, became law. As the political culture becomes increasingly pro-life, we can expect the grassroots pro-life movement to be encouraged in their harassing and violent tactics.

One of the primary challenges for an ethnographic project is access to the desired community — and this is expedited through personal connections (Lofland and Lofland 37). The investigator must acclimatize to the social situation by participating to a certain degree so that she can begin to blend into the context. In such a politically polarized circumstance, the participants are insistent to know "which side" the researcher adheres. Those who attempt to remain politically neutral by refusing to hold signs provoke endless inquiry: "I know that you are neutral, but what do you *actually* believe?" My allegiance — as a women's studies professor — was not a question. I entered the field through previously established networks — MCAP and the women's studies program at FIU. As my participation intensified, I recruited interested students to attend the event and write about it within the context of our academic research on reproductive rights. It was their very first taste of social activism.

The participant observation consisted of many long hours spent in a lawn chair, holding a "keep abortion legal" blue round as the only source of shade, through the hot, South Florida summer. Occasionally, a brief reprieve from the blistering sun would occur — heavy, tropical downpours. In addition to the weather, we endured the Catholic prayers in both Spanish and English, chanted trance-like, for endless hours. Over several months, we physically battled over turf. A small grassy area in front of the clinic became the center of this battle; it lined the clinic driveway and provided close access to patients entering the clinic. Each week we vied to arrive earlier than the opposition, in hopes of establishing our banner barriers first, an hour and a half before daybreak. Once positioned, one side took the offensive, and tried to intimidate the other out of position. The police hovered across the street; they avoided intervention until necessary. It became increasingly necessary as the sides became vitriolic and were eventually separated. Then, the opposing sides would alternate weekly their place on the center swale. This separation placed a damper on the hostile activity and shouting matches.

I conducted in-depth, videotaped interviews with many MCAP members, gathering "narrative texts" from which I could construct a sequence of events for the clinic defense (Franzosi 519; Woliver). This follows ethnographer Michael Burowoy's advice:

> It is absurd for social scientists to debate the subjects' situation without letting the subjects speak up for themselves. The ideal, then, is to give the subjects a voice in the academic world [Burowoy 267].

This interview process "seeks to *discover* the informant's *experience* of a particular topic or situation" (Lofland and Lofland 18). One of the findings of the in-depth interview is to establish the psychological "frames" on which the interviewee bases her or his understanding of the social world. Francesca Polletta states that "frames foster a sense of injustice, identity, and collective efficacy — cognitions that a situation is wrong, that it is not immutable and that 'we' can battle 'them' in order to change it" (421). These cognitive frames provide the organizational pins that hold together these collective identities. Hence, propagandizing is central to clinic protests and defenses. It is not enough for the pro-lifers to present their opinion through their graphic signage — they are out to change minds and save babies. This encourages them to continue to cross the line, literally, onto the property and physically interfere with the patient's private decisions. Equally for the pro-choicers, they are willing to utilize their physical bodies to shield the patient from intimidation and harassment.

The sub-discipline of visual anthropology aims to add images — photographs, video, artwork, and film — to the traditional written forms of ethnographic presentation (Mead). While anthropologists such as Margaret Mead utilized images in their work during the early 1900s, this practice soon fell into disuse in the middle of the century. Filmmaking was cumbersome and required a film crew. But with the advent of digital video, it is possible for the lone fieldworker to produce high quality images on small cameras and with nonlinear computer editing (MacDougall 15; Asch and Asch 343; Schaeffer 255). Timothy Asch and Patsy Asch suggest that "the ethnographer should be able to 'sit around' with the camera as she or he sits around with a note pad" (Asch and Asch 343).

Margaret Mead disagreed with some anthropologists about the physical use of the camera. Should it be placed on a tripod, a neutral observer of social fact, as Mead argued? Or should the camera be engaged, in hand, a social participant in the activities itself, recording intimate detail and directed speech, as her colleagues argued? This methodological difference arose at A Choice for Women. While I "sat around" with my camcorder in hand, clinic defender Gordon volunteered each week to perch his camcorder on a tripod, distanced from the action, silently recording the larger picture, while missing the details of verbal debates and personal interactions. Which camera provided more insight or neutrality? Which captured the "truer" essence of the story? Each perspective provided a particular insight. David MacDougall argues that "the image is affected as much by the body behind the camera as those before it," and, I would add, if *no body* is behind it (27).

The Pro-Life Grassroots Movement

Cristina Page has argued that the pro-life movement is primarily an anti-sex and anti–birth control movement and that abortion becomes the moral justification for this stance. She points out that none of the pro-life groups support "the use of birth control" (9). Ironically, while the pro-life groups claim to be against abortion, their tactics do nothing to reduce the number of abortions, and in fact, their anti–birth control stance increases the instances of abortion (5). Pro-life politics became the dominant political orientation under President Bush, who has promoted notoriously ineffective abstinence-only policies and cut financial support for women's reproductive healthcare. At the end of Bush's governor term in 2000, "Texas ranked dead last in the nation, fiftieth out of fifty, in the decline of teen birthrates among fifteen- to seventeen-year-old females" (70). The United States is the only rich nation that ranks among Third World countries for teenage births, "ranking just behind Thailand and directly before Rwanda" (Page 80). In addition, these are policies that the United States exports. Globally, programs receiving U.S. dollars are banned from speaking about birth control and family planning methods. Pro-life organizations, such as the Abstinence Clearinghouse Website, discourage condom use in African countries that have the highest rates of HIV (Page 87), deeming condoms "unreliable." Teenage pregnancy rates are responsive to and reflective of social policy: in Holland, for example, the country has been able to reduce "its teenage birthrate by a staggering 72 percent in thirty years while also having the lowest teenage abortion rates in the industrialized world" (Page 80).

According to Jennifer Strickler and Nicholas L. Danigelis, "people with passionate pro-life views are more likely to translate their beliefs into political activism that are those with equally extreme pro-choice beliefs" (200). Since *Roe v. Wade*, the Christian Right has organized an impressively vigilant grass-roots pro-life movement (Rozell and Wilcox 293) that has targeted the "local delivery of abortion services" (Ginsburg 44). This grassroots movement is strongly supported by the church infrastructure that can provide social net-working, materials, communication, ideology, and people (Ginsburg 44). In 1988, Operation Rescue burst on the scene, popularizing pro-life activism through the use of civil disobedience. When the founder, Randall Terry, organized his week-long siege on women's clinics in Atlanta, resulting in 134 arrests, both he and his organization were catapulted to overnight fame (Faludi 410). At the local abortion clinics, the pro-life activists often confront the female patients with posters depicting aborted fetuses in large, graphic detail. These activists label their activities "rescues" and "sidewalk counseling" (Maxwell 440). Patricia Donovan states that the Catholics United for Life describe their techniques of sidewalk counseling in this manner:

> as a peaceful, sensitive effort to persuade women to rethink their decision by pro-viding them with information and with offers of help. In reality, sidewalk coun-seling often fits another description provided by its originators, which says that it is "a last-minute confrontation" with a woman who is about to enter an abortion clinic [6].

When signs of bloody fetuses and sidewalk counseling fail to rescue women, they are often attacked with other denigrating signs. Comparisons of abortion clinics to Hitler's extermination camps and Nazi Germany, abound. "Clinics are labeled 'aboratoriums,' clinic employees are denounced as Nazis, swastikas appear on protest signs, and speakers often refer to Dachau and Auschwitz in their condemnation of abortion" (Donovan 8). The Holocaust provides a popular and inflammatory reference for pro-life protesters (Blanchard 97). This apocalyptic, holy damnation rhetoric is not the final tool in the pro-life arsenal. Their actions have also included extreme clinic violence — fires, bombings, and outright shootings of several people (including clinic staff members, doctors, and clinic defenders) (Deflem 805; Kolbert and Miller 106; Page 102; Ginsburg 50; Fried 209). This violence has been successful in creating an atmosphere of intimidation for abortion providers and staff members. With the rising cost of security measures, insurance, hostile landlords, emotional stress, and lack of training in medical programs, the number of providers has declined to 1,800, servicing 1.3 million women annually (Joffe 31; Page 147).

The Pro-Choice Grassroots Movement

The contemporary pro-choice movement has its roots in the women's movement of the 1960s, before abortion was legalized in 1973. While difficult to ascertain exact numbers due to the illegal and clandestine nature of illegal abortion, it is estimated that 5,000 women died annually pre–*Roe*. In 1969, the First National Conference on Abortion Laws was held, at which the National Association for the Repeal of Abortion Laws (NARAL) was established. Also in 1969, the New Yorkers for Abortion Law Repeal was established (Ginsburg 39). These organizations practiced both direct action and legislative campaigns to fight the criminalization of abortion. Some of the 1960s feminist groups participated in abortion referral services, where they found underground doctors for women (Staggenborg 49). The feminist group Jane eventually took matters into its own hands and trained its members to perform abortions themselves. Under growing pressure to legalize abortion, the Supreme Court decision *Roe v. Wade* was decided in 1973, legalizing abortion under the constitutionally protected right to privacy. It was a great victory for the women's movement. Overnight, women were no longer forced to subject themselves to dangerous, back-alley abortions. Once abortion was legalized the struggle became one of enforcing the law. However, "movements typically subside after winning a major legal or political battles, and ours has not escaped this cycle" (Borgmann and Weiss 40).

The pro-life movement did not suffer its defeat passively — it went on the offensive and attempted to re-criminalize or restrict abortion access through lobbying; connecting issues into a broad "family values" platform, and strengthening the grassroots organization of the Christian Right. Restrictions on abortion were soon enacted. In 1977 the Hyde Amendment was passed, which denied Medicaid and other federal funding for abortion (Staggenborg 94). Abortion foes continued to pass legislation that restricted access to abortion; and the pro-choice movement was again on the defensive, both legislatively and in grassroots defense of clinics (Wilder 74). In South Florida, Carol Cohen, a clinic defender at A Choice for Women, started the non-profit organization Women's Emergency Network (WEN) that provides financial aid to women in need of abortion services. Cohen described the needs of her clients:

> Well, let's talk about the women who come to us. Surprisingly, most of them are not teenagers. Only about one in five is a teenager. ... Most of the women who come to us are single mothers struggling to rise out of poverty. A significant proportion is homeless or has experienced domestic violence. A number of them are battling physical or emotional illness, including cancer, heart disease, bipolar disorder, HIV/AIDS, they run the gamut.

The Women's Emergency Network was closely associated with the Choice for Women clinic, and when Cohen "heard they were being picketed, we felt that it was our duty to defend them."

Clinic Defense

In the late 1980s, Operation Rescue was founded by Randall Terry to utilize civil disobedience and mass arrest to shut down women's health centers. In 1988, Operation Rescue organized a civil disobedience action in which hundreds were arrested as they demonstrated against a clinic in Atlanta, Georgia, during the Democratic National Convention. In 1991, the "Summer of Mercy" was organized in Wichita, Kansas, at which the clinic operated by George R. Tiller was blockaded during six weeks and culminated in a rally that filled Cessna Stadium. In response to these attacks, clinic defense groups began to organize against Operation Rescue and other pro-life protesters (Ginsburg 236). These clinic defenses often utilized escorts that would "shield their patients from sidewalk counselors" (Donovan 6). Many clinic defense organizations were developed nationally in the 1980s, including the Clinic Defense Network in Chicago, the 1980s Clinic Defense Committee in the Bay Area, the Washington Area Clinic Defense Task Force, the New York Clinic Defense Task Force, and the Feminist Majority Foundation's National Clinic Access Project. The Miami Clinic Access Project was also established in the early 1980s to protect Florida clinics from pro-life protesters. The group reunited over the years in response to clinic harassment.

Clinic defense and clinic escorting are comprised of volunteer activists' intent on shielding patients from harassment as they enter and exit clinic property. If patients must park and walk onto the clinic property through the protest site, then escorts — wearing fluorescent-colored mesh vests — walk with patients and physically shield them from the onslaught. At A Choice for Women, the patients are able to drive onto clinic property. Therefore, interactions are limited to pro-lifers approaching cars with literature, and peering over the hedges to yell at or videotape patients, as a practice of intimidation. Therefore, clinic defenders are stationed at the driveway entrance and shield approaching cars and the property. Because of nationwide clinic harassment, legislation, including the FACE Act, has been enacted to keep protesters a prescribed distance from clinics, and to limit their engagement with patients. However, the FACE Act is not preventative, but only safeguards the clinic and patients after an infraction has occurred; it does not regulate a buffer zone before an offense has been committed. Pro-life protesters picket hundreds of clinics annually, yet their activities do not reduce the number of clients, nor change the mindset of women "who have made their own decisions to have an abortion" (Diamond). The privacy rights that *Roe v. Wade* was founded upon continue to be eroded through the pro-life picketing of clinics.

Conclusion: Reproductive Rights Education

At the end of the semester, the students in the Introduction to Women's Studies course presented their activity paper, describing a women's event they had attended. Several spoke about their experiences at the clinic defense. For all the student participants, this was their first experience with social activism (Edwards). One student observed, "I see that those people were trying to impose their belief on us" (Andrade). For many, this was a familiar experience, growing up in a Catholic dominated region; yet their perspective was fresher, more socially conscious and critical. Nicole Acosta, a student journalist who was successful in having the clinic defense action written up in the student paper, experienced her Catholic background and budding feminist consciousness in an acute antagonism. As she described in a video interview included in the documentary *Defending a Choice for Women*:

> As my assignment for Intro to Women's Studies, I started to go to A Choice for Women where they were having clinic defense. I ran into this Catholic priest.... [transition to Nicole speaking at the clinic] The priest that is here today, I have been watching him, and he looked very familiar. Then I decided that I knew who he was, he was the very same priest that did my communion and confirmation, when I was eight years old and then thirteen years old. And this very same priest just came up to all of us early in the morning and said that we are misguided and confused.

Other students identified with the clinic patients and defenders. As one student recounted for the class:

> What really shocked me was that most of them were our age or younger, and the vast majority was with their boyfriends coming to pick them up and driving them off. And if not that, their parents, and one girl, her dad had picked her up [Lopez].

These ethnographic lessons were explored in conjunction with academic scholarship about the constitutional protection of choice, institutional political power, and the power of material resources (Roberts; Correa and Petchesky). The historic abortion restrictions and contemporary abortion issues were covered in their textbook; and they were surprised to discover that women did not always have the right to make decisions, or have access to resources impacting their body, life, and educational options. As we learned about *Roe v. Wade*, they were indignant to discover that women's access to clinics continued to be impeded. They were impressive in their righteous anger as they screamed back at pro-life picketers' biblical condemnations, their blue rounds held high above their head. "The personal is political" became more than an historical mantra from the 1960s women's movement about which they read; it applied to them as well. They experienced unanticipated resistance to their interest in Women's Studies from family and friends, and they excitedly spoke up as we discussed concepts such as "lesbian-baiting" and stereotypes of feminists. They discovered that it was impossible to keep their lessons inside the classroom and away from their personal lives as they dealt with nonplussed fathers and boyfriends. Furthermore, they were encouraged to conduct ethnographic fieldwork and experience feminist activities firsthand. For their presentations, they incorporated non-textual materials to engage our senses — photographs, video clips, and music. Visual anthropological/sociological methodologies were easily incorporated in the interdisciplinary Women's Studies classroom. Had they not experienced firsthand the pro-life picketers at the clinic engaged in patient harassment, they might have written off the importance of *Roe* to historical footnotes. Had they not seen the documentary *Defending a Choice for Women*, they might have believed that the Catholic picketers were politically inconsequential or harmless. However, it was the combination of these historical textbook lessons, and the ethnographic fieldwork in feminist activism which provided an engaged education in women's reproductive rights and health.

Works Cited

Asch, Timothy, and Patsy Asch. "Film in Ethnographic Research." In *Principles of Visual Anthropology*. Ed. Paul Hockings. New York: Mouton de Gruyter, 2003, pp. 335–360.

Baird-Windle, Patricia, and Elanor J. Bader. *Targets of Hatred: Anti-Abortion Terrorism*. New York: Palgrave, 2001.

Blanchard, Dallas A. *The Anti-Abortion Movement and the Rise of the Religious Right: From Polite to Fiery Protest*. New York: Twayne, 1994.

Borgmann, Caitlin, and Catherine Weiss. "Beyond Apocalypse and Apology: A Moral Defense of Abortion." *Perspectives on Sexual and Reproductive Health* 35(1) (January–February 2003): 40–43.

Burowoy, Michael. *Ethnography Unbound: Power and Resistance in the Modern Metropolis*. Berkeley: University of California Press, 1991.

Correa, Sonia, and Rosalind Petchesky. "Reproductive Rights and Sexual Rights: A Feminist Perspective." In *Culture, Society, and Sexuality: A Reader*. Eds. Richard Parker and Peter Aggleton. New York: Routledge, [1999] 2003, pp. 298–315.

Deflem, Mathieu. "The Boundaries of Abortion Law: Systems Theory from Parsons to Luhmann and Habermas." *Social Forces* 76(3) (March 1998): 775–818.

Donovan, Patricia "The Holy War." *Family Planning Perspectives* 17(1) (January–February 1985): 5–9.

Faludi, Susan. *Backlash: The Undeclared War Against American Women*. New York: Anchor, 1991.

Franzosi, Roberto. "Narrative Analysis — or Why (and How) Sociologists Should Be Interested in Narrative." *Annual Review of Sociology* (24) 1998: 517–54.

Fried, Marlene Gerber. "Abortion in the United States — Legal but Inaccessible." In *Abortion Wars: A Half Century of Struggle, 1950–2000*. Ed. Rickie Solinger. Berkeley: University of California Press, 1998, pp. 208–226.

Ginsburg, Faye D. *Contested Lives: The Abortion Debate in an American Community*. Berkeley: University of California Press, 1998.

Gold-Steinberg, Sharon, and Abigail J. Stewart. "Psychologies of Abortion: Implications of a Changing Context." In *Abortion Wars: A Half Century of Struggle, 1950–2000*. Ed. Rickie Solinger. Berkeley: University of California Press, 1998, pp. 356–373.

Joffe, Carole. "Roe v. Wade at 30: What Are the Prospects for Abortion Provisions?" *Perspectives on Sexual and Reproductive Health* 35(1) (January–February 2003): 29–33.

Kolbert, Kathryn, and Andrea Miller. "Legal Strategies for Abortion Rights in the Twenty-First Century." In *Abortion Wars: A Half Century of Struggle, 1950–2000*. Ed. Rickie Solinger. Berkeley: University of California Press, 1998, pp. 95–110.

Lofland, John, and Lyn H. Lofland. *Analyzing Social Settings: A Guide to Qualitative Observation and Analysis*. New York: Wadsworth, 1995.

MacDougall, David. *The Corporeal Image: The Ethnography, and the Senses*. Princeton, NJ: Princeton University Press, 2006.

Maxwell, Carol J.C. "Coping with Bereavement through Activism: Real Grief, Imagined

Death, and Pseudo-Mourning Among Pro-Life Direct Activists." *Ethos* 23(4) (December 1995): 437–452.

Mead, Margaret. "Visual Anthropology in a Discipline of Words." In *Principles of Visual Anthropology.* Ed. Paul Hockings. New York: Mouton de Gruyter, 2003, pp. 3–10.

Page, Cristina. *How the Pro-Choice Movement Saved America: Freedom, Politics and the War on Sex.* New York: Basic, 2006.

Pheterson, Gail, and Yamila Azize. "Abortion Practice in the Northeast Caribbean: 'Just Write Down Stomach Pain.'" *Reproductive Health Matters* 13(26) 2005: 44–53.

Polletta, Francesca. "Contending Stories: Narrative in Social Movements." *Qualitative Sociology* 21(4) 1998, pp. 419–446.

Roberts, Dorothy E. "Punishing Drug Addicts Who Have Babies: Women of Color, Equality, and the Right of Privacy." In *Abortion Wars: A Half Century of Struggle, 1950–2000.* Ed. Rickie Solinger. Berkeley: University of California Press, 1998, pp. 124–155.

Ross, Loretta J. "African-American Women and Abortion." In *Abortion Wars: A Half Century of Struggle, 1950–2000.* Ed. Rickie Solinger. Berkeley: University of California Press, 1998, pp. 161–207.

Rozell, Mark J., and Clyde Wilcox. "Second Coming: The Strategies of the New Christian Right." *Political Science Quarterly* 111(2) (Summer 1996): 271–294.

Saletan, William. *Bearing Right: How Conservatives Won the Abortion War.* Berkeley: University of California Press, 2003.

Schaeffer, Joseph H. "Videotape: New Techniques of Observation and Analysis in Anthropology." In *Principles of Visual Anthropology.* Ed. Paul Hockings. New York: Mouton de Gruyter, 2003, pp. 255–284.

Staggenborg, Suzanne. *The Pro-Choice Movement: Organization and Activism in the Abortion Conflict.* New York: Oxford University Press, 1991.

Strickler, Jennifer, and Nicholas L. Danigelis. "Changing Frameworks in Attitudes Toward Abortion." *Sociological Forum* 17(2) (June 2002): 187–201.

Van Maanen, John. *Tales of the Field: On Writing Ethnography.* Chicago: University of Chicago Press, 1988.

Wilder, Marcy J. "The Rule of Law, the Rise of Violence, and the Role of Morality: Reframing America's Abortion Debate." In *Abortion Wars: A Half Century of Struggle, 1950–2000.* Ed. Rickie Solinger. Berkeley: University of California Press, 1998, pp. 73–94.

Woliver, Laura R. "Ethical Dilemmas in Personal Interviewing." *PS: Political Science and Politics* 35(4) (December 2002): 677–678.

Get Out of My Uterus!

A Manifesto Against Reproductive Politics in the Academic World and in the World at Large

Domnica Radulescu

The fabricated images of bloody mangled fetuses the size of newborn babies, the signs saying "Abortion stops a beating heart," the gigantic crosses looming over highways, the more recent pre–2008 election signs saying "Obama Nation — Abortion Nation" — you've seen them at one point or another in your lifetime if you live in America and you move around. So must you have seen the crowds of emboldened women of all ages marching down the streets of our nation's capital or of large American cities holding signs saying "Keep abortion legal!" There is one pro-choice sign in particular that says in slogan form that which I will try to develop in this manifesto: "I shouldn't have to be here!" And I shouldn't have to be writing this essay.

As co-founding chair of the Women's and Gender Studies Program at my institution I should not have to advise the students in the organization affiliated to my program to come up with their own pro-choice speakers, activities, and forums in order to stand up to the barrage of "pro-life" speakers and events organized by our Students for Life organization. Yet as a thinking, lucid, educated, emancipated woman, feminist and professional of the twenty-first century I have no choice but to do just that, and no apologies for the intended pun! I shouldn't have to try to match pro-choice speakers to the line of anti-choice speakers that the Students for Life organization tirelessly keeps bringing to campus and to try to convince liberal colleagues who maintain that "we should hear both sides of the debate," or "engage in dialogue," that the two sides of the debate are *not* equal, that what goes on in a woman's uterus, fallopian tubes, genital organs is nobody's business but that of the woman who is the sole possessor of those organs and body parts and that when it comes to political issues of ethnicity, race, freedom of speech, they wouldn't really want to support a speaker who advocates a return to slavery, institutionalized anti–Semitism, preventing women from getting an education or someone who supports dictatorial systems of governance or taking away the freedom of speech amendment from the citizens of the United States. That simply we, they, none of us should have to be "here," in the place of a public discussion in the middle of our university campuses, in the middle of a discussion that debates whether or not it is all right to create policies deciding on the movement and division of cells inside that much idealized, fetishized, too often abused and not enough respected with the distance and neglect it deserves female part: the uterus, or poetically and even mythically, or religiously called "the womb."

Most American university campuses have "pro-life" and pro-choice student organizations that bring their own speakers, are funded by the universities, their alumni and boards of trustees, and organize events, forums, make posters or tee-shirts and engage in activism for their respective causes. From large state universities like Arizona State to Ivy leagues like Princeton, Yale, or Harvard, to my own small liberal arts university in Virginia, students "for life" or "right to life" student organizations are relentless in their activism. And, to be fair, so are pro-choice student organizations, or pro-choice coalitions, from Advocates for Choice at the University of Wisconsin, to the Penn for Choice student organization, to University Choice Coalition at the University of Minnesota, to my own small liberal arts university's students for choice organization. An interesting phenomenon, nationwide, is that of pro-choice religious organizations such as Catholics for Choice or Kentucky Religious Coalition for Reproductive Choice; these organizations hold the view that it is precisely their religion and their belief in the sacredness of a woman's right to make decisions that govern her own body that motivates their pro-choice activism.[1]

Inversely, the newest movement of "pro-life" groups is that of Feminists for Life, whose president, Serrin Foster, graced even our small campus with a visit and a talk several years ago. The move to appropriate a feminist face and slogans such as "women deserve better," a feminist rhetoric such as the "right to choose of the unborn baby," and the use of the denomination "feminist" itself have emerged as the new tactics of "pro-life" groups in an attempt to attract young, hip, emancipated students on university campuses and trap them with the lure of "feminism." This continues the move started already in the seventies when anti-abortion activist Joseph Scheidler was urging in his *Closed: 99 Ways to Stop Abortion:* "[R]arely use the word 'fetus.' Use 'baby' or 'unborn child.' You don't have to surrender to their vocabulary.... They will start using your terms if you use them." "At anti-abortion demonstrations, 'The baby has to have a choice!' became a favorite chant," notes Susan Faludi (405). It turns out that the ruse of the "pro-lifers" is a double one: use words like "unborn child" for a microscopic set of cells scientifically called an embryo or for the fetus but also appropriate the feminist language where suitable in order to make a "pro-women" argument to the undecided, the young and naïve, such as young and vulnerable university women for instance. The ruse is the pretense of a non-threatening, apparently reconciliatory feminism — certainly not the one which on campuses like my own is still often used pejoratively, derisively because it uncompromisingly stands for certain inalienable rights of women in society — but a feminism that allows women to be "real" women, to accomplish their maternal urges before they even graduate from college, a feminism that intrudes into those fetishized or demonized female body parts by wishing and acting to create policies that would allow states, the government, churches, husbands and fathers to have control over what happens inside those body parts and private female spaces.

During the talk given on our campus, Serrin Foster looked around the room and wondered out loud at some point why she didn't see more babies on our campuses? Hmmm, let's see, maybe because men and women normally go to university campuses in order to obtain a solid and highly priced education with which to secure their future and not to turn these campuses into huge daycare centers? Could that be the reason why our campuses may be lacking in the all too heart-warming spectacle of women students pushing along baby strollers or carrying snuggles with new-born babies hanging around their necks in the front while their school backpacks with their French or chemistry textbooks are hanging on their backs?

These initiatives belong to the new "pro-life" campaign to turn what is often perceived as the severe face of no-nonsense, pro-choice feminists to the benevolent sexism of what Susan Faludi calls "faked emotions — pity for single women, worry over the fatigue level of career women, concern for the family" (72), or that of even more pricelessly phony sentiments of someone like Phyllis Schlafly, a Harvard educated lawyer "who opposed the ERA 'because it would take away the marvelous legal rights of a woman to be a full-time wife and mother in the house supported by her husband'" (Faludi 239). This is a campaign to use pretense "worry," for women, for family, for the "crisis" of the family, and create an illusion of concern for women's bodies, welfare, lives. On my university campus, the night when the Women's Studies Program brought to campus Lisa Johnson Firth, a feminist human rights international lawyer, to speak about the violence against women perpetrated as a result of human trafficking and abuses of female migrant workers in Western countries, our student "pro-life" organization brought to campus none other than Phyllis Schlafly and scheduled her speech exactly at the same time as that of the feminist human rights activist. Could the message of that strategic scheduling have been something like this: the violence perpetuated against women's bodies is not really that important, what is really important is to make sure we convince the young women on this campus that their education is for naught, or maybe just good enough so they can entertain their husbands or better raise their children as they savor their "marvelous legal rights" "to be a full-time wife and mother in the house supported by her husband?" And let us not worry about violence or sexual violence against women, too much is made of that anyways, as much as we might "worry" about the welfare and health of the women who have not yet taken full advantage of their reproductive apparatus. And let us not worry about the legal protection women sometimes need from the very husbands who care for and support them. "Let us worry about women's welfare," the unspoken but clear underlying message seems to be echoing in my mind as I think of that evening of the two parallel talks, by making sure they at least reproduce in a healthy and abundant way and keep taking advantage of that marvelous right to be mothers and housewives, all while we also make sure that were women ever to go out and earn their living and put this education to some use, that they are not equally paid, just so that they can see it's a tough world out there. And as for you, young aspiring women dreaming maybe of both a career and motherhood, you are better off just not exposing yourselves to the harshness of that unequal world, where you are paid less than the men in your field, because really you shouldn't be out there in the first place.

That is the clear message I got from that strategic scheduling, and from that disturbing overlap between a feminist international human rights lawyer working to protect women against physical and sexual violence and a pseudo-feminist who tells women they should forget about claiming all the rights that actually made it possible for her to be there giving that talk in Lee Chapel, on that schizophrenic night on our campus, the very year we were celebrating twenty years of co-education and of women having access to our university's resources.

As part of the "feminists for life" agenda, the turn of the century American Suffragette Susan B. Anthony is often invoked, as she was during Foster's speech at Washington and Lee, and as she is looming large on the website of the organization, together with a quote by her on the necessity to create "a better state of things for mothers generally." Who in their right mind wouldn't agree with that? Only that taken out of context and yanked away from the totality of Susan B. Anthony's life and of the even larger work of the first American feminists' work and principles, which were unequivocally supportive of women's freedom and possession of their own bodies, including the freedom to refuse sex to their husbands, the quote — just like the feminist rhetoric or bits of feminist statements used by anti-choice groups — is manipulated to serve the larger agenda of "feminists for life." This agenda in turn corresponds to the larger agenda of anti-feminists and corresponds to the very agenda of the Phyllis Schlaflys of America and ultimately to the agenda of patriarchal values that oppose, undermine, stand in the way of the full participation of women in all aspects of social and political life.

Let us be clear about a couple of issues: the philosophical/religious controversy over when does personhood or life start, over whether the life of a grown living woman may be less or more precious than that of a utopian cluster of divided cells, may make for an interesting controversy in a philosophy or history of religions class, or at a cocktail party, but it has no business in the making of policies and in university activities, if universities and colleges are to remain places of learning, acquisition of and respect for knowledge and critical thinking. And let us be equally clear about another issue: the "pro-life" groups and feminists for life organizations are after one thing and one thing alone: keeping women tied to those "marvelous legal rights" "to be a full-time wife and mother in the house supported by her husband." As was the agenda of the Catholic Church over the centuries, as was the agenda of the New Right leaders in the seventies, as was Franco's agenda in Spain,[2] as is the agenda of the evangelical and extreme right leaders and advocates right now in the two thousands in the United States of America.

A woman's ability to complete an education, to pursue a career, to even as much as take an occasional weekend trip or go to a movie by herself, let alone pursue public office all are dependent to a significant degree upon her ability to be in charge of her reproductive choices. Faludi says it quite eloquently:

> All of women's aspirations — whether for education, work, or any form of self-determination — ultimately rest on their ability to decide whether and when to

bear children. For this reason, reproductive freedom has always been the most popular item in each of the successive feminist agendas — and the most heavily assaulted target of each backlash [414].

The agenda of anti-choice groups, organizations, movements and ideologies is unequivocally an anti-woman and anti-emancipation agenda. The most flagrant proof of it is that their activism does not stop with abortion, but targets all forms of contraception, as well as science-based and realistic sexual education in schools and among young and sexually active people. We now have pharmacists who refuse to fill out prescriptions for birth control based on their religious beliefs, insurance companies like my own that cover nothing or close to nothing toward women's birth control medication but do cover erectile dysfunction medication such as Viagra for men. Federally funded sex education programs were dwindling or disappearing under George W. Bush and were being replaced by abstinence-only programs in the face of which even the daughter of rabid anti-choice politician Sarah Palin laughed on national television, saying they are inefficient. In fact, since 1997 until President Obama took office, the federal government had spent more than one and a half million dollars on abstinence-only programs that not only have proven ineffective time and again, but also impart erroneous information to young people about sex and sexuality. Finally, and thankfully, President Obama actually removed funding for such inefficient programs and increased funding for comprehensive sex education programs that have proven effective in both preventing teen pregnancies and sexually transmitted diseases. And then Pope Benedict goes to Africa and tells people that condoms actually contribute to the spread of AIDS.

The ultimate target of any anti-choice group or movement or ideology is *women*, their sexuality and their self-determination. It is also these same groups, as well as anti-choice politicians, senators, governors, justices, people who hold the reins of the law, of policy making and governance in this country and who have often voted against federally funded programs to support single mothers, or to create and fund daycare centers, or to prevent teen pregnancy. Their worry isn't really the growth or protection of the embryo or fetus, it isn't even life, but really women's self-determination.

There are certain values which, in a supposedly democratic society, we have come to take for granted and ignore universities, these revered, both ancient and modern institutions of liberal thinking, respect for knowledge and science, upholders of democratic principles, are not sponsoring or debating any longer; these are values that no longer need debating *because* they are part of our accepted sense of equality, secularism, and most importantly, on policies based on science and pragmatic evidence. For those discussions, not even the country's most conservative institutions and student groups set aside time, physical space and money. The day when I see five-week-old embryos walking down the streets of my town or holding their mother's hands or playing in the park down the street, talking, laughing, running, that day, I might consider having a debate about a woman's right to the integrity and decisions that regulate her body versus the independent right to life of that half an inch gnome trotting down my street — which no mistake about it — can be the most adored cluster of divided cells in the world *if* and *when* desired by the woman carrying it. However, until that day comes that is still in the realm of science fiction, and "I shouldn't have to be here."[3]

I am not arguing here the pros, the strengths, the righteousness, the necessity, for women's lives of the pro-choice agenda versus the so called "pro-life" agenda. I am arguing that we shouldn't have to be here, and that we shouldn't have to argue for a right that in any true democracy should be taken for granted. I am arguing that the biological activities that may or may not go on inside women's uteruses and reproductive apparatus should not be politicized, and least of all should it be the target of campus activism. But that we have to do it just like we have to defend ourselves and fight for our life if we were attacked in our home in the middle of the night. If someone intruded in our intimacy, in the very cocoon of what we consider our most sacred right — that to our privacy — and put a knife to our throat or a gun to the back of our head and asked us to repeat the Lord's prayer after them, or to give them access to our bodies, or to swear that we believed in what *they* believed in, wouldn't we fight back with all our might? Or would you just give in and go ahead and say the lord's prayer even if you didn't believe in it, just to save your life? But then what if he/she wanted more, what if he/she wanted you to do anything that his/her God might be telling him/her to make you do at that point in time?

And another thing: would you like to have a dialogue with that intruder and try to see his/her point of view at the late hour of the night when he/she has barged into your home trying to rob, rape, kill or convince you of the righteousness of his/her God? Would you like to listen maybe to his/her position about why he/she is trying to rob or force his/her convictions literally down your threatened throat? Would you be interested in hearing that they were doing that because maybe he/she had a sad childhood or even more formidably, because God just spoke to him/her and guided him/her to do just what they are doing: stand there at 2:00 A.M. with a knife stuck to your pulsing jugular and force you to say the Lord's Prayer? And this intruder might be in a hurry too, because he/she might have to get up early for a Sunday mass in order to shoot Doctor George Tiller right in the middle of those alleluias resounding in a good old American town filled with God-loving Christians, in Wichita, Kansas, for example?[4] Don't these people have any idea of semantics? Don't they know that killing someone just because you don't agree with their politics, isn't really a life-affirming gesture? Would you truly be interested in what that person had to say and would you want to hear "both sides of the story," other than maybe if you were possessed by a wild anthropological curiosity to see how far human irrationality can reach?

I grew up and lived in the most oppressive of Communist dictatorships behind the notorious Iron Curtain during the 60s, 70s and early 80s before I escaped and made my way to the United States as a political refugee. In 1966, when I was only a few years old, abortion was made illegal, as were all forms of contraception. Women had to reproduce and bring up children for the Communist utopia that we had to attain under our "beloved" leader Nicolae Ceausescu in Romania. Children were "the future" not only of the country but of Communism itself, wouldn't you know it. Yet women, par-ticularly those living in urban areas and working full-time as most women did, somehow kept falling short of that Utopia and instead risked their lives, often lost their lives or remained damaged for life, in dark hospital rooms, basements, alleys, someone's apartment late at night, having illegal abortions performed onto them or performing them with their own hands. If caught, the doctor performing it would face many years or life in prison at best, or face capital punishment at worst. It was not in the name of a Christian God whispering in the ears of our leaders that women's most basic rights to have control over their reproductive apparatus were all taken away, but in the name of the state. "[M]arriage between demographic concerns and nationalist policies, turned women's bodies into instruments to be used in the service of the State" (quoted in Parrot and Cummings, 28). Women's lives "became less important to the greater social good" (Parrot and Cum-mings, 28). Between 1966 and 1989, nine thousand four hundred and fifty five women died from illegal abortions in Romania (Kligman 1992, 405–19).

Gail Kligman, in her ethnography *The Politics of Duplicity: Controlling Reproduction in Ceausescu's Romania* brilliantly testifies, through interviews with women and physicians, the multifarious and nefarious ways in which the Orwellian reproductive laws of Communist Romania tragically affected the entire texture of society, not women alone, but also men, children — everybody. In 1989, after the revolutions that tore down communist walls, curtains, systems and dictators, an entire world looked in horror at Romania's post-revolution children — blank eyed, or tear faced orphans staring from behind bars of insalubrious orphanages or crying in the streets of Romanian cities, often AIDS-ridden, drugging themselves by sniffing glue, pitifully skinny and uncared for. The *New York Times* couldn't get enough of Romania's children for a while following the 1989 Revolution, as if, only blocks away from their offices, a world full of starving, abused or killed in drive by shoot-outs children did not even exist. Just leafing through the pages of photographs in the book *Ceausescu's Children*, by Kent Klich (photographer), recent Nobel Laureate Herta Muller, and Chris Steele-Perkins (photographer), one cannot but be shaken, angered, brought to tears at the sight of Ceausescu's nightmarish legacy of abandoned children. Gail Kligman has got the right answer and poses the right question, while the *New York Times* went around the right question and answer: "What are those desperate children the result of?" They are nothing more or less than the tragic offspring of Ceausescu's reproductive laws, of policies that intruded deep inside women's uteruses for decades, and that were the cause of ten thousand women's deaths from illegal abortions and unwanted pregnancies. When the State, the church, husbands, fathers, governments are equipped with laws that regulate women's reproductive apparatus, that's what you get: Dantesque spectacles of abandoned, suffering, dying children, and of women bleeding to death in back alleys or on hospital tables with doctors looking at them but not touching them so that they not be accused of having performed an abortion.[5] The first Human Rights Watch report after the Revolution, in December of 1990, also lucidly links the 100,000 orphans who, according to the report lived in "Dickensian institutions" with Ceausescu's pronatalist laws instituted in 1966 and then strengthened in 1985 by the law of "demographic command bodies" according to which women had to undergo periodic gynecological exams at their workplace to make sure they were not pregnant, and if they were, to make sure they did not abort.[6]

In the history of the Catholic Church, starting with Saint Augustine and Thomas Aquinas,[7] to Pope Pius XI and up to today's Pope Benedict, any form of contraception has been regarded as sinful and condemnable, since it encourages fornication without conception and abortion has been considered an even greater sin, akin to that of murder. Though inspired by

Christian faith and century-old teachings to which new cults and agendas have been overlapped like a formidable palimpsest of interdictions and requirements placed on the female body, the "pro-life" groups, organizations, or individuals in the United States, whose fierce activities were intensified in the seventies after the *Roe v. Wade* verdict, are actually not different in the substance and scope of their actions and ideologies from those of the Communist dictatorship I grew up under or from those of Franco's Spain in the late forties, fifties, and sixties. In fact, if that proverbial gun or knife mentioned earlier were pointed at my head or jugular and if by some *reductio ad absurdum* I were to be asked to choose under which system of laws governing women's bodies would I prefer to live — the far right one of the type we see in the United States, or the far left one under my good old Communist dictatorship — I believe that, were I not to have enough courage to just say "shoot" or "strike," and were I to choose life in that fraction of a second, as images of the two beautiful and brilliant children I have raised would flash before my eyes, or of the multitude of human and intellectual riches that had made my life worthwhile till that point, were I to choose life in that millisecond, I believe I would go for the Communist dictatorship all over again. At least, there is a concrete pragmatic, palpable motivation in the Communist interdictions on reproductive freedom: that people bring up lots of young people in order to serve, work and create that new Utopian State, no matter how absurd and how oppressive that State may be. I can understand the idea of work force. But that's just my personal taste.

The personal is political? Watch out what you are wishing for. The notion that the "personal is political," first launched in the article with the same title by radical feminist and founding member of New York Radical Women, Carol Hanisch, in 1969 emerged when feminists were rightfully trying to make the argument that the domination, abuse, inequality, violence that is perpetrated by men upon women is not simply a matter of personal life, but one of "gendered inequity," and therefore, in order to repair that inequity, political action was required. Germaine Greer also strengthened the notion of the personal as political by developing the thesis that the oppression of women starts in the most intimate place, namely that of their relationship with their bodies. This notion however has become worn and used too lightly by feminists themselves and thus much of its original and profound meaning has come to be distorted or banalized or even turned into its opposite. Really, in the presence of laws recognizing and regulating issues of gender inequity, violence against women, protecting women and their bodies from violence and providing the necessary reproductive freedom to their bodies, the personal should stay personal, in the sense of the private, the intimate, the area where we don't want the State, the Government, the Church interfering and telling us what to do. The "personal" needs to become political however, whenever women's bodies are *not* protected by the law against abuses and violence, whenever their reproductive choices are *not* protected by the law, because then really the personal *is* a matter of gender inequity and therefore a political issue. But when politics enters our bedrooms and uteruses in order to control them, that is when the personal needs to remain as such by being protected under laws that depoliticize it. As Catharine MacKinnon has pointed out, the situation of a woman being raped or sexually abused needs to be treated politically and judicially. A society needs to take that violence outside the realm of the personal and the private, and make it a legal matter, establish a policy against that violence, so that the woman's intrinsic right to the integrity of her body be protected and so that the man, who uses his social power as the privileged gender to dominate the woman as the unprivileged and unprotected one, can be prevented from violating that woman's humanity and the integrity of her body in the private space.[8]

In 2009, at Washington and Lee, another Feminists for Life talk graced our campus. The announcement indulged in the same ruse discussed above: using feminist rhetoric to envelop an anti-choice agenda, and using "faked emotions" and "care" or "concern" for women's welfare to envelop that same agenda: "Karen Shablin will address the impact of healthcare policymaking on abortion, including the controversial implementation of the family cap in welfare reform. Ms. Shablin, Feminists for Life of America speaker, will present 'Abortion: A Betrayal of Feminism.'" Karen Shablin is a former NARAL member turned feminist for life who has lead events such as the Walk for Life in San Francisco. Like the other feminists for life who have paraded on our campus, such as Serrin Foster or Phillys Schlafly, she uses feminist rhetoric in order to take away the bottom line element of feminism itself: choice. The 2010 Walk for Life march that is being prepared puts forth the following slogans: "Abortion does violence to women and to their children, both physically and emotionally. It harms women and men; it divides families and society. Women — and all people — deserve better than abortion." The ruse here is that this rhetoric presents abortion as an obligation, not as a right, an option, an alternative, as part of the panoply of reproductive choices women should have in any society. From these slogans, you would think pregnant women were being taken by force from their homes and made to have abortions. Secondly, it sensationalizes abortion in the way it connects the idea of violence with a medical procedure that is less painful and invasive than a man's vasectomy, and has fewer threats to a woman's health than the repeated use of erectile dysfunction medication for men, such as Viagra or Cialis, whose side effects range from dangerous levels of blood pressure, to dizziness and nausea, to death. Thirdly, it banks on myths about abortion and unscientific information such as "post-abortion syndrome" of women who have undergone abortions and of which *no* evidence was found by the American Psychological Association. Actually Nada Stotland, MD and former president of the Association of Women Psychiatrists, noted in an article in *Journal of the American Medical Association* that: "The incidence of diagnosed psychiatric illness and hospitalization is considerably lower following abortion than following childbirth."[9]

The fact that the chair of the women's and gender studies program at my university was approached and asked to advertise or attend the event, is part of the ruse, of course. I was traveling in Turkey at the time when I read the announcement on my laptop, and I couldn't help wondering at the following paradox: while women were strikingly absent from certain public spaces, particularly in the old section of town in Istanbul, and while many were wearing the Turkish scarf on their heads, some the burka, despite the interdiction started by the progressive president Ataturk,[10] I found out that abortion and contraception are legal and not a source of political controversy in Turkey. At the same time, the streets and public spaces of our American large and small cities are equally filled with men and women, yet at every moment, those of us in the millions who care about keeping our reproductive rights, have to constantly keep vigil that our uteruses aren't under attack, aren't subject to political controversy, subject of talks on the campuses we work or study at. At least Turkish women did not have to worry about their reproductive rights. Which one would you rather have, I asked myself in that same perverse *reduction ad absurdum* game: would you rather have to wear a silk scarf on your head or have the state dictate the number of children you must have? I'd go for the silk scarf. The irony baffled me as I saw the email announcement. A chain of emails was generated after I responded from my Turkish hotel whose hostess was a feminist woman writer, with a message objecting to the very farce of the Women's and Gender Studies program being asked to advertise the event and to the very use of the word "feminist" in the context of an anti-choice agenda. I will quote here one faculty member's response, which I think best supports this very manifesto and which I also believed was the most eloquent response to my liberal colleagues supporting the "let's have a dialogue and hear both sides" argument:

> On this issue, the feminist position is defined by individual choice to have an abortion or not on a case-by-case basis. It is "pro-choice," or, less unapologetically, democratic. The anti-feminist position is defined by its paternalistic, absolutist rejection of choice for all under all circumstances. It is "anti-choice," or, less euphemistically, totalitarian. "Women who do not support the right to an abortion" and whose "deeply felt reasons" for doing so doubtlessly include sectarian religious dogma (again absolutist and paternalistic) cannot qualify as feminist on this issue because they oppose the (definitive) exercise of individual choice. I find it hard to support the rights of people who don't support mine or others,' and I don't feel obligated to tolerate the intolerant. I also don't think an educational institution is obligated to give "equal time" to proponents of error, superstition and/or mendacity. If it were, we would be inundated with "intelligent" designers, holocaust deniers and free marketeers.

How ironic, I thought to myself while pondering on these exchanges, as I was strolling down the streets of Istanbul, that my university is sponsoring and hosting talks that undermine women's reproductive freedom, with only twenty years of co-education behind, and still with faculty, students, alumni and trustees who deplore co-education, feminism, the very Women's and Gender Studies Program that I chair and view them all as a threat to the "values," "traditions," or the honor system of our university. You don't even have to be a feminist to see the agenda: instill in young women the idea that their place isn't really in a university, in public office, in law firms as associates or in hospitals as medical doctors. On the other hand, right here in Istanbul, women cannot be vendors in the Egyptian Spice Bazaar or in the Grand Bazaar. Whether I want to buy some paprika or a scarf or a necklace or an item of underwear, I have to buy it from a male vendor who is practically forcing me into his store, shoving ten items under my nose at the same time and making me feel like a prisoner in his colorful and nice smelling boutique. But then the women cooking for them at home don't worry about reproductive choice. On yet another hand, the women amidst whom I grew up in my native Romania, worked full time, built careers in all professional domains, but were terrified of their own sexuality because it came with the possibility of unwanted pregnancy, or died in illegal abortions, or were left damaged for life from the same illegal procedures, being among the "lucky" ones to have survived. If you are a woman, is it better to live in Turkey, I wondered, in my newly democratic Romania, where contraception and abortion are now as available and affordable as a bar of chocolate, or in the United States? Is there no place on this earth where women can work, have control of their bodies, enjoy the home and the public space and where they can have all the basic rights all on the same side of a national border and at the same time in history? Maybe Norway and Sweden, I thought, just as I escaped the harassment of yet another Turkish vendor trying to pull me into his boutique and sell me some carpets.

I will conclude this manifesto with the following suggestions for American university campus feminists to fight the intrusion into women's bodies by pro-life groups.

1. Certain principles are non-negotiable and not subject to debate — the intrusion of state, church, government, men into women's uteruses and reproductive apparatus is one of them — hold on to your non-negotiable, non-compromising position, the same way you would if you had pro-slavery proponents or Holocaust deniers who wanted to speak on your campus. Ask yourselves: would you want to have a public discussion financed and sponsored by your university or organization in order to bring such people or groups to your campus?

2. Lucidly and consistently uncover, unveil, denounce the ruse, the farce, the false rhetoric of expressions as "feminists for life," of the sensationalizing and scientifically erroneous language used by anti-choice groups, or of downright offensively erroneous language such as the use of the term "Holocaust" to refer to aborted embryos or fetuses. Check out the history, etymology, and data about the actual Holocaust in case you may need reminding. The use of such terms is offensive to the very victims of the Holocaust.

3. Resist using the term "pro-life" in relation to what really are anti-choice groups, reveal the ruse and speak the truth any chance you get: pro-choice advocates are not "pro-abortion," but just that, pro choice, we believe in the right to reproductive freedom of women and men in society. We also stand for policies and programs that help and support single mothers, children of single working mothers, the creation of daycare centers, support for AIDS-infected, economically disadvantaged or abused children, the lives of grown women and mothers, and comprehensive, scientifically sound sex education to prevent teen pregnancies and sexually transmitted diseases. The so called "pro-life" groups and individuals often stand against such

programs, initiatives, thus contradicting the very notion of "pro-life." Furthermore the bans on unscientifically named procedures such as "partial birth abortions" and initiated or carried out because of the activism of these groups, often do not even leave an exception for the life or health of the mother. Who said "pro-life" means actually supporting, helping, facilitating life here on earth? Uncover the farce, reveal the ruse, any chance you get!

4. Inform yourselves and have pragmatic and scientific data that both demystify abortion myths and that illustrate the damage done to women, children and men, to whole societies when reproductive freedom is taken away (i.e., statistics of women who died from illegal abortions under totalitarian regimes or before *Roe v Wade* in America, or on numbers of abandoned children living in squalor or dying of Aids, such as the 100,000 of Ceausescu's legacy).

5. Use scientifically correct language about the stages of life, such as embryo and fetus, and do not adopt the language of the anti-choice groups, including the denomination "pro-life" which pro-choice advocates such as myself place between quotation marks, including expressions that have by now wrongly become part of legislative language under George W. Bush such as partial birth abortion, which was never recognized by the American Medical Association as a scientifically valid term for the procedure.[11]

6. Do not forget that "we shouldn't have to be here," we shouldn't have to defend our bodies from attacks by religiously fanatic groups who try to force their religious ideas upon our minds and body. It is religion that is just as personal as our bodies are. But that at times, given the constant attacks we "have no choice" but to defend our bodies. Wouldn't religious people defend their religion if the State told them they can't worship the way they wish to? Which is more personal to you, your body or your religion?

You may think this manifesto is too radical. Should you think so, do take a look at the data and at the historical evidence of countries, societies, regimes both in our modern era and throughout history that tried and succeeded in taking away women's reproductive freedom by criminalizing forms of contraception and abortion and controlling women's bodies, and, after you have done that in all earnestness, scientifically, non-sentimentally, do let me know what you really think of those many hundreds of thousands of women who have taken the law in their hands and exerted their own reproductive freedom in exchange for painful deaths; let me know what you really think of those gaunt, blank-eyed smeared faces of children staring at you from orphanages or streets in a Romanian city; let me know what you really think of those thousands of children from across the world from Brazil to Zimbabwe to the United States, dying from starvation, street violence, AIDS, sexual trafficking and abuse. And I would like to hear how that picture may possibly be a life-affirming one, if you consider yourself "pro-life." And until our American society renders you obsolete the way the societies and legislations of many Western and now even post–Communist East and central European countries and governments have done it, just know there still are many of us, in the thousands, if not millions, who do not buy your ruse, your feminist rhetoric, your concern for life particularly when you invade our university campuses where women and men come to be educated and to develop that which your fanaticism has rendered entirely dormant: a critical thinking.

But mostly, this manifesto is for liberals out there who think we should hear "both sides of the debate" and who have stopped manifesting in justified self-defense with a loud scream saying: "Get out of our uteruses" just like you would do if you were attacked in your own home in the middle of the night and would scream: "Get out of my house!" Shouldn't your body be even more sacred than your house? I am addressing all of you defenders of democratic values who on the reproductive freedom issue start your debate a sentence too late, instead of where that pro-choice slogan of young women in the streets of our nations starts it: "We shouldn't have to be here!"

Notes

1. Carol Walker Bynum and other Christian feminist theologians have in fact argued that in his teachings, actions, gestures about and toward women, Jesus of Nazareth was deeply respectful of a woman's body, her physical integrity and reproductive cycles.

2. During the Franco regime in Spain, the ban on abortion and contraception did not stop thousands of women from getting illegal abortion. The punishment for health professionals providing abortions and for the women getting them was imprisonment, "regardless of any risks to herself or the foetus, or of whether she had been a victim of rape or of incest." See Anny Brooksbank Jones' book *Women in Contemporary Spain* (85–87).

3. Actually the rabid anti-feminist and anti-choice activist Randall Terry used to carry around to his meetings an embalmed fetus dressed in miniature clothes and placed in a shoe-box "coffin" (Faludi 408).

4. Dr. George Tiller, who used to perform abortions, was shot and killed during a religious service in Wichita, Kansas, on May 31, 2009. The following other people were also killed in anti-abortion violent acts: in 1998, Dr. Barnett Slepian was shot and killed in New York and officer Robert Sanderson was killed in a planned parenthood

clinic; Dr. John Bayard Britton and his escort James H. Barrett were shot and killed in Pensacola, Florida, in 1994; and Dr. David Gunn was shot and killed in Pensacola, Florida, in 1993.

5. This was a common practice in Romania. Often when women were brought to an emergency room or a hospital because of a spontaneous miscarriage, doctors did not attend to them so that they could not be charged with inducing abortions.

6. See the part of the report: titled "Romania's Orphans: A Legacy of Repression," 2–4.

7. See Margaret Miles, *Carnal Knowing*, and her discussion of the ways in which the Catholic Church has viewed and tried to regulate women's sexuality and bodies in the Middle Ages and the Renaissance.

8. See MacKinnon's recent book *Women's Lives, Men's Laws*, and the arguments regarding the ways in which the laws of men need to be reframed in order to bring about true equality and to treat abuses against women as human rights violations.

9. See Stotland's article and quote in: "The Myth of the Abortion Trauma Syndrome."

10. President Ataturk was the creator of the modern and secular Republic of Turkey in the 1920s and 1930s.

11. The correct term is intact dilation and extraction, and the procedure is done when the health or life of the mother are in danger. However, in April 2007, the Supreme Court decided that the previous decision stating that the law was unconstitutional does not violate the Constitution. Justice Ruth Bader Ginsburg reacted to the lack of a health exception for the woman, pointing out that the decision would jeopardize both women's health and place doctors in a difficult bind. See also the July 7, 2009, *New York Times* article and interview with Justice Ginsburg, "The Place of Women on the Court."

Works Cited

Bazelon, Emily. "The Place of Women on the Court." *The New York Times*, July 7, 2009.
Bohlen, Celestine. "Romania's AIDS Babies: A Legacy of Neglect." *The New York Times*, February 8, 1990.
Brooksbank Jones, Anny. *Women in Contemporary Spain*. New York: St. Martin's, 1997.
Faludi, Susan. *Backlash: The Undeclared War against American Women*. New York: Doubleday, 1991.
Hanisch, Carol. "The Personal Is Political." In *Notes from the Second Year: Women's Liberation*. Eds. Shulamith Firestone and Anne Koedt. New York: Radical Feminism, 1970.
Human Rights Report. "Romania's Orphans: A Legacy of Repression." December 1, 1990. http://www.hrw.org/en/reports/1990/12/01/romanias-orphans-legacy-repression.
Kligman, Gail. "Abortion and International Adoption in Post–Ceausescu Romania." *Feminist Studies* 1992, 18(2):405–19.
_____. *The Politics of Duplicity: Controlling Reproduction in Ceausescu's Romania*. Los Angeles: University of California Press, 1998.
MacKinnon, Catharine. *Women's Lives, Men's Laws*. Cambridge, MA: Belknap Press of Harvard University Press, 2007.
Miles, Margaret. *Carnal Knowing*. Boston: Beacon, 1989.
Muller, Herta, and Kent Klich. *Children of Ceausescu*. New York: Umbrage, 2002.
Parrot, Andrea, and Nina Cummings. *Forsaken Females: The Global Brutalization of Women*. Lanham, MD: Rowman and Littlefield, 2006.

Perlez, Jane. "Romanian 'Orphans': Prisoners of Their Cribs." *The New York Times*, March 25, 1996.
Stotland, Nada. "The Myth of the Abortion Trauma Syndrome." *Journal of the American Medical Association* 268(15) (1992): 2078–2079.
Walker Bynum, Carol. *Jesus as Mother: Studies in the Spirituality of the High Middle Ages.* Los Angeles: University of California Press, 1984.

Teaching to Spite
Your Body

ROBIN M. LEBLANC

I have invented a new drinking game for middle-aged women. The rules are simple, but you'll need to, as they say, "preload" for this one. Drink a few (the less you eat, the faster this goes), and then say: "Cunt." The more ways you can say the word, the more sentences you can put it in, the more you can own it — as in, "my fucking cunt" or "because, frankly, I'm just a cunt" — the more you win.

What do you win? You'll be heard. Nobody at the table will turn away. No one will talk over you, disbelieve you, amend you, correct you, moderate you, mock you, or simply fail to notice you. Because of what you have to say, your voice will have authority. I've been a teacher for nearly 20 years. I can think of many other ways of forging a position of authority from the resources available in the circumstances around me, but the "Cunt Game" is by far the easiest path I know to the elusive thrill of being listened to. Say the word, lie back, be heard.

You might wonder how I came up with this gem of a drinking game. The truth is I borrowed the idea from students at my university. A little more than a year ago, a "humorous" article in one of our two student newspapers mimicked the national college basketball championship's March Madness playoff bracket by ranking students by name in categories such as "pretentious slut" and "most likely to come out of the closet." Among those of us faculty with a few years of service under our belts, the incident was depressingly unsurprising if still much debated. In a typical year, I might have let it slide to the back of my mind once I had written my usual protest letter and joined colleagues in asking the predictable sets of questions of administrators. But one part of the bracket article rankled so badly I have not been able to let it go.

45

In their section ranking women by alleged sexual exploits, the authors described our campus as a "Cuntry Club." The very personally directed and appallingly obscene discussion of female students' purported sexuality was, of course, a worse thing than the use of "cunt" in the description of the university. Still, the Cuntry Club reference bothered me in a way the student rankings did not. I think it was because I saw the meanness directed at students as limited to students in ways I could not understand the Cuntry Club labeling of the entire institution to be. I could stick up for students by calling the article authors bullies, and I did. But because I also now worked at an institution that some number of male students considered it funny to call a Cuntry Club, I felt that I, too, as a possessor of the genitalia referenced, had been attacked. I needed to stick up for myself, as well as for the students, and for various reasons — but mostly because I am a teacher — I found that hard to do.

I could and did complain vociferously in print and in person that "cunt" is not the sort of word that should be allowed in a student newspaper at a private college that prides itself on its traditions of "civility" and "honor." But what I could not say, except to a few friends, is that because I am a woman, the article had dangerously plastered me with my cunt-ness. I walked around campus wondering if male students were thinking: "There goes another cunt," or "That's the cunt I had for intro." Moreover, I suspected that if I made it clear to my campus audience that I felt offended because I am a woman, then I took the risk of becoming a female teacher forever linked to her cunt. Students would think "cunt" every time I played devil's advocate in class discussion (something I do a lot because I teach courses such as Introduction to Political Philosophy and Gender and Politics). Every time I frustrated students with critical comments on their work, they would think "cunt." Eventually the students who liked me, perhaps especially the female students, would be loath to admit as much to their peers. Every time they mentioned me, they would cringe, waiting for the ugly word: "Cunt." Until recently, I was the only woman in the Politics Department, which is part of the overwhelmingly male Commerce School. My students are more frequently male and more frequently conservative than they would likely be at another liberal arts college. I worried that if, in that context, I pointed out how personally harassing I found the Cuntry Club notion to be, I would suffer a crucial loss of position.

When I thought my way through the peculiar significance I had given the Cuntry Club reference, I saw that my instincts revealed a surprising antipathy toward my femaleness. Despite nearly twenty years of "growing into my own skin" as a teacher, despite similarly long years of careful research on the relationship between gender and power, despite my own articulate critiques delivered in the classroom and beyond of the problematic ways in which we link assumptions about competence with gendered notions of the body, and despite real professional successes, I have not moved very far in my own consciousness raising. In some ways, although I am now in my forties, I am still the new college professor I was in my late twenties, envying seemingly more confident male colleagues who disguised their own youthfulness with professorial-looking goatees.

What I was thinking when I agonized over how to respond to "Cuntry Club" was that if "cunt" became (or already was) a standard way of viewing women at my institution, then I was stepping out onto a crumbling cliff every time I walked through the door of a classroom. The inescapable presence of my genitalia which might at any moment be acknowledged (in a student-to-student note, in an under-the-breath comment, in a throat-clear sort of half guffaw) made my professional status tenuous. Experience counted for nothing; the ability to grow a beard still counted for a lot.

Taking a step back, I can see how unable I have been to let go of gendered notions of competence. I have, if partly unbeknownst to myself, been eager to measure my own professional bearing and my skills as a pedagogue against masculinist standards. I might have spent the last two decades studying the problematic epistemology of male privilege, but when it comes to living my own life, I have worked quite hard to seem less female. Perhaps in my male-dominated discipline of political science, my masculinist aspirations were necessary. Yet, now that I see how easily I had assumed my professional success was dependent upon my capacity to make my students and colleagues forget my genitalia, I am taken aback by the problem of pedagogic authority more generally. I have started to ask new questions about it.

For example, instead of asking how, as a small woman, I might secure the sort of easy student confidence in my authority as a professor that I have seen some male colleagues bolster with beards, big bodies, and deep voices, I am now asking myself why I think I need that confidence. Instead of envying male colleagues who are not in danger of having their cunts erupt into their classrooms, I have started to ask if there are things students might learn from such a rupture. I ask if I would be a better teacher if I were working less hard to be a like-a-male professor and what, then, "better" would mean. And I find myself asking what male professors might find it hard to learn about teaching precisely because they do not have to work so hard to legitimate their professional position. I have come to wonder if I could put the cunt's authority to use in something other than a drinking game.

* * *

My teaching career started inauspiciously in graduate school when, at 23, I was handed my own section of Introduction to American Government. I looked younger than most of my students. I scrambled before every class to find a few things in my meager wardrobe that looked professional. I had been assigned an oblong, windowless room with acid green carpet. I felt I had to run back and forth across the front of the classroom seeking eye contact with the students flung out to the far edges. As I ran, I struggled breathlessly to shout above a noisy air-handling system pitched at the same frequency as my voice. My command on the rangy subject matter seemed weak to me, and when my dissertation adviser came to observe me, he noted that I repeated the word "OK" more than 100 times in 50 minutes. At the end of the term, my evaluations were as weak as expected. The only mystery was a student comment that claimed I had "ruined the lives of 35 people." I had 70 students, so I have always wondered what happened to the other 35.

I sought counsel from another faculty member, famous among under-graduate and graduate students alike for his inspiring teaching. He shook his head over my evaluation results. "I don't get it," he said. "You're so smart. You shouldn't have trouble with this." I must have looked up at him with scared puppy eyes because he didn't push the conversation much farther. "Try speaking from the diaphragm," he suggested.

The advice wasn't useless. In focusing on my diaphragm, I distracted myself from some of the terror I felt in big university lecture halls, and I probably came across as more confident. I could make myself heard above the roar of air conditioner fans. I pulled my evaluation scores into the low end of the university's average spread and somehow pulled myself through several more courses as a graduate-student teacher.

My first full-time teaching job was at a small liberal arts college with small classes and a friendlier atmosphere than that I had confronted in the 100-level courses in a big state university. The students called me "Dr. Le Blanc," and they were starting to look younger. I had passed all of my grad-uate school exams with distinction, and I had written an award-winning dissertation. I was more comfortable with my competence in the subject matter. I began to relax a little, which if nothing else, made speaking from the diaphragm a lot easier.

One issue with which I continued to struggle was how to manage peri-odic challenges from large, class-clown-type males. I would sometimes get one or two in class who would make a show of not paying attention, or insisting quite openly that I did not know what I was talking about, or who would, with inappropriate laughter or vigorous head shaking or nudges to the guys sitting next to them, try enlisting their classmates in mocking me. Having long been a student myself, I sensed danger when a student of mine acted up like that. I thought that I if I couldn't assert myself against them effectively, I might find my entire class drifting into their mocking posture, seeing more value in fitting in with the alpha dogs among their peers than participating earnestly in my discussions of Socratic dialogues or the comparative justice of different electoral systems. I wanted to tamp those alpha dog students down, but I had trouble imagining how I might do that. I sensed that my gender was somehow involved, but I couldn't figure out how to neutralize it.

I had seen male authority in the classroom, but I had not had a female political science professor. As an undergraduate, I had also studied English as well as political science, and there and in language classes I had studied with a few female professors. Most of those classes were dominated by women students, however, and the kind of guys who really enjoyed the power play involved in open challenges to a teacher's competence weren't very common in the English major. Plus, I had the vaguely guilty sense that I, too, had been the sort of student who preferred male professors (confident, not bitchy) to female professors. I suppose I had unaccountably assumed that by the time I became a college teacher, I would have also been blessed with male traits.

After a particularly frustrating encounter with a truculent male in one of my classes, I shared the story with Isabel,[1] a female English professor whose office was a few doors down the hall from mine. Unlike male colleagues who often professed alienating surprise when I revealed uncertainty about my teaching, Isabel listened to me recount the troubling episode, nodding in sympathy. She was small like me, but more feminine in her flowing skirts than I thought I was in my tailored dresses and pantsuits. Her graying, curly hair billowed about her narrow-featured face, and she was pure in demonstrations of enthusiasm whenever a student or colleague said something she liked. When she shared an opinion of her own, she would stutter just a bit as if parting reluctantly with each juicy tidbit of thought, not infrequently sliding off along the way into asides that knit her brow as she spoke as if they were about to steal from her any possibility of coherence. When I first met her she seemed to me a bit wispy, as if she had become the elusive poetry she had taught for many years. She captured my imagination, but if anyone had asked me, I would have expressed real wonder at her ability to manage a classroom effectively. And yet she was a popular teacher, respected by students and colleagues, alike.

On the day I told her my story about the obnoxious male student, she startled me by snapping into an uncharacteristic firmness. "I used to have that problem, too," she said. "I'll tell you what you have to do. You have to humiliate those guys." Then, without asides, without a stutter, without any whimsy at all, she offered up a list of possible tactics. I think they were moves such as calling out the names of late students in sarcastic tones, firing impossibly difficult questions at troublemakers, moving down the aisle to teach while standing over their desks if they were pretending to ignore me, or simply acting maddeningly as if the offending student were not in the room.

In truth, Isabel had so many ideas, and over the last 15 years, I have taken her advice so completely to heart, that I can no longer separate in my memory what she suggested to me and what I invented for myself as my capacity to dish out strategic humiliation evolved with my growing maturity as a teacher and with my move to a different institution. However, no matter which of the tools in my arsenal are properly Isabel's and which I fashioned later to fit my own needs, I will always credit her as the mentor who was finally willing to put it to me baldly. Women professors are sometimes threatened simply because they are women, but they can fight back, lowering the defenses of their opponents and asserting control over their classrooms.

Over the years, I've become a better teacher than I was when I started, and my expanded confidence and aging face have made it easier for me to command authority in the classroom, even from skeptical males, without resorting to humiliation very often. Nonetheless, on occasion I've had to whip out Isabel's advice. Some of those times are memories I relish.

One fall, when our introductory sections of political philosophy all filled up, I entered my classroom at the beginning of the second week of the term to find a student who desperately wanted to add the course sitting on the floor. I had hoped for a few drops to make room for this student, but I was literally out of seats. I told the student on the floor to stay put for the class period because I was still mulling out how I might manage an addition. Could the dean find me another room? An extra chair?

As our class discussion began, I noticed a male student on the front row who did not seem engaged. He was lying back in his seat, his legs spread and stretched out as far as they would go. We were working carefully through a passage in John Locke's *Second Treatise*, but I didn't see a book on this student's desk.

"Where's your book?" I asked.

"I haven't bought it yet," was the reply.

"Did you get a syllabus last week?"

"Yes."

"So you knew what the reading was but you haven't done it?"

"I guess not."

I made my voice softer, deeper, firmer. "Get up," I said.

"What?" he asked, somewhat startled.

"Get up. We need your seat. We have a student here who wants to add the course, who has bought the book and done the reading, but we don't have enough seats. You are taking a seat we could use. Get up and give us your seat."

"What am I supposed to do?" he asked, half rising.

"Drop the course. We need your seat. Now." I said.

Looking confused or slightly scared, he gathered his things and left the room. I turned to the student on the floor and told him or her (oddly, I don't remember who the lucky student was) to take the empty seat.

The class was silent and a little reluctant for the rest of that period. During the remainder of that term I had no trouble from students who were not well prepared; they all did the reading. Occasional dramas of that sort have given me a reputation at my university as an "intimidating" professor as well as a general level of compliance from my students that I would have envied when I was younger. I have this reputation as a tough teacher even though, truth be told, my grade point averages are in the top half of those dealt out by department colleagues, I'll almost always give in to requests for exceptions to due dates, I usually give more generous participation grades than I probably should, and I generally hate the elements of higher education that pressure us to maintain a competitive atmosphere.

Still, knowing that I have pulled off power plays like the mid-class period seat switch has lent me useful confidence in less contentious situations. For example, when I was a guest lecturer at another institution in a class taught by a Japanese man, he expressed surprise at the ease with which I took command over students he had seen as somewhat resistant to his efforts toward engagement. When he took me into his classroom, I saw his approximately 30 students spread out among desks in tiers that might have held closer to 100 if the room were fully occupied. He mounted a podium at the front of the room, a small-boned, almost aristocratic looking man, and gave me a soft-spoken introduction. The students looked unimpressed as I took my place at the lectern.

I filled my lungs with air. "All right everybody, stand up!" I told them in my professor-in-charge voice.

I indicated a compact area at the front of the classroom where I wanted them to sit. "Move on down!" I ordered, fully from the diaphragm. Then, I joked around a bit. "I've got great seats going for cheap in the front row."

In a matter of minutes, the students gathered into a manageable space at the front of the room; the classroom atmosphere, shaken up a bit by all of the moving and my blustery orders, had gone from almost sullen to a bit bemused. Buoyed by the early success with the seating, I strode across the podium with authority and delivered my lecture on gender in Japanese elections with energy. Students asked good questions at the end. Admitting that when it came to connecting with American students he felt a bit at a loss, my restrained Japanese colleague told me I was a great teacher. I still remember that lecture as one of my best.

I have learned how to be a man or, at least, how to establish an authority that is like manliness in my classroom. Most of the time neither I nor my students worry I will lose control over my classroom, and that allows all of us to focus more fully on the content matter I am teaching. My course evaluations reveal as much where, in great contrast to the evaluations from my first years, questions that ask about my competence — about the organization of the course, my preparedness, or my seeming knowledge about the content matter — I am usually ranked quite highly. Now a more common worry for me is that I am too controlling. I work on ameliorating the notion that I am intimidating, reminding myself to smile more often (something I don't do when I'm concentrating), pausing frequently to express my appreciation for student competence instead of working so hard to demonstrate my own. Of course, these are also often strategies for dealing with my students' and my own gendered judgments of teacher behaviors. I'd like to be described appreciatively as "tough," but I am constantly aware of the possibility that I will be read negatively as "harsh." The label "harsh" reminds me painfully of female professors I evaluated critically, and I do what I can to avoid it.

If students had not chosen to describe my current university as a Cuntry Club, efforts to improve my classroom management techniques might still be largely devoted to working the balance between the tactics that earn me classroom authority and those that allow the students to see me as not harsh but appropriately (and not too much that way) nurturing. I dare say, that would be an undertaking shared by many of my fellow college teachers, and not one without value. Of course, many other issues of pedagogy remain outside the mere establishment of a professor's authority to profess — how to balance the urge to cover a large quantity of subject matter with the value of allowing students time to fully digest and explore a smaller quantity, how to construct writing assignments that encourage independent thinking while disciplining polemic natures, when to dispense with messy class discussions for a lecture and when to let a discussion ramble a bit while students find their own way toward the crux of an issue, for example. Moreover the culture of my masculinist discipline of political science is likely more concerned with classroom authority than are many others. Still, my own conversations with young women just starting out in academe in fields as distinct as history, anthropology, and mathematics have led me to believe that establishing authority in the classroom is still seen as fundamental to a successful teaching career, the many scholarly efforts to critique this sort of authority notwith-standing.[2]

Having had a certain amount of success employing my strategies and tactics for quelling doubters and inspiring confidence in myself and in my students, I might have moved cheerfully through my career assuming that one day I would perfect the balance between speaking from the diaphragm and softening my face into a smile. Forced to confront my inability to banish my cuntability from the classroom, however, I began to doubt the whole authority building enterprise. My fear of the cunt made me realize how much I had understood the challenge of winning my students' faith in my competence as something I could do *despite the fact* that I am living in a woman's body. My teacher self was something I performed *as if I were not a woman* so as to be recognized as *not-a-mere woman*.

I am no essentialist about my own womanhood; I once told a masculinities class in Japan that my most comfortable gender identity is gay male, and I meant it. Perhaps that is why I was willing to do what it took to subdue aggressive male students in my political science classes. I wanted to be the most powerful man in the room. Still, being forced to see my womanness as something I was working everyday to overcome was painful for the part of myself it suggested I might be losing in my striving toward masculine freedom from the cunt. The realization was still more painful for showing me the outlines of a male privilege I was unlikely to ever achieve. Finally, my terror at my cuntability was deeply embarrassing because it revealed that, although I had come to think of asserting my authoritative position in the classroom as a way of being a feminist role model for my students, I was actually engaged in precisely the naïve effort to obscure gendered difference that I am always cautioning my students to avoid.

In the spirit of the Girl Scouts' motto — "Be Prepared" — I have tried to think about what I could recover of my pedagogic self if the worst happened and cuntness ruptured my classroom authority. I cast about for models of how this ruptured teaching would work. I ask if there have been times when the cunt and I have happily shared a classroom, but if there are, I've repressed them in a far, dark chamber of my unconscious. What I find instead is a model of learning that comes from the most terrifying and exhilarating part of my scholarly life.

I am a political anthropologist who studies gender in the world of non-elites in Japan. I use participant observation and interviews to investigate how ordinary people understand, describe, and interact with political institutions, organizations, and movements in their communities — and to learn, as well, why people often fail to interact with politics at all. My participant-observer approach means that when I am in the field collecting data about my research subjects, I am constantly walking into unfamiliar situations and asking awkward questions in a difficult language that I will never speak like a native. I am daily making stupid mistakes.

Because Japan is such an affluent and literate country, I cannot even fall back on an old-fashioned anthropologist's notion of superiority to the natives. Many of my subjects are better educated and better established than I am. They are perfectly capable of discerning that I am affiliated with a small, Southern school they've never heard of, not Harvard, or Princeton, or MIT. Some of them openly laugh at me and my odd ways of phrasing things and my weird questions; most of them have only the most minimal confidence that I am capable of understanding them. I think the majority of them see me as a fairly ordinary woman, smarter and better educated than most, more adventurous than many, earnest, even likable, but decidedly not a figure of authority. This sort of judgment of me is usually intensified by the fact that I am often quite nervous when I approach informants. Also, since I see winning their acceptance of me as a benevolent person as more important than establishing my professional status, I work harder at projecting myself as a proper (i.e., well behaved) woman and as a polite and unassuming interlocutor than as a successful academic.

That position suits me fine when I'm doing fieldwork because it is a great one from which to ask for my informants' explanations of everyday life. Because my competence is seen as dubious, I am often underestimated, but when I am underestimated, I am also allowed to repeat my questions and to ask for interpretations of what is considered obvious. And in the study of politics in particular, my lack of authority is also a kind of certification of benign intent. Activists, elected officials, and bureaucrats don't get as defensive as they might with someone who seemed more clearly powerful. With my clumsy grammar, mediocre professional pedigree, and cheerful female face, I do not seem to pose much of a threat. I have had politicians tell me the most extraordinary things, including one who opened his private ledgers to show me long lists of illegal funeral gifts he had given his constituents. The "ordinary" people I study often confide that I "don't seem like a professor at all." I'm not sure, but I believe that view of me makes them more confident that I will not judge them harshly if they share their complicated feelings about the world around them.

I find fieldwork exhausting precisely because, in order to do it, I must operate in a world where I am accorded less appreciation for my professional acumen than I think I deserve. I have to suppress the discomfort brought on by an endless barrage of little injuries to my ego. I cannot use my diaphragm or my arsenal of small humiliations to render my subjects more appreciative because their capitulation would also end our frankest conversations. Much of what I am thinking I cannot (or should not) impart. I imagine this is what teaching in a cunted classroom would feel like for me. I keep doing the fieldwork because it rewards me enormously. Pressing down my ego is a discipline that not only allows me access to informants; it also opens me to new ways of thinking things I thought I already knew. I suspect this is why periods of fieldwork are also usually intellectually fertile. I read different sorts of things, traverse disciplinary boundaries, find myself seeing the questions of my academic field with renewed clarity.

In the field, I do what I tell my students they must do if they really want to read something, to humble themselves before the text, to work meticulously at "getting it" while striving to hold off on judging it. Every once in a great while, a student follows that command and comes back to me in awe. The book spoke to her, the thinker she has now encountered is a new one, relevant to her life in so many unexpected ways. At first she was troubled; she couldn't sleep. Now she sees things. She has so much to say. She is not stuck for what to write, but only how to write it. These conversations are the best sorts of encounters. I go home feeling not like a teacher, but like a pure power, an intellectual beacon, a soul mate for readers everywhere. If there is an eroticism peculiar to teaching, this encounter with the bruised and humbled reader is when I feel it.

Thus, I wonder, if I can see the awkward researcher in the field as an allegory for the teacher in the cunted classroom, would it also be possible for me to imagine the threatening failure of my pedagogic authority as an invitation to triumph? What would it mean for my students to see *me* humbled before the text rather than commanding their humility? What would it mean to accept an expressed lack of confidence in my competence with a cheerful smile? To even invite it? To hold back on some of what I might impart to them in order to avoid revealing my mastery? To let them see me as "just another cunt" rather than a wielder of the power to which my credentials have entitled me? Some of them would laugh, right? I would see the effects of my dis-authorized voice in more negative course evaluations. Some of them would complain; they would want me to take charge, to manage their obnoxious peers, to hold us all to a true line. Some would insist that their own credentials were diminished by my failure to insist on mine. But would these be significant losses for anyone in the long run? What if some of my students, just out of boredom or perverse curiosity, tried sitting still before their texts or began questioning me, digging through the things I hadn't thought to say for something really worth knowing? What would these students learn?

As I offer these speculations, I am reminded of my favorite teachers during my student years. I am developing the sneaking suspicion that they were at their very best on the days they approached their classrooms with their authority somewhat in check. Of course, my favorite teachers were all men, and so it never occurred to me that their classrooms could be ruptured by a threatening cunt. In that sense, perhaps what I am trying to envision goes beyond something I have seen — or at the least beyond what I have been willing to appreciate. Still, I'd like to think about what it would mean to aspire to be a like-a-woman professor instead of a like-a-man professor. I doubt it would seem any more natural to me than mustering my diaphragm for an authoritative voice or meting out minor punishments to the bully in row three seemed when I first began to teach. I am doubtful that like-a-woman teaching would disrupt male privilege in the college classroom in any major way. I can well imagine how, as a result of its seemingly unnatural quality, a male's like-a-woman approach might be viewed as a more genuine effort at engaging students than a female professor's similar, "only natural" efforts would. But perhaps we might still see something to be gained in the way the like-a-woman approach emphasizes learning over knowing and highlights the tenuousness of the professional guise rather than reinscribing its centrality.

*   *   *

Last fall I endured a shocking assault on my professorial authority. On the Friday of Parents' Weekend, a number of my students' parents had taken advantage of the University's blanket invitation to attend classes with their children, and my Gender and Politics seminar was packed with unusually giggly students and their proud mothers and fathers. I had chosen to discuss a set of brief philosophical essays examining the case that might be made for the value of government-sanctioned marriages. We had been working on marriage for a week or so, and the essays I had chosen were neither the most conservative nor the most radical of the readings I had assigned for the unit. I wanted to show the parents how well their children functioned in a class discussion with a little bit of controversy, but I didn't want to offend anyone. I had miscalculated.

In order to get the discussion started, I asked a few questions reviewing an essay we had discussed earlier in the week in which Iris Marion Young argued that government plans to improve the circumstances of children in the homes of single mothers by encouraging their mothers to marry was shortsighted. In response to my query, a student dutifully presented Young's perspective. Pushing marriage on single mothers would not solve the real social problem, the poverty that women and their children were often forced into as a result of gender discrimination in the work force and inadequate social services. Plus it would leave women dependent on men who could sometimes be violent.

Suddenly, a father sitting quite near me leaned in at me across the table. "Don't you know children are better off when raised in two-parent homes?" he shouted out.

It is true, those children are less likely to fall victim to the many ills of poverty, I acknowledged, but I pointed out that, as a feminist, Young could not countenance forcing women to be even more reliant on men for their welfare.

The father's face colored. "Don't you know what the research on this says?" he asked, in a very big voice, and then "Have you read anything at all?"

Beside him, his already shy daughter slid low in her seat.

I took a deep breath. I could sense the other parents watching me, wondering what I would do now. I wanted to tell him just how many things I have, indeed, read. I wanted to ask him what kind of fool he was for taking a professor on in her own classroom. But I didn't. I thought verbal sparring would only dignify his attack. Instead, I tried to smile knowingly.

"Sir," I said, as if talking to a young child, "I'm going to have to ask you to follow along with the discussion and see if this becomes clearer to you as we continue."

He harrumphed and scooted back in his chair. I launched back into discussion questions, but the man was not satisfied. As we were nearing the end of the hour, he again leaned over the table, making audible noises of disapproval. He opened his mouth as if he were about to shout another commentary on my competence in the area of the class discussion. I pushed my arm out full length in the direction of his face, my hand in a traffic cop's "stop" position. I tightened my diaphragm and firmed up my voice.

"Sir, I'm going to have to ask you to remain quiet," I said, just as a state trooper might invite a drunk driver to step outside his car. The man shut up. The class ended.

I taught the next section somehow, and then I went back to my office. I sat at my desk in the pantsuit I had so carefully picked out that morning to highlight how easily I rested in my hard-won professionalism, the sweater jacket that was supposed to be feminine but not girly pulled tight around me. I wanted to cry, but nothing came out. I knew I had done the best I could. "You handled it better than I would have," my dean said to me later. Still, the attack was terrible, I thought. To be at this point in my career and yet still required to answer for my position as if I could not possibly have deserved it, even if only to an angry ideologue, appalled me. Reminding myself of my coolheaded and effective use of my authority arsenal did not really ease my misery because what hurt was knowing I would never earn a permanent exemption from such unjust challenges.

I couldn't help but think about the students' Cuntry Club article from a few months earlier. I found it difficult to imagine the clearly traditionalist father who had attacked me using the kind of obscene language those students used. Yet in the way the man's ire had been provoked by my review of a feminist text and in the way he used his big body and loud voice without any apparent consciousnesses of having crossed the boundary into my rightful space of authority, I felt that he had cunted my classroom nearly as fully as the Cuntry Club article had threatened to do. I kept remembering how a male student two seats down from the angry father had shaken his head and sort of laughed during the episode. I wondered what that student had been thinking. Was he laughing at the father's outburst, or at me, the small, erstwhile feminist in the sweater jacket, whose class presence was not impressive enough to forestall the attack? I felt I had been humiliated in front of my students. I was intensely angry and hugely sad. My vulnerability was almost physically intolerable to me.

Only now, more than six months later, am I capable of turning the angry father's outburst carefully around in my mind, of considering alternative responses. When the man leapt into my classroom discussion, I first tried a neutral response, offering him further information about the particular feminist perspective of the author we were reviewing. When that only drove him to a greater level of intensity, I had tried a mild humiliation tactic, implying he had much to learn before he spoke. Finally, I had simply resorted to a brute assertion of my authority; speaking from the diaphragm had saved my class discussion from the chaos he would have introduced. Throughout the encounter I had remained calm; my voice and posture had been strong. I find it hard to believe that, if I were a man, the angry father would have taken me on the way he did. Still, as a like-a-man professor, I limited the damage he might have done to my professional stature before my students. The event was proof that I learned my mentors' lessons well. I am smart, and I am experienced. Still, I was angry at the fact that I must always run the risk of such encounters because I am a woman and that I will always wonder about the reaction of the student two seats down from the irate father. At times like this, the classroom authority game seems exhausting and pointless.

What if I had tried something completely different? Instead of stalling and then marginalizing the angry father, I could have responded to his most insulting questions in a gentle way. When he asked me if I had read "anything at all," I took a deep breath to restrain the vicious response I wanted, instinctively, to give him. I'm proud of that restraint. But after that deep breath, instead of asking him to follow along with the discussion I was leading, I might have responded much more positively. For example, I could have said, "You know, sir, I obviously haven't read the research that has formed your perspective. Why don't you tell me what you've been reading?"

I am not sure what his reaction would have been. Possibly, he would have mumbled something like "Forget it, we'll talk about it some other time." Or he might have taken me up on my offer and shared the source of his conviction. If I was successful in suppressing my irritation at the right-wing politics I suspect he would have offered up, I might have engaged him in a series of questions just as I do the political activists I interview for my research in Japan. In order to keep the conversation going, I would no doubt have to resist the tendency to dissect his claims to reveal their problematic assumptions or faulty data. Instead, as in an interview with an informant from my field, I would want to let him give full voice to a perspective on marriage and family that would likely include some insults directed at feminists, academic elites, and single mothers, all categories into which I, personally, fit. One of my favorite theorists, Young, would be misinterpreted and unfairly criticized. I would sustain wounds in order to sustain the angry father's faith in the possibility of winning me or my students over with his superior understanding of American families. Countering my own personality and years of training, I would work hard to come across as a nice, like-a-woman professor in order to keep the man talking.

Thinking about the encounter this way intrigues me. I can't help but think that, if I had ceded him more space, the angry man would have done a much better job than I could ever do at representing a certain stalwart element of gendered public discourse about American families. Given that I wanted to teach my students the contours of the marriage debate into which the feminist authors we were reading were launching their arguments, I can, with hindsight, see how valuable that man's anger could have been for my students if only I had lent him my bully pulpit. Instead of restricting our investigation of gendered discourse to bits of philosophic texts that students had difficulty seeing as significant, I could have opened my classroom up to the field site that lay within it. The angry father was, incarnate, the problem our authors were worrying. How often do the political phenomena about which I teach actually march in amongst my students' desks the way this man had? How could I have turned him aside?

I know why I did. I saw that cunt coming at me. I feared her authority. But I should have let her speak.

Notes

1. Not her real name.
2. Clarissa Rile Hayward provides a rich review of this literature in her study of teachers' management of authority in two public elementary schools (Hayward 2000).

Works Cited

Hayward, Clarissa Rile. *De-Facing Power*. New York: Cambridge University Press, 2000.

Running the Gauntlet

Battling Sexism in Academia
with Greasepaint, Bed Sheets
and Mardi Gras Beads

NORMA BOWLES

As the artistic director of Fringe Benefits Theatre, I have had the opportunity to take techniques I've developed for collaboratively devising activist theatre to universities and communities throughout the United States, and in Australia, Canada, Spain and the United Kingdom. Our workshops, residencies and plays have addressed a wide variety of issues including racism, sexism, classism, "looks"-ism, homophobia, and transphobia, and have helped promote immigration rights, marriage equality, and the employment of formerly incarcerated women. In this essay, I will share stories about, and questions raised by, five different Fringe Benefits Theatre for Social Justice workshops, residencies, and/or projects addressing sexist discrimination in academia.

Fringe Benefits

Fringe Benefits is a groundbreaking social justice theatre company with an eighteen-year track record of collaborating with school and community groups to create plays that promote constructive dialogue about diversity and discrimination issues. Our first community collaborations in the early 1990s engaged homeless lesbian, gay, bisexual and transgendered (LGBT) youth in the development of tolerance-promoting theatre and performance art. Through discussion and improvisation, the youth worked together to transform their experiences with homophobia into powerful plays which premiered at Highways Performance Space, were subsequently published, and which also became the subject of the award-winning documentary film *Surviving Friendly Fire*, narrated by Sir Ian McKellen. Following the theatrical release of the film in 1997, Fringe Benefits began to develop a broader mission: to create theatre in collaboration with ever-expanding community of youth, educators, parents and others wrestling with a wide range of social justice issues. Fringe Benefits' theatre activism workshops and residencies, the two published anthologies of our plays, *Friendly Fire* and *Cootie Shots: Theatrical Inoculations Against Bigotry*, and the *Surviving Friendly Fire* documentary, have earned the commendations of educators, youth, parents, and community leaders. In 2009, we produced *Mitos, Ritos y Tonterías* (Myths, Rites and Silliness), a Spanish-language film based on a script we developed with a team of thirty Latina mothers who asked us to work with them to create a show to help their community understand the harmful impact of gender bias and homophobia on children.

From 2004 through 2009, my Fringe Benefits colleagues and I led twenty-five Theatre for Social Justice Institutes in which we brought together diverse groups of university theatre students, faculty and staff, along with campus and community organizations to create and tour plays addressing a wide variety of social justice issues. We worked with First Nation youth and University of Winnipeg students and faculty to devise and produce a Forum Theatre play which will be used in Canadian high schools to help generate dialogue among students about racism. The play we developed in North Carolina with homeless youth, Time Out Youth, Davidson College faculty, and the Charlotte Actors Theatre helped the youth obtain emergency housing. After seeing our Freshman Week Show at Kent State University in Ohio, all but two of the 282 students surveyed expressed increased motivation to educate themselves and others or to serve as allies for LGBT persons. The Southwestern University students we worked with in Texas were inspired to form their own campus-based theatre for social justice company. In spring 2005, we worked with Miami University of Ohio students and faculty to devise a play advocating the overturn of Ohio's discriminatory, heterosexist marriage laws. The following fall, they toured the play to 21 classes, and used it to draw press and progressive allies to a state senator's speech against health benefits for domestic partners. Four years later, they still receive requests to tour the play.

Fringe Benefits' process for collaboratively devising activist theatre is shaped by the following questions: "What is the specific problem — the social

Karla Burgos, Glenda Torres, Ruben Garfias (sitting), Carlos Martínez and Alejandra Flores in *Mitos, Ritos y Tonterías (Myths, Rites and Silliness)* (Photograph by Norma Bowles).

justice issue—we want to address?"; "Whom do we feel we need to reach in order to begin to resolve this problem?"; "What is the most effective way to reach this target audience?"; and "What measurable outcome should we aim to achieve?" Typically, over a period of several months, I work with representatives from the university and community groups with which we are partnering to articulate some preliminary answers to these questions. I also work with these fellow project leaders to recruit a diverse group of 30 to 50 or more university and community members to devise and produce a play that meets our collective goals. Once we are all assembled, I co-facilitate a series of workshops in which the group creates the play through story-sharing, discussion and brainstorming, and through collaborative play-structuring, improvisation, writing and editing. All voices are included and engaged, as we create work for, by and about the community. As Lani Guinier has articulated so eloquently, "By assembling a diverse team of people, each of whom has different skills and different expertise," together we can "collaborate, brainstorm creatively, put the big issues on the table and come together as a community so that we can convert what could have been a tragedy into a triumph" (Guinier lecture).

Battling Sexism in Academia

As one might imagine, in the course of conducting antidiscrimination workshops and residencies with university students, faculty and staff, I've heard many — too many — women[1] on the frontlines of countless university "Theatres of Operation" share their first hand testimonies about sexist assaults.[2] Our story circles and theatrical collaborations function at times like boot camps, helping armed participants with verbal and physical, individual and collective strategies for contending with seemingly inevitable battles with sexist bigotry. More often, however, we function like a consciousness-raising, radicalizing USO troupe, preparing a show either for "the good guys" (innocent targets of sexist behavior), for "the bad guys" (sexist discriminators), or for bystanders, who actively or passively collude with sexist behavior. The specific target audience and modality/battle plan of our collaboratively devised activist theatre is always determined by the diverse group of people who gather together in order to find an artful, constructive and effective way to address sexism on their campus. But regardless of the intended outcome of any specific collaboration, our itinerant theatre company seems to operate somewhat like a M.A.S.H. (Mobile Army Surgical Hospital) unit, creating, at least for a moment, a relatively safe space where healing can begin.

In our "intelligence gathering sessions," we've learned that, whether pursuing an academic degree or tenure, just trying to pay the rent, or just trying to cross campus, university women must run gauntlets of sexist abuse.[3] The specific manifestations of sexism in academia reported in these sessions include everything from puerile joking to vicious sorority hazing practices, and from chauvinist, exclusionary treatment of female colleagues to date rape.[4] In several universities, male faculty not only routinely exclude female faculty from conversations and departmental decision-making, and exclude mention of their female colleagues' work in faculty meetings, news publications and Web sites, but in a number of instances, they also prevent their female colleagues from doing the very work (teaching and artistic) for which they've been hired. In a number of universities, students spoke of on-campus, on-line and published systems assigning degrading "grades" to female students. Everybody seemed keenly aware of the overall "grade" assigned to the women on their campus, especially as male students often derided the women about their low "grades," and used the system to manipulate women into accepting their sexual advances. Also at a number of universities, students, faculty and staff agreed that sexual assaults and rape, especially date rape, were greatly underreported. In one university, members of the crisis line said that callers never referred to sexual attacks as anything more than "sexual assault," and never as "rape." At that same university, however, both male and female students had found another, very disturbing use for the word: a workshop participant said that she heard a female classmate exclaim ecstatically, "I totally raped that test!" Other participants said they'd heard similar uses of the word. And, of course, double standards still persist: the male student returning home the morning after a date is cheered as a "stud," while his female counterpart is sneered at as she treads the "Walk of Shame."

Unfortunately, too, as one might anticipate, women of color, queer, bi, lesbian and transgendered women, women of size, and any women who do not conform to white, sexist and heterosexist "norms" are subjected to additional degradations. Students on several campuses reported that, throughout the year, but especially during Freshman Orientation Week, male students will perch together on a sofa, or on the wall or stairs of a centrally located building and loudly comment on the "fuck-ability"[5] of passing girls. Women who are larger than average, wear shorter hair, don't dress in very stereotypically feminine clothes, carry books on feminist topics, and/or who dare to hold hands with each other, are verbally abused and laughed at as they are compelled to run this gauntlet. Some have had garbage thrown at them. White women who try to distance themselves from overtly sexual advances at dances are called "dyke" or accused of having a "dried up, dusty old pussy." Women of color, especially African American women, on the other hand, are often scorned as "slutty" when they dance. For days afterward, the men joked and bragged about their "clever" maneuver. Many of us wondered if the men would have treated a group of white cheerleaders in such a mean-spirited, humiliating manner.

Boot Camp

On several occasions, the university women with whom I've worked have elected to dramatize their experiences with sexist behavior as Forum Theatre. Forum Theatre is one of Augusto Boal's Theatre of the Oppressed techniques, which "begins with the enactment of a scene ... in which a protagonist tries, unsuccessfully, to overcome an oppression relevant to that particular audience. The joker [facilitator] then invites the spectators to replace the protagonist at any point in the scene that they can imagine an alternative action that could lead to a solution. The scene is replayed numerous times with different interventions. This results in a dialogue about the oppression, an examination of alternatives, and a 'rehearsal' for real situations" (Schutzman and Cohen-Cruz 236–37). In a couple of instances, the people with whom I've worked have been graduate students who wanted to use Forum Theatre in a fairly traditional way to explore possible strategies for responding to sexual harassment from male colleagues and supervisors in their student-placement jobs. Another time, I worked with a group of professional women involved in a variety of different fields, including academia. While these women were quite keenly aware of the oppressive circumstances in their workplaces, they were generally unwilling to explore any potentially risky tactics for combating the sexist attacks, even in the context of a theatrical improvisation with an audience of supportive female peers. They were almost unanimously in agreement that putting up with sexist, chauvinist behavior was just part of the game, just what you have to be willing to do if you want to "play with the big boys." If you challenged the system, your victory would only be pyrrhic: you could lose your chance at a promotion, or your job, and you might even ruin your career. You might win the battle, but you were certain to lose the war.

While the weeks I spent with the aforementioned group of women made me more painfully aware of the professional dangers one must be willing *and able* to hazard if one wants to battle against institutionalized sexism, the experience also gave me an interesting idea for an Anti-Sexism Boot Camp Drill. One of the participants had distilled the sexist abuse at her job into a short scene comprising a series of brief, increasingly brutal interactions with colleagues: a "blow-off" from a peer in lunch room, a brusque command from a supervisor in his office, a lewd comment from a client in the hallway, et cetera. In the workshop, we set up the space to replicate her office complex, and stationed participants in each of the areas to play the sexist colleagues. At first, the woman on whose experiences the scenario was based played the role she had scripted for herself, following fairly closely what she actually had said and done in life. Then, other workshop participants took turns taking her place and exploring a variety of approaches to responding to the sexist attacks. After a few people had tried out their ideas, and we were all beginning to feel a bit tired and "punchy," one woman ran the gauntlet like Lucille Ball. She responded to the "blow off" with a goofy retort, the brusque command, with an annoyed "take" to an invisible camera, the lewd comment, with a pratfall, et cetera. We were rolling in the aisles. Now, everyone had renewed energy to run the gauntlet ... as Mae West, Margaret Cho, Mo'Nique, Katharine Hepburn, and other "Fast-Talking Dames."[6] The chance to let the sexist male co-workers "have it," to shoot from the hip, with both barrels, was liberating and uproariously cathartic, and lifted our spirits like a liberal dose of laughing gas from a M.A.S.H. unit. At the same time, we were surprised by the fact that this playful approach generated a number of rather cunning, effective and practical strategies for tackling the oppressive behavior.

On a later occasion, I was invited to work in New Orleans with a group of feminist professors who were interested in exploring how theatre might be used to tackle sexism in academia. The gauntlet exercise immediately came to mind. Then I started thinking a little more about the city where we would be working, New Orleans, the birthplace of jazz, the haunting setting for Williams' *A Streetcar Named Desire*, and perhaps the Mardi Gras capital of the world. Mardi Gras ... the street celebration during which women and girls are enticed by men cruising past them on parade floats to "show their tits," and rewarded with doubloons and strands of shiny, plastic beads for colluding with this lewd, sexist, debasing practice. Hmm. And one of the figureheads for the New Orleans Mardi Gras revelries is a Jester, close-cousin to the "Joker," the term by which Augusto Boal refers to a Forum Theatre facilitator. Hmm. Perhaps this ritual could be played with, subverted, turned inside out and upside down to good effect? Perhaps we could set up a gauntlet of sexist jeers and taunts, through which our female participants could pass, as if parading down Bourbon Street. But our Joker/Facilitator would reward them with beads for standing up to the sexist onslaught, rather than for col-luding with it! And so, after the workshop participants had shared stories about their *many* encounters with sexism in academia, we set up a "parade route" along which we stationed several participants to play the antagonists and recreate the scenes the women had described —

> Two male colleagues exclude a female colleague from their discussion about a department issue.
> When asked by a female professor if he will be taking her spring course, a student responds that he would "rather have his balls in a vise than take another course in 'feminist *anything*'!"
> A male colleague asks a female colleague who will be choreographing his musical production to "Be sure to find lots of girls with big tits for the show!"

Participants were then invited either to take on these diverse adversaries seri-ously, "realistically," and/or as they imagined one of their favorite female comedians might. The resulting improvisations were something of a cross between Boal's rapid-fire version of Forum Theatre, a boot camp drill with high heels, champagne and cream pies, and a WWF Smackdown between

Xena and Mardi Gras. We all played enthusiastic celebrants/spectators for each other. Dressed in the traditional purple, green and gold, three-pointed Mardi Gras Jester's hat, I played the joker/facilitator, cheered the loudest, and tossed the contestants strand after glittering strand of beads to honor their revolutionary efforts.

USO Show #1: The Singing and Dancing Trojan Horse

We also used a very broad, comedic approach to raise awareness about sexism in academia for an audience of students, faculty and staff at a small, very conservative liberal arts college. In this instance, I was invited to create a short *Commedia dell'arte*[7] play about the issue with a group of undergraduate French Theatre students. I began by introducing the students to *Commedia* characters, *lazzi*[8] and performance techniques. We then worked on physical and vocal characterization, comic timing, economy of movement and dramatic structure. As we continued the performance training, we started to share stories about discriminatory, sexist behavior on campus. The students' experiences ranged from professors ignoring female students' comments in class to date rape. We dramatized the stories using characters inspired by Balinese *topeng* (masks) and traditional Italian *Commedia* masks. Through the use of *Commedia* devising techniques, we created such scenarios as "The Boys' Club," "Double Standard Girlz," and "Capitano and the Date Rape Cocktail," among others. In the latter, Capitano was outsmarted by a female character much like the sixteenth-century actress, scholar, and writer Isabella Andreini's brilliant character Isabella, described by Domnica Radulescu as a "powerful, independent, resourceful, and, at times, cunning woman who broke the accepted boundaries of the feminine for her time" (Radulescu 89).

The show, *Point/Contrepoint*, wove these scenes together in a narrative that was at first crisp and light but which, by the end, turned grotesque and dark, following the all-too-frequent trajectory of discriminatory behavior that moves from "joking" to hate crimes. The performance style of the show was largely physical rather than verbal, and the spare lines of dialogue, devised along with the movement through improvisation, were all in French. While it must be said that I was invited primarily to teach the students *Commedia* performance and devising skills, I believe that our performance style enabled us to crack open a door and instigate discussions about sexism in a highly fortified bastion of patriarchal ascendancy. (We had been discouraged even from using the words "Sexism," "Sexist Discrimination," and "Gender Bias" in our flyers advertising the show.) Still, perhaps like a Lipizzaner version of the Trojan Horse, our highly stylized, broadly comedic, foreign language sketches amused and beguiled some of our stuffy, conservative audience members long enough to get them to drop their guards a little and allow in a few stealthy critiques of their chauvinist attitudes and sexist behavior.[9]

USO Show #2: Not-So-Friendly Fire

In another university-based Theatre for Social Justice Workshop, the participants shared some sickening stories about navigating a minefield of sexist discrimination on their campus. They gave accounts of male professors laughing at female students' comments in class, calling female students on the phone with warnings about how hard their classes would be, and even playing with their female students' hair during hallway discussions. The participants also described a particularly disturbing but all-too-familiar, sorority and fraternity scene including physically dangerous, and generally abusive and vulgar "Rush," hazing and "partying" practices. As with countless universities where I've worked throughout the country, party themes played into pervasive cultural stereotypes, with men always "on top," such as: "CEOs & Office Hos," "Millionaires & Trophy Wives," "Barbies & Barbarians," "School Girls & Dirty Old Professors," and the ever-popular "Playboy Mansion." One student told us that, every fall, one of the fraternities hosts a Jello wrestling match for charity, to which each sorority is invited to send a team. A faculty member reported that a student had come into her office, closed the door and burst into tears. She'd gone to a fraternity party, asked for a drink, and was told, "If you want a beer, Bitch, Get on your knees!"

What seemed particularly disconcerting to this group, however, was the "friendly fire" to which sorority members subjected each other as well as prospective members throughout the year, but especially during Rush Week. One sorority's hazing process included forcing new recruits to strip down to their undergarments and sit on a running clothes dryer. Their "sisters" used permanent ink pens to mark any and all parts of their targets' bodies that jiggled. Many freshman women anxious about upcoming Rush Week degradations such as this, were heard to say they were "not going to eat during Christmas break!" So, although we agreed that this university's male professors, staff and students clearly needed to be educated about sexism, the Theatre for Social Justice group decided that they wanted to start by grappling with problems on the "home front," with the female students. The group felt it was important to make the sororities, and prospective freshman members, aware of how they were colluding with the dehumanizing, sexist objectification of their bodies and their worth when they participated in these degrading traditions and practices. "Hazing" rituals such as this have a destructive impact that can be immediately felt, but can also desensitize both the female targets and the female perpetrators to sexist thinking and behavior, leaving them more vulnerable to direct attacks from male perpetrators, more likely to comply when commanded, "If you want a beer, Bitch, Get on your knees!"

The Theatre for Social Justice group determined that a good way to reach an audience of sorority members and Freshman women would be through a satirical dramatization of Rush Week as an exceptionally nightmarish version of *America's Next Top Model*. A panel of "bitchy" judges could put contestants through a series of increasingly dehumanizing "challenges," and scrutinize and pass judgment on them, both to their faces and behind their backs. The audience could be made privy to the destructive impact of the challenges and judgments through "confession booth" testimonies from and "backstage" conversations with the contestants. The workshop participants also explored how real and fictional commercials and PSAs (public service announcements) could be interpolated into the show to provide crucial information about resources and crisis centers, as well as to underscore the absurdity of some of the sexist and looks-ist thinking exposed in the central drama. Some of the commercial parody concepts discussed include:

> A take-off on the Dove "Real Beauty" campaign in which a young woman emerges from her dorm bed in the morning sporting "perfect" hair and makeup, and wearing ball gown.
> A commercial advertising "Oxygen! The Best Diet in the World!"
> Another commercial promoting "A Bowl of Ice Cream for Dinner. Your finger for dessert."

Near the end of the workshop, the group began to consider whether to conclude their "Not-So-Friendly Fire" show with someone getting gravely injured, with one of the judges experiencing a change of heart when she hears a particularly affecting confessional, or with the rejected women banding together to form a new sorority with progressive, feminist values. There was a great deal of enthusiasm about continuing to work on the play and performing it for sorority members and freshman women, ideally during Freshman Week. Many wanted to create a spring term Theatre and Women's Studies course through which they could devote more time to researching and writing the play, and to developing pre and post show curricula and handouts. Everyone agreed that "Sometimes we're our own worst enemies," and that it is "important that women support each other."

USO Show #3: Changing Channels

My final report from the field concerns a counter-sexism theatrical "campaign" currently being waged in a state university in the Midwest. Several years ago, when my Fringe Benefits colleague and I parachuted in to work with members of the university to create our play addressing discrimination based on gender, we encountered an unfortunate obstacle: our collaboration had inadvertently been cross-scheduled with a collaboration designed to address the issue of restroom access for transgender people. While our project site liaisons had contacted members of the organizations co-sponsoring this other project, they had asked only them to pass along information about our project. We had neglected to work with these other organizations either to co-develop a project or even to work out a mutually agreeable schedule. In the best of all possible worlds, we all could have worked together to create a play promoting progressive approaches to gender issues including, perhaps even giving primary attention to, the issue of bathroom accessibility. In addition to causing us to forfeit an opportunity to join forces with these LGBT and allied organizations, this unfortunate planning misstep also cost us a lower than average turnout of LGBT members for our project, and, consequently, a paucity of LGBT related stories of sexist discrimination. Still, our Theatre for Social Justice Institute was wonderfully productive despite this fact. I mention this because I strongly believe that, no matter how narrowly one focuses the scope, goals and outcomes of a project, the importance of collaboration, *deep and broad* collaboration, in planning and producing the work cannot be overstated. Deep and broad collaboration is imperative vis-à-vis creating work that is inclusive, that truly embodies a complex understanding of the issues, and that both literally and figuratively reaches its audience. Moreover, it is important to remember that, "Cultural patterns of oppression are not only interrelated, but are bound together and influenced by the intersectional systems of society,"[10] and that working in coalition with other communities is a life-saving defense against pervasive divide and conquer strategems.

What greatly strengthened the development of our anti-sexism campaign at this university, however, was the participation of a racially/ethnically diverse team of students, faculty and staff, including members of the theatre department and of the university's diversity committee. Everyone shared accounts of harrowing first and second-hand experiences, including a chilling number of sexual harassment, sexual assault, date rape and beverage-drugging stories. While one young woman was delivering an oral presentation in class, a male classmate wrote: "CUNT!" on the chalkboard behind her. A young man went out drinking with his friends and woke up naked the next morning with lewd comments written in ink all over his body. Several students had friends who had survived experiences with "date rape cocktails." One young man told us that when he'd confronted some of his fraternity brothers who'd drugged his girlfriend's beer, the men responded "Oh, we're really sorry.... We didn't realize the two of you were dating!" And everyone talked despairingly about a yearly tradition at the school of greeting incoming freshman with extremely crude and mean-spirited "Welcome" signs painted on sheets hanging from men's dorms all over campus. After the first workshop during which the participants shared these and other equally grim stories, members of the diversity committee informed us that more than a third of the incidents described were under litigation, and so we would not be able to include them in our play.[11]

After reflecting on the particularly crude and sophomoric proclivities of our target audience, we all decided to fight fire with *MAD TV/Saturday Night Live*-style fire. We created *Changing Channels*, a dark, sketch comedy show, designed to be shown during Freshman Week in the residential halls. The central characters are two students, male and female, who are watching television together. As they flip through the channels, they — and the audience — witness fictionalized reenactments of the true stories shared by the Institute participants: a CSI parody of the chauvinistic "Walk of Shame" attitudes towards women who return "suspiciously" late from their dates; a horror movie style treatment of the drunken, zombie-like behavior of students from Thursday afternoon through Sunday nights; a clever subversion of the demeaning *Girls Gone Wild* commercials; and more. Following is the "Marla Steward" approach we used to introduce the topic of date rape cocktails:

And we're back! While our Oysters Rockefeller en Croute are browning....
We have just a moment to respond to the veritable avalanche of e-mails & phone
    calls we've received requesting a reprise of our "Get Lucky" drink mixes!
I'd like to thank all the inquisitive undergraduates out there
who take such an interest in our program!
So, here it is, one of my favorite For-Guests-Only treats:

"The Thursday Night Home Run"!
Let's start with equal parts fresh-squeezed orange juice, pineapple juice
and pink grapefruit juice,
add a splash of POM (pomegranate juice),
and our favorite vodka (Grey Goose works for me) cold, cold, COLD,
and just two ... maaaaybe three drops of "Get Lucky"—

(She shows the vial with skull and crossbones on it.)

— for that extra-special kick: complete loss of memory and clothing!
This is great for those dates who are really sweet, and really cute ...
but REALLY not into getting down to business!
Just garnish with a bit of mint and serve!
You're in for a night *you'll* NEVER forget ...
but *your date* will never remember!

We used each of the "TV" sketches to spark dialogue about sexism between
the two main characters. And we followed the entire play, with a post-show
discussion with the audience about sexist jokes, sexual harassment and sexual
assault.

I'd like to conclude this section with another brief sketch from *Changing Channels*: a "QVC"-like commercial satirizing the young men's practice,
mentioned above, of hanging lewd, sexist bed sheet signs from their windows during Freshman Orientation week. Remember, this is all based in
FACT!

"Full of Sheet"

SPOKESPERSON: It's the first week of classes and you have a big decision to make:
Go out and party!! ... or stay home and come up with catchy phrases for a
Freshman Orientation welcome sign? Really do you have the time to buy the
materials AND paint the sheet? And who can compete with last fall's classy
signs?!—

DRUNK SHEET, MALE: "Free STD's!" "Don't worry, Mom, we won't make her
sleep on the floor!" "15 Pounds of CUM sold here!!"

SPOKESPERSON: No worries, man, with—

SEXY FEMALE VOICE: —"Full-of Sheet"! *(moan)*

SPOKESPERSON: You'll be all the envy of Pine Street.

SEXY FEMALE VOICE: Uh-huh.

SPOKESPERSON: Choose from a variety of pre-printed "Full-of-Sheet" statements,
like—

DRUNK SHEET, MALE: "Freshman girls are welcome! Free facials ANYTIME!"
"WANTED: FRESHMAN PIE! REWARD: A TON OF CREAM!!"

SPOKESPERSON: And the infamous—

DRUNK SHEET, MALE: "Freshmen!! Get them while they're skinny!"

SPOKESPERSON: Display your "Full-of-Sheet" sign from the second floor of your
house. Or use it as a toga, a curtain, a picnic blanket. Or the all-time classic—

SEXY FEMALE VOICE: ... as a bed sheet.

SPOKESPERSON: All "Full-of-Sheets" are created with spanking white, 150 thread-count cloth, hand-woven and hand-painted in vibrant, eye-catching colors by small children in some third world country. No back pain, no brain-strain for you! Just two easy payments of $19.99 each! But wait there's more!! We'll throw in —

SEXY FEMALE VOICE: — Two for the price of one!

SPOKESPERSON: You get not just one, but TWO Pre-Printed —

SEXY FEMALE VOICE: "Full-of-Sheets"!

SPOKESPERSON: — for the price of one! But wait there's more! Call in the next ten minutes and we'll throw in the ever-popular —

DRUNK SHEET, MALE: "Dad, make sure you have the number for Planned Parenthood, 'cuz your daughter's gonna get FUCKED!"

SPOKESPERSON: Don't worry, ladies, we have Full-of-Sheets for you too.

DRUNK SHEET, FEMALE: "Free Pussy Here! Oh, yes, ... and we have drinks, too!"

SPOKESPERSON: Warning — purchase and use may elicit egging, unwanted visitors, angry parents, irate neighbors, potential eviction and lawsuits.

(Spokesperson holds up bed sheet with first phrase)

SEXY FEMALE VOICE: Make sure everyone knows you're ... "Full of Sheet!"

After viewing this "commercial," Mike and Cynthia, the central characters of the play have an animated discussion about the bed sheet sign tradition at their university. Ironically, it's Mike who turns off the television in disgust and exclaims, "That's gross! Can you believe that crap?!" and Cynthia who admits that she found some of the signs funny. But then they both dig a little deeper and agree that the signs create a hostile and unsafe environment for women on campus. After the show, the cast invited the audience to share their thoughts and feelings about the signage, and to propose solutions. It gives me great pleasure to report that the painted sheet tradition ended less than a year after our show premiered on campus. I'd like to be able to say that this is entirely due to the salutary, consciousness-raising effect our show had on student audiences. To be honest, though, the practice ended because the university and community worked together to develop a procedure for vetting and clearing signage. Still, it is quite possible that our anti-sexism theatrical campaign might have played at least a small role in this wonderful change, especially as the tradition had continued for years before our intervention.

At Ease

And here is where I'll conclude my war stories. For now. And I still have so many battle metaphors to torture and explode! I can't believe I didn't find a way to work in "Operation Restore Hope," "collateral damage," "soft targets," or ... heavens-forefend ... "booby traps"! Criminally negligent, isn't it? And isn't it problematic in the first place to use war terminology in an essay addressing sexism in academia? Perhaps this blunder, this shameless series of misfirings, will only serve to prove, yet again that "the master's tools will never dismantle the master's house." (Lorde 112) Still, I hope I have been able to execute this strange little tactical verbal maneuver with sufficient humor and irony to "hoist" the sexist, militaristic language and thinking with its "own petard."[12] Just as, to achieve certain ends, sometimes a woman might do well to wear pink "with irony."[13] Perhaps when battling sexism in academia, a feminist combatant might similarly do well to "take up arms with irony"?!

The "Call to Arms" I recommend is a call to speak up in opposition to discriminatory comments, behavior, "traditions," and policies. It's Audre Lorde's call "to stand alone, unpopular and sometimes reviled, and [...] to make common cause with those others identified as outside the structures in order to define and seek a world in which we can all flourish." (112) These are some of the kinds of interventions we rehearsed in our Theatre for Social Justice "Boot Camps" and modeled in our "U.S.O." plays. And, while I've used military metaphors to describe both the sexist hostilities at numerous universities, as well as the strategies we employed to resist those hostilities, I must emphasize that our theatrical approaches to "battling sexism" were not combative or confrontational. More often than not, our battle cries were laughter and humor. Our armaments were "greasepaint, bed sheets and Mardi Gras beads." Our shield was the Perseus' mirrored shield reflecting the reifying sexist gorgons' bigotry right back at them. We laid down our own gauntlets and said, "Enough."

Notes

1. Fringe Benefits program participants have included people of many different gender identities. I use the words "woman," "women" and "female" to refer to all participants who express a desire to be identified as women — whether that was the identity assigned to them at birth, or not. I use the words "man," "men" and "male" similarly. I use "Genderqueer," "Two Spirit," "FTM" or "MTF" if and when the individual to which I am referring wish to be identified in that way.

2. While Fringe Benefits programs have addressed a wide variety of social justice issues, this essay will focus exclusively on sexist discrimination in academia. Stories of heterosexist and transphobic discrimination are not included, as such accounts were shared almost exclusively in our programs addressing LGBTQ issues, and, although explicitly welcomed, only very rarely shared in our programs addressing sexism. Discussions of prejudice, stereotypes and discrimination are generally enriched and illuminated by the inclusion

of an examination of the points of connection and disconnection between various "isms" and identities. Still, for the sake of brevity and in order to remain completely within the parameters of this volume, this essay's sites are narrowly set on sexism in academia.

3. "Run the gauntlet. 1. Go through an intimidating or dangerous crowd, place, or experience in order to reach a goal: *they had to run the gauntlet of television cameras*. 2. *Historical*: undergo the military punishment of receiving blows while running between two rows of men with sticks" (Jewel and Abate 703).

4. In our workshops and residencies, participants shared their stories and experiences in a context wherein confidentiality was mutually agreed upon. After hearing each others' stories, the assembled participants had the right to determine democratically how, if at all, the stories would be dramatized and presented to an outside audience. In this essay, therefore, the identities of all participants, witnesses, targets, discriminators and bystanders, as well as the names of the universities (or potentially identifying information such as street names) and other organizations with which they are affiliated have been changed or disguised.

5. After some reflection and discussion, the editors and I have decided to include, unexpurgated, the derogatory language reported by project participants and/or used in their plays. We thought it was important that people feel the full semantic weight of the discriminatory language.

6. Just an admiring "tip of the hat" allusion to Maria di Battista's text.

7. "Also known as *commedia all'improviso* (improvised comedy), *commedia delle maschere* (comedy of masks), and *commedia dei zanni* (comedy of servants), the *commedia dell'arte* is exclusively an actors' theatre that emerged and thrived during the sixteenth and seventeenth centuries in Italy, France, and later in Spain, England, and Germany. The term *arte* is used in its ancient meaning of skill and professionalism, calling to mind the medieval guilds of specialized groups of professionals. The complete definition of this theatre is given by the very names it has acquired: it relies entirely on the actors' professionalism and imagination, it is largely based on improvisation, [and] most of the characters wear masks" (Radulescu 87).

8. *Lazzi* are "comic interludes and actions performed by the Italian actors meant to link scenes and to entertain the public" (Radulescu 96).

9. As no formal evaluation instruments — such as postshow surveys or interviews — were used, we cannot be certain to what extent attitudes and/or behavior were changed.

10. "Examples of this include race, gender, class, and ethnicity" (Collins 42).

11. One of our contractual requirements for our Theatre for Social Justice Institutes is that the host organization include a someone with legal expertise in the play devising team. We do this to help insure that our plays accurately represent relevant laws and policies, do not run afoul of slander, libel or copyright laws, and fit appropriately within the language and content parameters of the institutions within which we perform.

12. I am borrowing from Shakespeare's now proverbial phrase "*hoist with his own petad*" from *Hamlet*. A rough translation would be *to cause the bomb maker to be blown up with his own bomb* (Shakespeare, Act III, scene iv, line 207).

13. "Fem(me) science questions the dignity and wisdom of anyone who would wear pink without irony, or a floral print without murderous or seditious designs" (McHugh 157).

Works Cited

Collins, Patricia Hill. "Gender, Black Feminism, and Black Political Economy." *Annals of the American Academy of Political and Social Science* 568:1 (2000).

DiBattista, Maria. *Fast-Talking Dames*. New Haven: Yale University Press, 2001.

Guinier, Lani. "Educational Opportunity and Democracy" lecture at the University of Wisconsin, Madison, February 11, 1998.

Jewell, Elizabeth J., and Frank Abate. *The New Oxford American Dictionary.* New York: Oxford University Press, 2001.

Lorde, Audre. "The Master's Tools Will Never Dismantle the Master's House" [comments at "The Personal and the Political Panel," Second Sex Conference, New York, September 29, 1979]. In *Sister Outsider: Essays and Speeches by Audrey Lorde.* Berkeley, CA: Crossing Press Feminist Series, 1984, pp. 110–113.

McHugh, Kathleen. "The Femme Manifesto." *Women and Performance: A Journal of Feminist Theory* 8:2 (1996).

Radulescu, Domnica. "Caterina's Colombina: The Birth of a Female Trickster in Seventeenth Century France." *Theater Journal* 60:1 (2008), pp 87–113.

Schutzman, Mady, and Jan Cohen-Cruz, eds. *Playing Boal: Theatre, Therapy, Activism.* New York: Routledge, 1994.

Shakespeare, William. *The Tragedy of Hamlet, Prince of Denmark.* Ed. G.R. Hibbard. Oxford: Oxford University Press, 1998.

Feminist Mentorship in the Academy

Revolutionary Feminism in Action

JENNIFER A. BOISVERT

This essay explores how feminist mentorship, as an expression of revolutionary feminism, can redefine the academy by shaping mentees' education and training. It reviews the literature on women's experience of the academia and feminist mentorship within it. Four central themes of feminist mentorship will be explored: role modeling and support, opportunities for personal and professional growth, developing of a feminist identity, and social activism and revolutionary feminism. Three narratives are used to illustrate these themes, showing how mentors can empower mentees in their education and training, encourage them to analyze critically social and political forces, and become agents of change in the academy and the larger community.

The Academy: A "Chilly Climate"

Academe has a patriarchal tradition emphasizing power, hierarchy, male domination, objectivity and distance, along with tactics of oppression, suppression, social injustice and status quo. Women encounter sexism, hostility and psychological violence in various forms, e.g., being silenced, degraded or intimidated. Women's experience in the academy, as faculty members and students, is riddled with power hierarchies, harsh competitiveness, and a lack of support. The marginalizing and devaluing of women creates a "chilly climate" in the academy characterized by discrimination on the basis of gender, race and class (APA; Crawford and MacLeod; DeMarco; Larsen and Boisvert;

hooks, *Ain't I a Woman?, Talking Back, Yearning, Where We Stand, Feminism Is for Everybody*; Nielson, Marschke, Sheff and Rankin; Osborne; Padula and Miller; The Chilly Collective). This hostile climate creates isolation, invisibility and divisibility of feminists. Feminists cope and survive this chilly climate by seeking out like-minded others for support and collective action (Hall and Sandler *The Classroom Climate* [1982]; *The Classroom Climate* [1984]; Franz, Cole, Crosby and Stewart; Gross, Kmeic, Worell and Crosby; Larsen and Boisvert; Osborne; Klonis, Endo, Crosby and Worell).

hooks, known for her feminist writings, survived the academy by speaking out about patriarchy and its influence in the education system. She theorizes (*Ain't I A Woman?, Learning Where We Stand*) that within the academy patriarchy produces and perpetuates oppression, domination and status quo. It disregards issues of race, class and gender, for example by marginalizing and devaluing Black women. She argues that academe as a system, with its roots in patriarchy and hierarchy, limits a feminist's ability to teach and mentor or to empower students in their learning of self, social action, and that academe is a system of oppression, domination and perpetuation of the status quo. Feminism in the academy needs to have a presence because otherwise it is a male-dominated and male-designed system. Feminists' teaching and mentoring of students, be they undergraduate or postgraduate, helps women to survive the chilly climate (Collins; Colley; Humble, Solomon, Allen, Blaisure and Johnson; Kmeic, Crosby and Worell; Stalker).

Feminist Mentorship in the Academy

hooks' assertion that "Feminism is a movement to end sexist oppression" (Feminism Is for Everybody, 6) and that "feminist liberation is linked to a vision of social change which challenges class elitism" (43), sexism and racism, brings a call to action that feminists should connect theory with practice. She and others (e.g., Hoffman and Stake) argue that feminists create change through pedagogical and political action. Feminist mentoring connects theory with practice vis-à-vis pedagogical and political action; it is a process grounded in feminist pedagogy and ethics. It encompasses ethical values and principles such as respect, fairness, integrity and collegiality in relationships, and is one of the cornerstones of feminist theory. hooks (*Ain't I A Woman, Teaching to Transgress*) and others (e.g. Rich; Worell and Johnson) argue for the need to challenge the status quo in order to create an environment that allows for transgression, the reconstruction of knowledge, reinterpretation of position and open expression of one's voice. Feminist mentorship is an expression of feminist pedagogy, political action and advocacy, representing a departure from the status quo and challenging the context within which it exists (Benishek, Bieschke, Park and Slattery). It offers the potential to facilitate and support feminists' efforts to "work toward a woman-centered university [with the awareness] if that [patriarchal] center of gravity can be shifted will women be really free to learn, to teach, to share strength, to explore, to criticize, and to convert knowledge into power" (Rich, 128). It can be a vehicle for increasing inclusiveness and diversity in the academy so that marginalized and devalued groups of women are recognized as equals, and they are acknowledged for their unique identities, and empowered in their learning process to discover and wield their power.

In feminist mentorship, both mentor and mentee have a personal and professional investment in the relationship. This is a fluid, didactic relationship that is formed between the mentor and mentee in which the teacher becomes the learner and the learner becomes the teacher (Atkinson, Casas and Neville; Baugh, Lankau and Scandura; Benishek et al.; Dohm and Cummings; Huang and Lynch; Humble et al.; Lark and Croteau). Mentors benefit from the relationship by role modeling such things as feminist values, principles and ethics, work/life balance, investing in a future colleague, supporting her/him in the achieving of academic and career goals, developing insight into complex professional issues, and providing a sense of validation and support in their academic work. As a role model, the mentor is an "experienced person who guides and facilitates the professional growth of the relatively inexperienced protégé" (Bogat and Redner, 851). A mentor facilitates professional development through "mutual empathy, mutual empowerment, mutual caretaking with a healthy degree of reciprocity, and authenticity marked by role flexibility" (Heinrich, 463).

A mentor has self-awareness and openly acknowledges strengths, limitations, assumptions, biases and stigmas on both personal and professional levels. On a personal level, mentors show how self-care is essential to maintain strength and resilience. Feminist mentoring, with its emphasis on relational, developmental, pedagogical and political dimensions is designed to meet students' needs for work/life balance, i.e., attending to family responsibilities but also excelling scholastically (Atkinson, Neville and Casas; Benishek et al.; Bruce; Humble et al.; Kalbfleisch and Keyton; Padula and Miller; Schweibert, Deck, Bradshaw, Scott and Harper).

On a professional level, mentors show that a commitment to social activism and advocacy is an ethical duty and a fundamental aspect of feminist pedagogy. They incorporate a political perspective into their work with mentees, bringing to the fore "the personal is political" tenet and the belief that education is not value-free. They acknowledge, examine and confront aspects of the academy reflecting systemic oppression, domination or status quo. Through role modeling, mentors show how to challenge the status quo and create systemic change. They strive to raise mentees' critical consciousness, awareness of social justice, and involvement in social activism and advocacy. They openly acknowledge strengths, limitations, assumptions and biases, enabling mentees to see what constitutes appropriate ethical and professional boundaries and how self-awareness might foster a passion for political and social change (Benishek et al.; Faunce 1990; hooks, *Teaching to Transgress*; Porter; Rave and Larsen). Mentees should be taught that they are a source of truth, knowledge and power, and that a strong, congruent sense of self is instrumental to change. Indeed, the mentor and mentee may use their relationship as a vehicle for change in the academy, despite systemic challenges or barriers.

Mentees benefit from the relationship by having a role model and by developing academic and career skills. The mentee can witness the mentor's confidence and competence, but also her uncertainty and humanness. The mentee becomes confident and competent because of this role modeling. At the same time, the mentor gains a colleague when the mentee learns to trust herself/himself as a person. The mentor collaborates with the mentee by bringing her/him into networks with colleagues, providing mentees with experience and involvement in professional activities. The mentor models what mentees are expected to learn as future colleagues and collaborators in revolutionary feminism; this is especially important for doctoral students as they prepare for post-doctoral work or career entry (Blankemeyer and Weber; DeMarco; Padula and Miller; Peyton, Martin, Perkins and Dougherty).

Feminist mentorship facilitates awareness of power differences and issues within academe (Benishek et al.; Cochran-Smith and Paris; Humble et al.; Tom; Roffman). Mentors strive to address these power differences in a variety of ways. For example, mutual disclosure by mentor and mentee might address power differences. Mentors should openly acknowledge power differences in the relationship and strive to empower the mentee. Tom described the "frame of the deliberate relationship" in which a mentor "acknowledge[s] the responsibilities of being in a position of authority in relation to students while working with them to challenge, question, and redistribute power to the fullest extent possible" (4). This suggests that the relationship can be both hierarchical in terms of knowledge and experience and mutual in terms of interaction and collaboration.

While there are many benefits to feminist mentorship, there are challenges caused by individual or institutional factors (Eby, McManus, Simon and Russell; Johnson "The Intentional Mentor," "A Framework"; Johnson and Nelson; Kite et al.; Seldin). Mentors are often faced with institutional stressors from teaching, research and committee activities that might limit the amount of time that they can devote to mentees. Mentors might also lack knowledge or experience of how to mentor because they themselves were not mentored. Their inability to set appropriate boundaries with mentees may result in abuses of power, unmet expectations and negative experiences. Mentees, too, may not have had the opportunity to think critically about such things as their academic or career needs, their expectations surrounding faculty-student relationships or the chilly climate of the academy. All of this may give rise to relationships with conflict or ethical dilemmas.

The Explorative Process: Approach and Methodology

This essay explores benefits and challenges of feminist mentorship from a mentee's perspective. These narratives represent my personal truth, views and experiences and a way of looking at the world that is unique. hooks often includes personal stories in her writings, though this draws criticisms from scholars for being "non-academic." These speak to the heart of her experience (see for example, *Feminist Theory*). Following hooks' example, I use narratives to explore my experience as a White woman who has received feminist mentoring in academic settings.

I agree with hooks' sentiment that "Everything we do in life is rooted in theory" (*Feminism Is for Everybody*, 19). Feminist theory, pedagogy and research focus on the experience and lives of women as a legitimate topic of study, highlighting the importance of context in enhancing our understanding of them (Belenky, Clinchy, Goldberger and Tarule; hooks, *Talking Back*; Reinharz; Richardson; Worell; Worell and Etaugh). Feminist research emphasizes reflectivity and the contextual and relational nature of knowledge. While reflexive narrative provides insights into social process and reflects a feminist commitment to constructed knowledge, i.e., knowledge that is informed by *both* theory and personal experience (Cancian; Clandinin and Connelly 1998; Connelly and Clandinin; Fonow and Cook; Lather; Manning and Cullum-

Swan; Olesen). This narrative approach has the advantage of highlighting "… the most important influences, experiences, circumstances, issues, themes and lessons" of what is being recounted (Atkinson, 125). Because the narratives reflect real life experiences, pseudonyms are used to protect privacy (Clandinin and Connelly).

Feminist Mentorship: Three Narratives

VERONICA

Veronica saw my vision and knew she could help make it a reality. A visionary herself, Veronica is a woman who combines vision with action. This commonality bonded us instantly. As an undergraduate, it was my vision to become a clinical psychologist who would help marginalized and oppressed persons, especially women. A white woman in her 50s, Veronica was committed to helping mentees and students achieve their academic and career goals. She believed she could ready me for graduate school by refining my research skills and "growth edges" and receive mentorship along the way. This opportunity was a one-year research internship at her non-profit foundation. This foundation was located on the campus of the university where Veronica was a faculty member in educational psychology.

Veronica connected teaching, research and practice and community advocacy. She did this by making people a priority, relating to them with integrity, and working collaboratively. I was inspired. During my internship, I linked teaching, research and community advocacy in many ways. I developed a knack for leadership and spirit for activism. I led a monthly community research group that sparked an interest in social activism and revolutionary feminism. I came to see article writing, public speaking and community events planning as ways to express social consciousness and engage in consciousness-raising. An avid photographer and writer, Veronica taught workshops on photography and wrote books about positive psychology. This was her expression of social activism. Her messages were thought-provoking and visually evocative. She touched others' lives in tidal waves, not ripples. She believed in diving below the surface of experience. She taught me how to shoot and print black-and-white photography so I could also dive deeply.

Through photography, Veronica taught me to appreciate the instrumental use of self in therapy; the therapist is her/his own best tool. I began to see peoples' lives and experiences through a new lens. She shared her wisdom by example, allowing me to observe individual therapy with clients. She also taught me to be ethical and real with others and myself. I learned to be respectful, non-judgmental, genuine and gentle. Her teachings are today apparent in my exchanges with students, mentees, research participants, therapy clients and colleagues. Veronica showed me how a professional functions and how a person functions as a professional, i.e., how one's personal and professional lives are intricately intertwined. I learned that being a woman professor requires one to "put on leather." That is, be tough-skinned to withstand the harsh academic climate. She revealed to me the softness hidden behind her "leather" hull. She said that I, too, had a softness that lay beneath a hard exterior that could serve me well should I choose to enter academia. She also said that because of my passion for research and scholarship, I was well-suited to academia, but like her, would be faced with hard choices that would test my character. She made it clear that, while being an academic has rewards, it also has pitfalls. Indeed, when I entered academia much later, I encountered ethical dilemmas that tested my character, strength and resilience, and my adherence to feminist values, principles and ethics.

Veronica taught me what it meant to be a scholar and to have "growth edges." In her view, imperfections, mistakes, disappointments and failures were launching points for growth. A skilled clinician, she exuded "possibility thinking" and reframed obstacles as opportunities for empowerment. She often shared her wisdom by drawing examples from her own life. She taught me how to take risks, conduct research on the leading edge, and think innovatively, resourcefully and holistically. I learned how to "color outside the lines" and challenge the status quo. Veronica taught me to be a teacher and mentor. She set up opportunities for peer mentorship so that her mentees and students could learn from one another in a safe environment. In this group, mutuality, reciprocity and support were emphasized. I witnessed how group interaction could lead to personal change. We "walked our talk" and put ideas into action. This experience led me to co-found a group for early career women psychologists that featured social activism (see Larsen and Boisvert).

Veronica challenged me to stretch my boundaries in a multitude of ways. A keen researcher, Veronica taught me to be guided by my own personal truth. She exposed me to a variety of qualitative research methodologies and to a new way of studying and understanding human experience. As a qualitative researcher, she taught me the importance of self-awareness, openness and experiential process. She encouraged me to engage in self-exploration and reflection. Having been trained in the empirical paradigm as an undergraduate, I found it difficult to grasp "subjective reality" as a concept and focus of study. Putting me to the test, Veronica provided me with an opportunity to conduct my own research study on the psychology of women. Because of this exposure to feminist research, my way of thinking was transformed.

The stretching of my boundaries paralleled those of our relationship, which grew in new and unexpected directions when Veronica was hospitalized. The uncertainty of her ability to mentor me for the rest of the internship was daunting. Insisting that I receive support and stay the course in my internship, Veronica arranged for one of her colleagues to supervise me. I was determined to help her regain her health, recognizing that she relied on me in small but significant ways. I took on new roles and responsibilities so that she could focus on her recovery. In a sense, I became the teacher, and she, the student. I regularly informed her of the progress of my study, the daily happenings at the foundation, and how I was, with her blessing, "running the ship" in her absence. Because of this, I developed autonomy, resiliency, flexibility and "possibility thinking." I learned to live in a place of hope. By the time Veronica recovered, mentorship had already given way to friendship.

Looking back, Veronica was the exceptional mentor I strive to be. She took time to congratulate others on achieving academic or career milestones. This included my being accepted into graduate school. Veronica had a gift for empowering others in graceful, respectful and powerful ways. She showed me that women professors needed to be tough in order to survive, but also soft in order to teach and mentor. Because of her, I have developed a deeper understanding of the chilly climate of the academy along with a healthy professional identity. I have also developed a deep passion for social activism, and its expression through such things as black-and-white photography.

Marcia

Marcia believed in me the moment she became my thesis supervisor. As a graduate student in clinical psychology, I was delighted to be mentored by her. Her belief in my ability to obtain my doctorate spurred me to leap the hurdles of program requirements. Her good qualities and research interests led me initially to approach her. Marcia had a caring and generous spirit. She was genuine, warm and heartfelt. She was sensitive to my academic and career needs. Her open discussion of department politics, power differences, and tactics opened my eyes to the reality of the issues that riddle the academy. She stayed out of the fray of faculty disagreements, lending her presence and energy instead to students and mentees. She saw the "big picture," believing it was more important to advocate for students and mentees, and advance their learning than it was to advance her own agenda. This belief set her apart.

An Aboriginal woman in her 40s, Marcia was a self-identified feminist and community activist. She openly acknowledged diversity issues. An astute clinician, Marcia taught me to be sensitive to diversity in therapy. She stressed the importance of being contextual in order to understand clients' psychological disorders or problems. Marcia also emphasized how community advocacy allows one to understand people and issues in their cultural groups and communities. I developed a keen awareness and understanding of the need for holism and humility in clinical and community work, especially with ethnic minority clients. Consequently, I applied for internships that would expose me to diversity issues.

Marcia shaped my identity as a feminist researcher-practitioner. She instilled confidence in my becoming a compassionate therapist and community activist. Drawing from her Aboriginal culture and her own life experience, Marcia helped me see that I was both a "healer" and a "warrior." According to Marcia, a healer was someone who walked with clients on their personal journeys and acted on their behalf when necessary. And, a warrior was someone who bravely fought for social justice and challenged the status quo. Marcia saw that I had a natural talent and gift for moving clients toward personal growth and healing while also honoring and advocating for them. As a result, I began to see therapy as both science and art.

Marcia opened my mind to the merits of an integrated therapeutic approach, describing how she incorporated Aboriginal traditions (teachings) into mainstream individual therapy approaches, e.g., psychodynamic, cognitive-behavioral. I learned about the Aboriginal medicine wheel and how to treat clients holistically, taking into account the physical, emotional, social and spiritual dimensions of their health and well-being. I gained awareness about Aboriginal ceremonies and rituals such as powwows, dances, storytelling, smudging (the burning of sweet grass to cleanse the spirit) and visiting with Elders (senior Aboriginals who are recognized by the Aboriginal community as possessing special knowledge, wisdom and sagacity). I understood from Marcia that Aboriginal women, although oppressed and marginalized by government policies, nevertheless create change in their own communities. She remarked on the enduring hope and spirit of these women as persons but also as a collective of Aboriginal peoples. My clinical work with Aboriginal women highlights their strength and resilience in the face of oppressive social and political forces, notably racism, sexism, classism and colonialism.

Marcia's feminist beliefs and values could be seen in her teaching and research. She approached research from a qualitative paradigm. She did so in a way unique to her — with heart. This was her expression of revolutionary feminism. She regarded these women and girls who were study participants as collaborators in the research process, using qualitative methods to understand their lived experiences of motherhood. She acknowledged cultural assumptions and biases, especially those involving Aboriginal women. She incorporated reflexivity, giving credence to the contextual nature of knowledge. In her eyes, women and girls' lived experiences should not be pathologized, but conceptualized to reflect an understanding of contextual factors such as social problems of racism, poverty and violence, or political forces of oppression, domination and status quo. She saw the "big picture" of women and girls' lives and experiences.

In my undergraduate training in an academic setting that emphasized patriarchy, hierarchy, objectivity and distance, I was only taught to conduct research in a quantitative paradigm. I regarded research participants as subjects and relied upon quantitative methods to study them. Marcia helped me see the limitations of this approach. I saw the merits and advantages of a qualitative approach, e.g., having more flexibility, diversity and creativity in the research process, and working collaboratively with participants. I grew to understand how qualitative methods reflect feminist values, principles and ethics, particularly community-based participatory research. Marcia showed me how these methods can embody the feminist idea that knowledge is grounded in community and that it is experiential. She helped me to understand how feminist and qualitative methods such as participant observation, focus groups, case studies and narratives could further community empowerment and social change. I also understood, however, that quantitative methods such as experimental social innovation, non-equivalent comparison group designs, and randomized field experiments could also achieve feminist research goals of social activism and change vis-à-vis gathering empirical data that supported feminist theory or informed institutional or governmental policy. As such, I acquired an appreciation of the breadth and depth of feminist methods.

Despite our initial difference in research approach, we had a common feminist research agenda. I appreciated Marcia's passion and commitment to research that could make a difference in the lives of women and girls. In her case, conducting community-based participatory research that focused on the prevention of teenage pregnancy and the experience of adoption. I appreciated Marcia's research passion and feminist commitment, and yearned to grow in this direction. Fortunately for me, Marcia assisted me in choosing a thesis topic that was close to my heart. I chose to test feminist theory through studying eating disorder symptomatology in women. She encouraged me to be creative in designing my study. Her mentoring style and research approach opened a door: a careful, flexible selection of mixed methods best suited to the research problem. I chose to use a mixture of qualitative and quantitative methods in my thesis research, broadening my feminist research repertoire. This balance felt comfortable to me as a feminist and as a researcher. Marcia said that I had all of the markings of a feminist researcher and affirmed my competency.

In addition to being a mentee, I learned from Marcia in the classroom as a student. She was enthusiastic and dynamic. Her class was a cooperative learning environment. She encouraged open dialogue among students by arranging the class seating in a circle so that students could interact as equals. This seating arrangement invited non-hierarchical discussion and debate. Marcia used talking circles, critical-thinking group discussions, conscious-ness-raising, reflective writing exercises, and culturally focused field trips. She had students take responsibility for their learning, inviting them to make class presentations on social justice and political issues. Marcia accepted her students as unique persons with different backgrounds, views, experiences and learning styles. Her values and principles of respect, equality, integrity, collaboration, justice and tolerance created a safe atmosphere for students to self-disclose and share experiences.

Marcia's role-modeling of feminist values, principles and ethics came into play when I was faced with systemic oppression and discrimination. Marcia was willing to intervene on my behalf. However, she reframed my experience, helping me to see it as an opportunity to recognize that "the personal is political" and to put feminist values, principles and ethics into action. From Marcia, I learned how to navigate the challenge of experiencing social injustice, oppression and discrimination in an academic environment by responding in a respectful, ethical manner. I gained confidence in my ability to problem-solve effectively and felt empowered. I resolved this situation on my own. Since then, this life lesson has come into play more than once in an academic setting. I am grateful for Marcia's support.

Looking back, Marcia's belief in me fueled my determination to achieve great things, especially my doctorate in clinical psychology. A powerful role model, Marcia embodied feminist values, principles and ethics like no other woman professor I have known. Feminism and activism are her lifeblood. Like Marcia, I ascribe to a feminist approach in mentorship and create respectful, collaborative and empowering mentoring relationships. I too, encourage mentees and students to achieve their fullest potential, to analyze critically the social and political forces that shape the academy and our society, and to see themselves as agents of change who have the power to transform the academy and the larger community. I have learned how to stay grounded and true to myself when faced with ethical dilemmas and systemic oppression and discrimination in the academy. Marcia has helped me become a healer and warrior whose aim is to create change — individual, institutional, communal and global.

Hannah

Hannah had confidence in my aptitude for achieving excellence in research. A faculty member in clinical psychology, Hannah supervised me in research and practice. A White woman in her 30s, Hannah modeled the importance of being ambitious and motivated in achieving academic and career goals, and the challenges of work/life balance. While working alongside her, I developed a healthy awareness of how professional and personal role demands and expectations can conflict, with stress and anxiety being filtered into work and professional relationships, including ours. I witnessed the difficulty she encountered in dealing with family responsibilities while excelling scholastically. From her, I learned to value self-care and to manage my time and energy to have a healthy, balanced personal life. This learning has been invaluable for my work in an academic setting and my relationships with others.

One of the challenges of our mentoring relationship was finding time to meet because of her academic demands and time pressures. This was problematic because I regularly required her feedback to proceed with various research and practice activities. It had a significant impact on our relationship. Although I was not aware of it at the time, I now see that Hannah's early career stage and status influenced her mentoring style. In contrast to my previous mentoring relationships, the relationship with Hannah was hierarchical. Power difference within a mentoring relationship was new for me. This difference presented its own challenges, such as different perspectives regarding the success of research studies or effectiveness of clinical interventions. These challenges pushed me to communicate effectively and assertively. I developed the language necessary to express my needs, wants and expectations about our relationship, and their importance in terms of achieving academic and career goals. Ultimately, I grew well-rounded in my professional identity and relational style.

Hannah role-modeled ethicality and excellence in research and scholarship. These were her strengths. She showed me that it was critical to be guided by ethicality. Ethicality threaded through her teaching, research and practice activities, and her relationships with other faculty members, mentees and students. She, more than any other mentor, helped me to see that ethicality is something that one integrates into their identity. Ethicality is now a core part of me. Because of her own academic demands and time pressures, she openly acknowledged her personal limitations, one of which was an inability to give more than she was capable of at any given time. She modeled assertiveness and boundaries by saying "no" to additional requests or demands. She articulated her assumptions and biases, cognizant of how these might come into play in the context of her research and professional relationships.

From Hannah, I learned the importance of translating research into practice. Like her, I identified as a researcher-practitioner, seeing myself as both scientist and therapist. I developed an appreciation of the advantages of a cognitive-behavioral therapeutic approach, the main one being its empirical basis. Hannah stressed the need for scientific rigor when conducting assessments and undertaking individual therapy, arguing that clients' presenting problems needed to be understood comprehensively and contextually. She emphasized the need for a systematic, detailed approach to data gathering to ensure that clients' presenting problems were accurately conceptualized and, in turn, diagnosed. She underscored that clinicians needed to be attuned to diversity issues in assessment and therapy, as these might influence clients' subjective distress, symptom presentation and/or level of functioning. This learning carried over into my clinical work with clients of diverse race/ethnicity, sexual orientation and religious affiliation. I understood more fully how to be a warm and caring therapist. Following Hannah's lead, I worked therapeutically with clients within a cognitive-behavioral framework, balancing the use of interventions and strategies with a display of empathy and compassion. I became adept at using the feminist approach as an adjunct to cognitive-behavioral treatment, especially in my clinical work with women with eating and weight disorders. Over time, I developed a therapeutic style that is reflective of feminist, person-centered and cognitive-behavioral approaches. This combination of therapeutic approaches is a comfortable fit. I have Hannah to thank for showing me how to be "hard-headed" and "soft-hearted" in my work.

To my surprise, shifting from graduate to postgraduate work led to a shifting in our relationship. With my graduation, our relationship was no longer hierarchical but collaborative and collegial. Hannah made it clear to me that becoming a doctor of philosophy meant that I had proven myself to be worthy of being accepted as a scholar. Now I relate to Hannah as a colleague, consulting about teaching, research and practical matters. Our relationship is one that is empowering and gratifying. The time and energy that she has invested in me, notably broadening and refining my research and practice skills, has paid off. I now have a fulfilling career as a feminist researcher-practitioner who also teaches and mentors.

Implications for Feminist Mentorship in the Academy

Looking within and across the three narratives, four central themes emerge: role modeling and support, opportunities for personal and professional growth, development of a feminist identity, and social activism and revolutionary feminism. These themes support earlier writings that suggest that feminist mentorship significantly influences mentees' achieving of academic and career goals, development of feminist consciousness and identity, and expression of feminist values, principles and ethics vis-à-vis social activism (Bargad and Hyde; Henderson-King and Stewart; Macalister; Stake and Gerner; Stake, Roades, Rose, Ellis and West; Stake and Rose; Worell, Stilwell, Oakley and Robinson).

In order to cultivate feminist goals and objectives globally, it is critical that feminists maintain a visible and active presence in the academy and the larger community. Feminists do not simply want to level the playing field of the academy; they want to reshape it to reflect better their values and visions (Kite et al.; Worell and Johnson). As Kite et al. assert, "the aim is not simply to help women succeed in obsolete patriarchal institutions but rather to reconstruct those institutions" (1080). Feminists, as faculty members and students, can improve the academy and the larger community by engaging in social activism and revolutionary feminism. Mentors can encourage mentees to refer to the writings of feminist theorists such as hooks (e.g., 2000c) to help them to put feminist theory into action, creating change within the academy and the larger community. As agents of change, mentors are aware of the contradictions and barriers while working in an environment where they challenge the status quo. They can transform the academy by drawing attention to political, social and economic forces that contribute to the chilly climate. They can provide gendered and political explanations about contradictions and barriers in academe and strategies for overcoming these through feminist-oriented change strategies such as consciousness-raising.

Mentors can help mentees to reflect and analyze critically their place in society and the choices available to them. Mentees should be encouraged to exercise feminist values, principles and ethics and challenge the status quo by virtue of exercising choices, recognizing that "one cannot be anti-choice and be a feminist" (hooks, *Feminism Is for Everybody*, 6). In addition to helping mentees become conscious in their choices and decisions, mentors can also help them to find their own voices. Mentees should be encouraged to demand alternatives to patriarchal aspects of education, encouraged to consider how "feminist liberation is linked to a vision of social change" (43). In doing so, mentors raise awareness about the absurdity of patriarchy in the academy from a systems perspective, prompting mentees to work collectively toward changing the chilly climate. Recognizing that feminism cannot succeed without men's participation in the movement because feminism is anti-sexism, not anti-male, mentees are apt to regard men as essential to changing the chilly climate of the academy. With this recognition, they will be better positioned to focus on problems such as sexism, racism and classism.

Mentors can encourage mentees to discover their own truth by writing a narrative about a unique academic life experience, taking into account their own biases and cultural assumptions supported by oppression — sexism, racism, classism, capitalism and colonialism. Mentees can then share these narratives in a group setting to stimulate discussion about forces, circumstances or policies that shaped their experience, and the feminist-oriented change strategies that can be used to create personal and social change. Aligned with the arguments of some feminist scholars (e.g., Belenky et al.; Reinharz) who contend that to be accurately understood, women's experiences must be told in their own words, enabling them to discover their voice, so too can mentors encourage mentees to use a personal perspective in their writing so that they might better understand patriarchy — its mechanisms and implications — on personal (individual) and political (institutional and communal) levels. Feminists recognize that essential to a feminist process is the empowerment of mentees in their ability to analyze their position in the academy and in society, encouraging the metaphorical use of voice as a vehicle to bring out truths. In this way, mentees might develop the language that is necessary to communicate this knowledge, with the end result being self and systemic change. Mentors can help mentees learn to voice their needs, expectations, desires or concerns related to their education and training, academia or the mentoring relationship, and to act on the things they articulate as problematic. This feminist process is consonant with a feminist pedagogy that encourages mentees to question, analyze and perceive their academic life experiences and personal histories as sources of knowledge, helping them to connect these experiences to social activism and revolutionary feminism (hooks 1989; Roffman 1996).

Conclusion

This exploration reveals that feminist mentorship is an expression of revolutionary feminism redefining the academy by shaping mentees' education and training. Feminist mentorship is very much about helping mentees to question power, become empowered, engaged in social activism, and committed to demonstrating revolutionary feminism by embodying "the personal with the political" tenet. As shown in this essay, narratives can provide a reflective space for mentees to discover their position as knowers and as agents of change and their experiences as sources of truth and knowledge. Further, these narratives can provide an entry point for exploring academic life experiences and/or personal histories and increasing knowledge about self and how patriarchy creates a chilly climate in the academy.

Mentees will benefit from being exposed to feminist mentoring at the undergraduate level so that they do not simply survive but thrive at graduate and post-graduate levels. Feminist mentorship has given me the wisdom and freedom to grow and change and the ability to develop a strong, resilient identity as a feminist. This identity reflects the integrity of my feminist values, principles and ethics, and shapes my professional work. As feminists, we must work collectively in our struggles to transform the chilly climate of the academy into one that is less harshly competitive and more supportive of all women. It is my hope that others, too, will explore their unique academic life experiences and personal histories, and experiment with possibilities for growth and change. As mentors, our words and actions hold power to redefine the academy.

Works Cited

American Psychological Association (APA). *Women in Academe: Two Steps Forward, One Step Back. Report of the Task Force on Women in Academe.* Washington: American Psychological Association, 2000.

Atkinson, Donald R. "The Life Story Interview." In *Handbook of Interview Research: Context and Method.* Eds. Jaber F. Gubrium and James A. Holstein. Thousand Oaks, CA: Sage, 2002, pp. 121–40.

_____, Antonio Casas, and Helen Neville. "Ethnic Minority Psychologists: Whom They Mentor and the Benefits They Derive in the Process." *Journal of Multicultural Counseling and Development* 22 (1994): 37–48.

_____, Helen Neville, and Antonio Casas. "The Mentorship of Ethnic Minorities in Professional Psychology." *Professional Psychology: Research and Practice* 22 (1991): 336–38.

Bargad, Adena, and Janet Shibley Hyde. "Women's Studies: A Study of Feminist Identity Development in Women." *Psychology of Women Quarterly* 15 (1991): 181–201.

Baugh, Gayle S., Melanie J. Lankau, and Terri A. Scandura. "An Investigation of the Effects of Protégé Gender on Responses to Mentoring." *Journal of Vocational Behavior* 49 (1996): 309–23.

Belenky, Mary Field, Blythe McVicker Clinchy, Nancy Rule Goldberger, and Jill Mattuck Tarule. *Women's Ways of Knowing: The Development of Self, Voice, and Mind.* 10th ed. New York: Basic, 1997.

Benishek, Lois A., Kathleen J. Bieschke, Jeeson Park, and Suzanne M. Slattery. "A Multicultural Feminist Model of Mentoring." *Journal of Multicultural Counseling and Development* 32 (2002): 428–42.

Blankemeyer, Maureen, and Margaret J. Weber. "Mentoring: The Socialization of Graduate Students for the 21st Century." *Journal of Family and Consumer Sciences* 88 (1996): 32–36.

Bogat, Anne G., and Robin L. Redner. "How Mentoring Affects the Professional Development of Women in Psychology." *Professional Psychology: Research and Practice* 16 (1985): 851–59.

Bruce, Mary Alice. "Mentoring Women Doctoral Students: What Counselor Educators and Supervisors Can Do." *Counselor Education and Supervision* 35 (1995): 139–49.

Cancian, Francesca. "Participatory Research and Alternative Strategies for Activist Sociology." In *Feminism and Social Change: Bridging Theory and Practice.* Ed. Heidi Gottfried. Urbana: Illinois University Press, 1996, pp. 187–205.

The Chilly Collective. *Breaking Anonymity: The Chilly Climate for Women Faculty.* Waterloo, Ontario: Wilfrid Laurier University Press, 1995.

Clandinin, Jean D., and Michael F. Connelly. "Personal Experience Methods." In *Collecting and Interpreting Qualitative Materials.* Eds. Norman K. Denzin and Yvonna S. Lincoln. Thousand Oaks, CA: Sage, 1998, pp. 150–78.

Cochran-Smith, Marilyn, and Cynthia L. Paris. "Mentor and Mentoring: Did Homer Have it Right?" In *Critical Discourses on Teacher Development.* Ed. John Smyth. New York: Cassell, 1995, pp. 181–201.

Colley, Helen. "Righting Rewritings of the Myth of Mentor: A Critical Perspective on Career Guidance Mentoring." *British Journal of Guidance and Counselling* 29 (2001): 177–97.

Collins, Patricia H. *Black Feminist Thought: Knowledge, Consciousness, and the Politics of Empowerment.* 2nd rev., 10th ed. New York: Routledge, 2000.

Connelly, Michael F., and Jean D. Clandinin. "Stories of Experience and Narrative Inquiry." *Educational Researcher* 19 (1990): 2–14.

Crawford, Mary, and Margo MacLeod. "Gender in the College Classroom: An Assessment of the 'Chilly Climate' for Women." *Sex Roles* 23 (1990): 101–22.

DeMarco, Rosanna. "Mentorship: A Feminist Critique of Current Research." *Journal of Advanced Nursing* 18 (1993): 1242–50.

Dohm, Faith-Anne, and Wendy Cummings. "Research Mentoring and Women in Clinical Psychology." *Psychology of Women Quarterly* 26 (2002): 163–67.

Eby, Lillian T., Stacy E. McManus, Shana A. Simon, and Joyce E. A. Russell. "The Protégé's Perspective Regarding Mentoring Experiences: The Development of a Taxonomy." *Journal of Vocational Behavior* 5 (2000): 1–21.

Faunce, Patricia S. "The Self-Care and Wellness of Feminist Therapists." In *Feminist Ethics in Psychotherapy.* Eds. Hannah Lerman and Natalie Porter. New York: Springer, 1990, pp. 123–30.

Fonow, Mary Margaret, and Judith A. Cook. "Back to the Future: A Look at the Second Wave of Feminism Epistemology and Methodology." In *Beyond Methodology: Feminist Scholarship as Lived Research.* Eds. Mary Margaret Fonow and Judith A. Cook. Bloomington: Indiana University Press, 1991, pp. 1–15.

Franz, Carole E., Elizabeth R. Cole, Faye J. Crosby, and Abigail J. Stewart. "Lessons From Lives." In *Women Creating Lives: Identification, Resilience, and Resistance.* Eds. Carole E. Franz and Abigail J. Stewart. Boulder, CO: Westview, 1994, pp. 325–34.

Gross, Rachel, Julie Kmeic, Judith Worell, and Faye J. Crosby. "Institutional Affiliation and Satisfaction Among Feminist Professors." *Psychology of Women Quarterly* 25 (2001): 20–26.

Hall, Roberta, and Bernice Sandler. *The Classroom Climate: Is it a Chilly Campus Climate for Women?* Washington: Project on the Status and Education of Women, Association of American Colleges, 1984.

_____. *The Classroom Climate: Is it a Chilly One for Women?* Washington: Project on the Status and Education of Women, Association of American Colleges, 1982.

Hazler, Richard, and Jamie Carney. "Student-Faculty Interactions: An Underemphasized Dimension of Counselor Education." *Counselor Education and Supervision* 33 (1993): 80–89.

Heinrich, Kathleen T. "Doctoral Advisement Relationships Between Women: On Friendship and Betrayal." *Journal of Higher Education* 66 (1995): 447–469.

Henderson-King, Donna, and Abigail J. Stewart. "Educational Experiences and Shifts in Group Consciousness: Studying Women." *Personality and Social Psychology Bulletin* 25 (1999): 390–99.

Hoffman, Frances L., and Jayne E. Stake. "Feminist Pedagogy in Theory and Practice: An Empirical Investigation." *National Women's Studies Association Journal* 10 (1998): 71–97.

hooks, bell. *Ain't I a Woman? Black Women and Feminism.* Boston: South End, 1981.

_____. *Feminism is for Everybody: Passionate Politics.* Boston: South End, 2000.

_____. *Feminist Theory: From Margin to Center.* 2nd ed. Boston: South End, 2000.

_____. *Talking Back.* Boston: South End, 1989.

_____. *Teaching Community: A Pedagogy of Hope.* New York: Routledge, 2003.

_____. *Teaching to Transgress: Education as the Practice of Freedom.* New York: Routledge, 1994.

_____. *Where We Stand: Class Matters.* New York: Routledge, 2000.

_____. *Yearning: Race, Gender, and Cultural Politics.* Boston: South End, 1990.

Huang, Chungliang A., and Jerry Lynch. *Mentoring: The Tao of Giving and Receiving Wisdom.* San Francisco: HarperCollins, 1995.

Humble, Áine M., Catherine Richards Solomon, Katherine R. Allen, Karen R. Blaisure, and Michael P. Johnson. "Feminism and Mentoring of Graduate Students." *Family Relations* 55 (2006): 2–15.

Johnson, Brad W. "A Framework for Conceptualizing Competence to Mentor." *Ethics and Behavior* 13 (2003): 127–51.

_____. "The Intentional Mentor: Strategies and Guidelines for the Practice of Mentoring." *Professional Psychology: Research and Practice* 33 (2002): 88–96.

_____ and Nancy Nelson. "Mentor-Protégé Relationships in Graduate Training: Some Ethical Concerns." *Ethics and Behavior* 9 (1999): 189–210.

Kalbfleisch, Pamela J., and Joann Keyton. "Power and Equality in Mentoring Relationships." In *Gender, Power, and Communication in Human Relationships.* Eds. Pamela J. Kalbfleisch and Michael J. Cody. Hillsdale, NJ: Lawrence Erlbaum, 1995, pp. 189–212.

Kite, Mary E., Nancy Felipe Russo, Sharon Stephens Brehm, Nadya A. Fouad, Christine C. Iijima Hall, Janet Shibley Hyde, and Gwendolyn Puryear Keita. "Women Psychologists in Academe: Mixed Progress, Unwarranted Complacency." *American Psychologist* 56 (2001): 1080–98.

Klonis, Suzanne, Joanne Endo, Faye J. Crosby, and Judith Worell. "Feminism as Life Raft." *Psychology of Women Quarterly* 21 (1997): 333–45.

Kmeic, Julie, Faye J. Crosby, and Judith Worell. "Walking the Talk: On Stage and Behind the Scenes." In *Women's Ethnicities: Journeys Through Psychology.* Eds. Karen Fraser Wyche and Faye J. Crosby. Boulder, CO: Westview, 1996, pp. 49–61.

Lark, Julianna S., and James M. Croteau. "Lesbian, Gay, and Bisexual Students' Mentoring Relationships with Faculty in Counseling Psychology: A Qualitative Study." *The Counseling Psychologist* 26 (1998): 764–76.

Larsen, Denise J., and Jennifer A. Boisvert. "Women's Professional Mentorship in Psychology and the Academy: One Group's Stories of Quilting and Life. In *Home/Bodies: Geographies of Self, Place and Space.* Ed. Wendy Schissel. Calgary: Calgary University Press, 2006, pp. 145–59.

Lather, Patricia. *Getting Smart: Feminist Research and Pedagogy With/in the Postmodern.* New York: Routledge, 1991.

Macalister, Heather E. "Women's Studies Classes and Their Influence on Student Development." *Adolescence* 34 (1999): 283–92.

Manning, Peter K., and Betsy Cullum-Swan. "Narrative, Content and Semiotic Analysis." In *Collecting and Interpreting Qualitative Materials.* Eds. Norman K. Denzin and Yvonna S. Lincoln. Thousand Oaks, CA: Sage, 1998, pp. 246–73.

Nielsen, Joyce McCarl, Robyn Marschke, Elizabeth Sheff, and Patricia Rankin. "Vital Variables and Gender Equity in Academe: Confessions from a Feminist Empiricist Project." *Signs* 31 (2005): 1–28.

Olesen, Virginia. "Feminisms and Models of Qualitative Research." In *The Landscape of Qualitative Research: Theories and Issues.* Eds. Norman K. Denzin and Yvonna S. Lincoln. Thousand Oaks, CA: Sage, 1998, pp. 300–32.

Osborne, Rachel L. "The Continuum of Violence Against Women in Canadian Universities: Toward a New Understanding of the Chilly Campus Climate." *Women's Studies International Forum* 18 (1995): 637–46.

Padula, Marjorie A., and Dana L. Miller. "Understanding Graduate Women's Reentry Experiences: Case Studies of Four Psychology Doctoral Students in a Midwestern University." *Psychology of Women Quarterly* 23 (1999): 327–43.

Peyton, Leigh A., Michal Marton, Molly M. Perkins, and Linda M. Dougherty. "Mentoring in Gerontology Education: New Graduate Student Perspectives." *Educational Gerontology* 27 (2001): 347–59.

Porter, Natalie. "Therapist Self-Care: A Proactive Ethical Approach." In *Ethical Decision Making in Therapy: Feminist Perspectives.* Eds. Elizabeth J. Rave and Carolyn C. Larsen. New York: Guilford, 1995, pp. 247–66.

Rave, Elizabeth J., and Carolyn C. Larsen. Eds. *Ethical Decision Making in Therapy: Feminist Perspectives.* New York: Guilford, 1995.

Reinharz, Shulamit. *Feminist Methods in Social Research.* New York: Oxford University Press, 1992.

Rich, Adrienne. *Toward a Woman-Centered University: On Lies, Secrets, and Silence.* New York: W.W. Norton, 1979.

Richardson, Laurel. *Fields of Play: Constructing an Academic Life.* New Brunswick, NJ: Rutgers University Press, 1997.

Roffman, Eleanor. "A Class Conscious Perspective on the Use of Self as Instrument in Graduate Clinical Training." *Women and Therapy* 18 (1996): 165–79.

Schweibert, Valorie L., Mary D., Deck, Monica L. Bradshaw, Pamela Scott, and Melanie Harper. "Women as Mentors." *Humanistic Counseling, Education, and Development* 37 (1999): 241–53.

Seldin, Peter, ed. *Coping with Faculty Stress: New Directions for Teaching and Learning.* San Francisco: Jossey-Bass, 1987.

Skovholt, Thomas M., and Michael H. Ronnestad. "Themes in Therapist and Counselor Development." *Journal of Counseling and Development* 70 (1992): 505–15.

Stake, Jayne E., Laurie Roades, Suzanna Rose, Lisa Ellis, and Carolyn West. "The Women's Studies Experience: Impetus for Feminist Action." *Psychology of Women Quarterly* 19 (1994): 17–24.

Stake, Jayne E., and Margareta Gerner. "The Women's Studies Experience." *Psychology of Women Quarterly* 11 (1987): 277–84.

Stake, Jayne E., and Suzanna Rose. "The Long-Term Impact of Women's Studies on Students' Personal Lives and Political Activism." *Psychology of Women Quarterly* 18 (1994): 403–12.

Stalker, Joyce. "Athene in Academe: Women Mentoring Women in the Academy." *International Journal of Lifelong Education* 13 (1994): 361–72.

Tom, Allison. "The Deliberate Relationship: A Frame for Talking About Faculty-Student Relationships." *Alberta Journal of Educational Research* 43 (1997): 3–21. Worell, Judith. "Opening Doors to Feminist Research." *Psychology of Women Quarterly* 20 (1996): 469–85.

_____ and Claire Etaugh. "Transforming Theory and Research with Women: Themes and Variations." *Psychology of Women Quarterly* 18 (1994): 443–50.

Worell, Judith, Doris Stilwell, Danielle Oakley, and Damon Robinson. "Educating About Women and Gender: Cognitive, Personal, and Professional Outcomes." *Psychology of Women Quarterly* 23 (1999): 797–811.

Worell, Judith, and Noreen G. Johnson, eds. *Shaping the Future of Feminist Psychology: Education, Research and Practice.* Washington: American Psychological Association, 1997.

Mothering Out of Place

Deconstructing the Maternal Wall in Academia

Jeanine Silveira Stewart

The Lessons of Motherhood

I would characterize my first decade and a half of mothering as a long, humbling adventure. In the first weeks of life with a newborn, there is constant, intense, around-the-clock work on behalf of someone who lacks the ability to show any overt sign of gratitude. Early on, the challenges of hauling my tot in her bulky, wheeled chariot increased my sensitivity to issues of physical access and the perils of un-cut curbs or steeply sloped parking areas. Later, volunteering in my daughters' pre-school and kindergarten classrooms and refereeing sibling interactions in my own home, I developed strategies for calmly encouraging a diverse and demanding group to become empowered, independent problem solvers. My mantra for a time was, "I know you don't have what you want, but do you have what you need?" More recently, I have found that adolescents demand more of my intellectual creativity, given the mismatch between their often child-like approach to risk assessment and their possession of full-sized adult bodies (and automobiles), not to mention their resistance of authority. On occasion I resort to the recommendation I could not abide in the newborn era. "Let them cry it out," seems to be more effective with teens who often find new routes to resolution of problem when I am unwilling or unable to offer up the cash that could immediately mollify a need. Admittedly, it is somewhat hyperbolic to compare the lessons of motherhood to the duties of an academic administrator, but I have found a sort of zen-like peace in the humorous parallels between my private and professional lives.

I taught undergraduate students full time for years before serving as a full time academic administrator. My role as mother is so much a part of who I am that, regardless of my professional role, I cannot avoid seeing clear connections between the skills I have developed as a parent and the demands of my work. I am often aware of daily applications for my abilities to work long hours with infrequent expressions of gratitude, to evaluate the accessibility of spaces, to empower others to contribute to solving problems and to assess their needs while setting aside at least some of their wants, to assist grown beings in evaluating and mitigating risks while navigating their resistance to authority, and to manage resources despite firm and persistent demands for liberal disbursements of cash. Not only do I see these oft-used skills as beneficial to my work, but I have also been lauded by many of my colleagues for demonstrating well-honed proclivities for thoughtful, fair-minded problem solving under pressure.

In addition to the skill set described above, two other types of benefits are often said to accrue to mothers in the workplace, although I submit that both apply equally to paternal and maternal figures. First, I cannot deny that my institution's contribution to the premium for family health insurance is a greater per-employee cost than its contribution to employee-only coverage. Other family friendly policies and practices often have no clear parallels among the benefits offered to non-parents. Second, I concede that "my child is sick" is a better excuse for canceling a class or moving a meeting than "I need to be home with my dog," or simply, "I need another day to finish the memo I promised the committee."

My goal in this essays is not to evaluate all of the tangible and intangible benefits and challenges of combining motherhood (or parenthood) with career. I will leave it to other authors to take on the debate of whether academic workplaces create a different set of equity issues by developing and implementing the so-called family friendly policies that make full career engagement more feasible for academics who are also parents. Rather, I will target this essay toward highlighting some of the assumptions that are made about mothers in the professional workplace, and the ways that those assumptions may unfairly limit the advancement potential of women who are custodial mothers (whose children are still young enough to require parental care). I see the key elements of this synthesis as having more to do with good intentions (moral intuition about what is "best" for the children or for the working mother) than with grand conspiracies. It is undeniable, however, that believing oneself to be well-intentioned does not un-do the very real discrimination that may result. So pervasive is the practice of limiting mothers' career progress when they reach a certain level in their workplace hierarchies, that the term, "maternal wall" has been coined to capture the phenomenon (Williams, "Hitting the Maternal Wall" 16). In this article I will share an overview of how this subtle yet destructive form of discrimination may play out in the academic workplace.

The Mommy Track and Academe

While relatively few investigations have targeted professors and other academic professionals, per se, there are two, non-conflicting schools of thought on factors associated with work-life balance that may drive the trend toward underrepresentation of women across the professions. Prominent works have developed plausible arguments that women are overwhelmed by their multiple roles in the workplace and at home, that mothers find the work of parenting more meaningful and rewarding than other paid work, and that many mothers, having made the choice to exit (even temporarily) the fast track in the working world find it difficult to impossible to maintain the respect of their colleagues or to return to lucrative paid positions in their professions (Hoschschild and Machung 31; Valian 272; Hewlett 43, 71). There seems to be a widely held view that women depart the workplace after becoming mothers due to the impracticality of managing most of the child care and household management duties along with the intensity of a professional career. This view is aligned with the set of issues subsumed by the title of the well known book, *The Second Shift.* In the updated edition the authors reported that as recently as the mid– to late–1990s, mothers tended to put in about 13 more hours per week household tasks than fathers did (Hochschild and Machung xxviii). While many authors have built upon the notion that working mothers are more likely than their male counterparts to be overwhelmed by the demands of their multiple roles, other prominent works have pointed out that professional mothers often find their work less important or become ambivalent toward their work after the arrival of their children (Valian 272). Another body of literature pertaining to work-life balance and the impact of women's choices goes along with the detailed analyses reported by Sylvia Ann Hewlett in *Off-Ramps and On-Ramps,* which describes the "non-linear careers" of professional women, and the challenges of shifting focus from career, to family, and back to career over the course of a professional trajectory (Hewlett 25–55). All of these works offer careful and well-considered treatments of complex work-life issues. Yet most authors emphasize the seemingly autonomous choices that women and their parenting partners make, either in the strategies they adopt for managing the household, or in decisions made to reduce or cease working outside the home. It often appears to be the case that professional mothers opt out of their full-time careers in order to avoid the long hours and interpersonal strain associated with the so-called second shift or because no paid work can compare to the rewards of active, hands-on parenting.

I was working on a postdoctoral fellowship in neuroscience when I gave birth to my first child. She was only four weeks old when my advisor called me back to the laboratory to continue data collection that had to occur under strict time constraints. He was the same man who had encouraged me earlier saying, "This is a great career, especially if you ever have children. A professor can work more flexible hours in the summer when the kids are home from school." Indeed, I found it possible to balance the demands of postdoctoral research and later, teaching and scholarship on the tenure track. Certainly the hours were long (especially during the years of daily commuting to accommodate my husband's desire to work outside the home), but the flexibility was helpful and I earned the respect of my students and colleagues on the way to earning tenure and a full professorship at a liberal arts college.

My former advisor is not alone in believing that the autonomy afforded academics appears ideal for working mothers. Yet, women in general, and mothers in particular are grossly underrepresented among the population of faculty on the tenure track at four-year colleges and universities ("Too Many Rungs on the Ladder?" 4), and in the senior academic and presidential leadership of academic institutions (Eckel, Cook and King 47). The reality is that my experience as a mother has generally enhanced my problem solving and interactional skills as an administrator. Yet, I now realize that I once held some very flawed assumptions about the limits of meritocracy in the academic workplace. Similar flawed assumptions may lead other female academics to push against invisible barriers, often triggering cultural biases that may contribute to patterns of differential and marginalizing treatment.

There is a growing body of literature suggesting that professionals who become mothers face subtle and overt forms of discrimination in the workplace. "Do Babies Matter?" queried Mary Ann Mason and Marc Goulden in the titles of their 2002 and 2004 articles in Academe (Mason and Goulden, Do Babies Matter? and Mason and Goulden, Do Babies Matter (Part II)?), answering in both with a resounding "yes." The authors analyzed data from the Survey of Doctorate Recipients, a longitudinal data set that tracks men and women with Ph.D.'s over the course of their adult lives, and they found that parenthood affects career trajectories very differently for men than for women. Among childless women hired on the tenure track, only one third will ever have children (Mason and Goulden, Do Babies Matter (Part II)). It may not be a dream of every female Ph.D. to become a mother, but additional data gleaned from survey responses of over 4000 faculty members in the University of California system revealed that 38 percent of the women (but only 18 percent of the men) reported having had fewer children than they had wished to have (cited in Mason and Goulden, Do Babies Matter (Part II)). There are certainly many factors that contribute to decisions about whether or when to combine parenting with a career, and it is unlikely that any two women's stories are identical. Still, after a decades-long struggle to diversify the professoriate, the senior ranks of tenured professors are predominantly male, and the majority of those women who are tenured (55 percent) are professionals without children (Mason and Goulden, Do Babies Matter (Part II)).

Babies matter not only to the extent that their presence in the lives of some female professors contributes to a realistic representation of modern demographics. The type of diversity represented by women whose life experience includes the parenting role is not better or worse than other forms of difference, but it is generally accepted that the goals of working groups and leadership teams are well served by welcoming a broad range of perspectives. It is curious that women are well represented in their graduate school cohorts but not among the tenured professoriate (Mason and Ekman, ix). The full impact of this loss of female academics begins to take shape in considering the trend toward conversion of tenure track faculty lines to contracted, impermanent positions, resulting in young women (under the age of 45) occupying a skimpy 5 percent of all full-time faculty positions at 4 year colleges, and 6 percent of the permanent positions at community colleges ("Too many rungs on the ladder?" 1). While it was possible for students in my cohort to complete a college degree without ever having a class with a female professor, students of today could complete degrees without taking a course with a fully employed female professor, and most faculty will never serve at an institution with female leadership.

Using the work of Mason and Goulden as a benchmark, women represent about 50 percent of the population of graduate students (21), but only about 35 percent of postdoctoral fellows (23) and only about 25 percent of the total tenure-line faculty (21; "Do Babies Matter?"). If I may be permitted the latitude to claim that it would be in the best interest of both the academic profession and the students of the future to retain more female scholars, including female scholars who happen to be parents, then it would follow that our profession must also examine the factors which contribute to disengagement of mothers from the more visible segments of academic life, despite the apparent benefits of the academic professional lifestyle to working parents.

Many people make assumptions about the commitment or professional capacity of women who are custodial parents, even when they share parenting duties with a full time partner. After a period in my administrative work that was filled with serious, confidential personnel issues requiring my delicate intervention, one faculty member reflected, "We could all tell that the pressure of meeting your children's needs along with this difficult job was wearing on you last spring. You looked so tired." To my kind colleague, it seemed only natural to assume that the weariness originated with a difficult work-life balance, rather than a hostile, covert attempt by a few of his colleagues to undermine my professional work.

With remarkable frequency, friendly, well-meaning colleagues offer sympathy or pity when they draw conclusions about normal reactions to the normal range of issues that arise in the workplace. In the minds of less charitable onlookers, such assumptions tally to create real risk for those who would highlight their parenting role. Academic workplaces are often highly politicized, and faculty members who give birth at an inopportune time of year often choose to return to work after shortened periods of leave, to continue work from home while recovering from birth or to forego other parental leave benefits entirely. Many institutions have shifted from offering family friendly policies as an option to making the policies automatic for anyone who qualifies. In those cases, instead of having to request activation of a policy, parental leave and other benefits are considered the default situation, and new parents must make a special request if they do not want to access the benefits.

In her article entitled, "Is Your Husband a Worse Problem than Larry Summers?" Linda Hirshman suggests that it would be better to address gender inequities in the distribution of domestic work, rather than to continue devoting academic institutional resources to the generation of myriad family friendly policies. She posits that the force behind the trend of educated young mothers opting out of their careers (in academics and other professions) is their hefty domestic burden. Sylvia Ann Hewlett and Carolyn Buck Luce surveyed women who had opted out of their careers to raise children and found that 93 percent hoped to return to their careers at some point (45), although only 5 percent of that group were interested in re-entering their particular workplace (52). In speculating about why 95 percent of their research subjects were hesitant to return to past worksites, Hewlett and Luce failed to consider the possibility that many may have been subjected to gender discrimination based on their status as mothers of young children. Neither did Hirshman in her piece contemplate that the opt-out option may hold appeal because it provides a socially acceptable exit from a professional world which is rife with examples of career-limiting bias against working mothers. Such bias has been described in the jurisprudential literature as the "maternal wall" (Williams, "Hitting the Maternal Wall" 16).

Deconstructing the Maternal Wall: Benevolent Sexism Couched as Concern

In the sphere of employment law, maternal wall cases typically arise out of clashing societal stereotypes regarding the ideal worker (committed 24/7 to the job) and the ideal mother (committed 24/7 to her children) (Williams, "Women's Work" 16). In decisions rendered since 2003 by the U.S. Supreme Court and the Second Circuit Court of Appeals, employers' use of motherhood stereotypes of female employees as well as "notions that mothers are insufficiently devoted to work [and] that work and motherhood are incompatible," all constitute gender discrimination under federal law (Euben B12). The fact that the high courts have had to rule recently on such matters demonstrates that employment discrimination at the intersection of gender and parental status is viewed as defensible by at least some employers.

It would be beneficial for those of us working in academic settings to consider how socially acceptable "benevolent" sexism in our workplaces ties to deeply held, implicit moral judgments about the appropriateness of working mothers' occupying high status or demanding positions at the upper levels of our organizations. Relevant vignettes collected over the past decade suggest that many of our female colleagues witness the erection of invisible barriers to their professional growth coincident with the timing of their family's growth:

> A part-time faculty member was discouraged from applying for a full-time position, "As your children get older their demands on your time will only increase." A female administrator whose work had been compromised after she was denied access to critical work-related information was told by her superior, "You just have so much on your plate. I didn't want to add to your burden." Mothers who volunteer for highly visible roles are sometimes met with tempered enthusiasm, "The symposium really is a 24 hour commitment, and we'll understand if as a

new mother you feel your priorities need to be elsewhere." Attempts at sarcastic humor demonstrate limited tolerance of the simple fact of being pregnant in the workplace, "If she would stop having babies we wouldn't have to deal with ..." fill in the blank — curriculum changes, university policy and benefit changes, the high cost of health insurance, etc. I have heard several versions of the collision of personal and professional domains, as in the story of one professor who testified against his female colleague at her child custody hearing and claimed that a serious scholar such as this woman could not possibly devote adequate time and attention to raising her children.

Comments such as these appear to convey collegial concern for the well-being of mothers, but they take on sexist overtones when they co-exist in an environment with hostile sexism, as is very often the case (Glick and Fiske, "An Ambivalent Alliance" 112). In a hostile environment, such discourse effectively undermines the professional qualifications, and ultimately the free choices of professional women; benevolently coercing their workplace conduct as they try to minimize or mitigate others' biased assumptions about their professional competence.

While research has shown no difference in productivity among female academics with children vs. those without (Valian 269), studies indicate that many people doubt that mothers possess the capacity to succeed professionally. Both employers and colleagues may question mothers' availability for work (e.g., given the normative assumptions that all mothers are primary caregivers, and that quality mothering requires intensive, focused attention leaving little time to focus on work). Mother status alters perceptions of work-related competence, potential for leadership, economic worth, and perceived appropriateness for holding positions of authority (Ridgeway and Correll 686). Social scientific data also demonstrate that mothers employed in jobs with heavy time demands tend to be subject to hyper-critical performance reviews relative to men or to women who are not mothers (694; Fuegen, Biernat, Haines and Deaux 748). The phenomenon of maternal discrimination does not appear to be generalizable to parental discrimination. One study demonstrated that employers actually show preferential lenience in employment evaluations toward fathers, who may be held to a lower performance standard (i.e. they actually benefit) because of their parental status (Fuegen, et al. 748). In many ways, therefore, one's status as a mother creates societal disadvantages that are distinguishable from those conveyed by female gender alone.

Benevolent sexism may originate from the paternalistic idealization of women in traditional, subordinate roles (Glick and Fiske, "Ambivalent Sexism" 491). The image of women as nurturers is a key stereotypical theme underlying patriarchal cultures, creating for females a role that is "the complement of male power [and] totally absorbed in the activities and qualities of caring" (Ruth 130). Both female and male behaviors are then prescribed by the stereotype, with women expected to focus on delicate or domestic work, and men expected to serve visibly as defenders of women. In the name of honor, then, men adopt chivalrous patterns, attempting to protect women from societal evils which may include (presumably) anything from cagier males to an excessive or burdensome workload, as in many of the examples offered above. In the social psychological literature, benevolent and hostile sexism are distinguished as follows:

> Benevolent sexism (a subjectively favorable, chivalrous ideology that offers protection and affection to women who embrace conventional roles) coexists with hostile sexism (antipathy toward women who are viewed as usurping men's power). Hostile and benevolent sexism are complementary, cross-culturally prevalent ideologies, both of which predict gender inequality (Glick and Fiske, "An Ambivalent Alliance" 109). Dominant groups prefer to act warmly toward subordinates, offering them patronizing affection as a reward for "knowing their place" rather than rebelling. Open antagonism is reserved for subordinates who fail to defer or who question existing social inequalities. (110)

Hostile and benevolent forms of sexism appear to be interrelated and mutually reinforcing, with benevolent strategies utilized primarily to maintain the privileged position of the dominant group, and hostile sexist interactions serving mainly to limit the ascent of subordinate individuals who threaten to gain power in the social hierarchy (Glick and Fiske, "An Ambivalent Alliance" 112). In the workplace, therefore, benevolent sexism directly or indirectly limits the potential for success of subordinate group members without engaging in more blatant forms of legally prohibited oppression. Clearly there is the potential for real harm to be done by those whose conduct is not overtly or even intentionally hostile, especially when respectful conversation about professional goals is replaced with subtle reference to maternal status. Open communication about work-life balance qualifies as mentoring, while oblique or tangential reference to maternal status is often marginalizing. Even enlightened academics may be prone to demonstrating subtle biases due to what some authors have referred to as "unexamined assumptions" about what roles are appropriate for mothers of young children (Crosby, Williams and Biernat 677).

Put another way, stereotypes provide an expedient mechanism for sorting people according to their degree of likeability or competence (Glick and Fiske, "Sexism and Other Isms" 194). In the case of mothers, for example, those who fit the nurturing stereotype are both liked and respected by holders of the stereotype. However, mothers who violate the stereotype by dividing their time between work and child-rearing are subject to one of two outcomes: if the mother works in a lower level or part-time job, then she may be viewed as likable (warm) but incompetent; if she works in a higher level or time-intensive job, she is likely to be viewed as unlikable (or cold) but competent (197). The net result of this societal ambivalence is a classic double bind situation, in which career advancement typically requires both social acceptance and competence, yet professional working mothers are virtually incapable of securing one while demonstrating the other, at least in situations where they are being evaluated by people who hold these common stereotypes.

Moral Intuition and the "Right Place" for Mothers

While it can be difficult to elucidate the hidden factors that drive widely held stereotypes, I propose that stereotypes associated with the maternal ideal are linked to moral intuition. In making a moral judgment, people often view a scenario as inherently and unequivocally right or wrong, and they make such judgments without consciously processing the decision. In fact, if asked to explain the judgment, people generally create post hoc explanations that do not appear related to the actual thought process involved in making the judgment in the first place (Haidt 814). Moral judgments tend to be associated with our most deeply held assumptions about how the world ought to be. We rarely hold these ideals open for debate.

Why might maternal stereotypes be derived from moral intuition? First, morality is a culturally embedded phenomenon (Haidt, Koller and Dias 613), and the vast majority of working adults in our society espouse the view that women will bear primary responsibility for child care (Valian 269), indicating a dominant cultural perspective that could serve as external validation for a moral construct. Recent studies of workers' attitudes in the U.S. show that 69 percent of over 1000 male and female workers surveyed reported that they believe a parent should stay home to raise children ("Life's Work" 4). Despite this prevailing view, the majority of mothers with young children in the U.S. are in the paid workforce (Halpern 397). Data from psychological studies suggest the presence of a societal myth holding that mothers in dual-earner families work to support consumerist behavior, rather than to meet essential needs of the family (Halpern 403). It seems reasonable to postulate that many in our society view mothers (but not fathers) who are engaged in active, professional careers as morally inferior.

Additionally, while most enlightened working adults are aware that they should not make statements excluding the candidacy of women in general for a particular job, it is still common to hear exclusionary language used with regard to mothers, as if the remarks represent incontrovertible facts (Williams and Cooper 860). Furthermore, in an experimental setting where the study's participants were all shown identical resumes each bearing either a male or female name, post-hoc explanations of judgments against female candidates tended to emphasize factors present on all resumes but viewed as pertinent only for the candidates who were mothers (Cuddy, Fiske and Glick 713). The stereotypical view of working professional mothers as "capable but overly ambitious and antisocial" (714) seems a likely example of a post-hoc explanation of a moral judgment that is applied only to women who are parents of young children. Unfortunately such explanations create very real and often insurmountable barriers to professional advancement for mothers in many work settings (i.e., a maternal wall).

Finally, personal observations suggest that professional limits seem most likely to be placed on working mothers when they attempt to enter privileged work domains, i.e. upper level supervisory positions, or highly visible and sought-after roles in the workplace. At such times, it becomes morally intuitive to intervene "for the good of the children." The degree to which people in a culture perceive that harm can come from a certain type of conduct plays into the culture's moral judgment (Haidt, Koller and Dias 624). Given the established significance of early childhood experience to later developmental outcomes, many people assume that mothers who work outside the home do so to the detriment of their children. In reality, psychological research conducted over several decades indicates that maternal involvement in the workplace provides children with substantial benefits and few, if any real risks (Halpern 399). Despite prevailing evidence, however, "morality draws its force from sentiment, not logic" (Haidt, Koller and Dias 626).

The Way Forward

Cultural change is difficult to incite, particularly when the popular culture lacks the ability to name a given, pervasive problem. If both moral intuition and stereotyping are in play when working mothers are evaluated on the job, what can be done to mitigate or remove harmful biases? Although some authors suggest that programming aimed at consciousness raising can encourage people to choose to abandon unhealthy stereotypes (Fiske 626), others have shown that such programming can lead to backlash from individuals with a strong tendency toward prejudice (Monteith, Devine and Zuwerink 321). Additionally, some scholarship suggests that even highly prejudiced individuals can move beyond their biases by learning to focus on the professional strengths of their diverse colleagues (Vescio 447) and on similarities that unite workers in striving for common goals (Dovidio and Gaertner 188). In every workplace, therefore, three things need to be in place:

1. A clear message about the communal benefits of healthy work-life balance, respecting those who engage regularly in child rearing, elder care, and other forms of significant community building;
2. strong, unifying leadership from senior administrators emphasizing the common goals sought by diverse work groups; and
3. well-crafted policies designed to limit behaviors that can cause harm, and demonstrating zero tolerance for all forms of discriminatory conduct.

The academic workplace is not immune to the type of stereotyping that views pregnant women and mothers as less competent, less committed workers, or potentially neglectful parents. Given that women are not represented in senior academic positions in proportion to their rate of degree attainment, and given the lack of opportunities for re-entry to an academic career after opting out to raise children, the support and retention of mothers in academic careers are critical goals. Additionally, it should benefit all of us who work in professional positions in academia to be able to name and understand phenomena that play a role in perpetuating destructive marginalization of working mothers in the academic workplace.

Works Cited

Crosby, Faye J., Joan C. Williams and Monica Biernat. "The Maternal Wall." *Journal of Social Issues* 60:4 (2004): 675–682.

Cuddy, Amy J.C., Susan T. Fiske and Peter Glick. "When Professionals Become Mothers, Warmth Doesn't Cut the Ice." *Journal of Social Issues* 60:4 (2004): 701–718.

Dovidio, John F., and Samuel L. Gaertner. "Stereotypes and Evaluative Intergroup Bias." In Diane M. Mackie and David L. Hamilton Eds. *Affect, Cognition, and Stereotyping: Interactive Processes in Group Perception.* New York: Academic, 1993.

Eckel, Peter, Bryan J. Cook and Jacqueline E. King. "The CAO Census: A National Profile of Chief Academic Officers." American Council on Education, February 2009.

Euben, Donna. "Working Mothers and Gender Discrimination." *The Chronicle of Higher Education* 51:38 (May 27, 2005): B12 (www.chronicle.com, accessed 11-02-2006).

Fiske, Susan T. "Controlling Other People. The Impact of Power on Stereotyping." *American Psychologist* 48:6 (1993): 621–628.

Fuegen, Kathlee, Monica Biernat, Elizabeth Haines and Kay Deaux. "Mothers and Fathers in the Workplace: How Gender and Parental Status Influence Judgments of Job-Related Competence." *Journal of Social Issues* 60:4 (2004): 737–754.

Glick, Peter, and Susan T. Fiske. "The Ambivalent Sexism Inventory: Differentiating Hostile and Benevolent Sexism." *Journal of Personality and Social Psychology* 70 (1996): 491–512.

_____. "An Ambivalent Alliance: Hostile and Benevolent Sexism as Complementary Justifications for Gender Inequality." *American Psychologist* 56:2 (2001): 109–118.

_____. "Sexism and Other "Isms": Interdependence, Status, and the Ambivalent Content of Stereotypes." *Sexism and Stereotypes in Modern Society.* Washington, DC: APA, 1999.

Haidt, Jonathan. "The Emotional Dog and its Rational Tail: A Social Intuitionist Approach to Moral Judgment." *Psychological Review* 108:4 (2001): 814–834.

_____, Silvia Helena Koller and Maria G. Diaz. "Affect, Culture and Morality, or Is it Wrong to Eat Your Dog?" *Journal of Personality and Social Psychology* 65:4 (1993): 613–628.

Halpern, Diane F. "Psychology at the Intersection of Work and Family." *American Psychologist* 60:5 (2005): 397–409.

Hewlett, Sylvia Ann. *Off-Ramps and On-Ramps: Keeping Talented Women on the Road to Success.* Boston: Harvard Business School Press. 2007.

_____ and Carolyn Buck Luce. "Off Ramps and On Ramps: Keeping Talented Women on the Road to Success." *Harvard Business Review* 83:3 (2005): 43–54.

Hirshman, Linda. "Is Your Husband a Worse Problem than Larry Summers?" *Inside Higher Ed,* 9 December 2005. <*http://www.insidehighered.com/views/2005/12/09/hirshman*>, accessed 23 October 2006.

Hochschild, Arlie Russell, and Anne Machung. *The Second Shift.* New York: Penguin, 2003.

Life's Work: Generational Attitudes toward Work and Life Integration (executive summary report). Cambridge, MA: Radcliffe Public Policy Center, 2000.

Mason, Mary Ann, and Eve Mason Ekman. *Mothers on the Fast Track.* New York: Oxford University Press, 2007.

Mason, Mary Ann, and Marc Goulden. "Do Babies Matter? The Effect of Family Formation on the Lifelong Careers of Academic Men and Women." *Academe* November–December (2002): 21–27.

_____. "Do Babies Matter (Part II)? Closing the Baby Gap." *Academe* 90:6 (2004): 3–7.

Monteith, Margo J., Patricia G. Devine, and Julia R. Zuwerink. "Self-Directed Versus Other-Directed Affect as a Consequence of Prejudice-Related Discrepancies." In Charles Stangor, ed. *Stereotypes and Prejudice: Essential Readings.* Ann Arbor, MI: Psychology, 2000.

Ridgeway, Cecilia L., and Shelley J. Correll. "Motherhood as a Status Characteristic." *Journal of Social Issues* 60:4 (2004): 683–700.

Ruth, Sheila. *Issues in Feminism: An Introduction to Women's Studies.* Fifth Ed. Mountain View, CA: Mayfield, 2001.

"Too Many Rungs on the Ladder? Faculty Demographics and the Future Leadership of Higher Education." American Council on Education. September 2008. <http://www.acenet.edu/AM/Template.cfm?Section=InfoCenter&Template=/TaggedPage/TaggedPageDisplay.cfm&TPLID=23&ContentID=29469,> accessed 13 August 2009.

Valian, Virginia. *Why So Slow? The Advancement of Women.* Cambridge, MA: MIT Press, 1999.

Vescio, Theresa K., Sarah J. Gervais, Swen Heidenreich and Mark Snyder. "The Effects of Prejudice Level and Social Influence Strategy on Powerful People's Responding to Racial Out-Group Members." *European Journal of Social Psychology* 36 (2006): 435–450.

Williams, Joan C. "Hitting the Maternal Wall." *Academe* 90:6 (November–December 2004): 16–20.

_____. "Women's Work is Never Done: Employment, Family, and Activism: Hibbs as a Federalism Case; Hibbs as a Maternal Wall Case." *University of Cincinnati Law Review* 73:365 (2004): 1–35.

_____ and Holly Cohen Cooper. "The Public Policy of Motherhood." *Journal of Social Issues* 60:4 (2004): 849–865.

Post-Tenure

A Performance of Blatant Subversion

Kathleen Juhl

On April 11, 1997, I was the first out lesbian tenured at Southwestern University, a small Methodist church-affiliated, national liberal arts college located in small-town Texas just north of Austin. My journey on the queer track to tenure took ten years. During the first four years, I held the rather elusive and tenuous title of "Visiting Artist" in the Department of Theatre and Communication. I was credentialed with a Master of Arts in Performance Studies and a Master of Fine Arts in Theatre, degrees not always considered "terminal" in academia. This made my position even more tenuous on one level and comforting on another — I wasn't sure at the time that "terminal academic" was something I wanted to be anyway. On top of all that I was ... and still am ... a lesbian, albeit "feminine" enough to "pass," but a lesbian all the same, with a partner and two daughters. I was thirty-three years old, in my first "real" job, and I was terrified, mostly, at first, about inadvertently "outing" myself.

Those first years were painful. I lied a lot about my personal life. I worried and worked harder than I probably needed to and even began a Ph.D. in performance studies at the nearby University of Texas at Austin. I thought that a Ph.D. would make up somehow for all the ways in which my position seemed frighteningly unstable. After four years, my visiting position became tenure-track and after competing with other applicants in a national search, I won the position and began my *official* journey towards tenure ... a little less fearful and very tired of the lies and the hiding and especially of everyone assuming I was heterosexual. So I started coming out to colleagues and a "safe" administrator or two.

In those coming out moments, my heart pounded, my face flushed, and my stomach flip-flopped, but somehow my theatre person's way of operating in present tense saved me from seeing the larger and scarier ramifications coming out might bring ... or maybe it was just denial or a pollyanna personality or just plain naivete. At any rate, I kept coming out and charging ahead in the new directions in which intellectual and artistic passions and desires were leading me. Through my Ph.D. course work, which I coordinated and wove into my work as an acting teacher and theatre director at Southwestern, I discovered play theories and feminist theories and gender theories and queer theories and the power of comedy and laughter in my work with students. Coming out and whether it would hurt my chances of getting tenure caused only occasional panic attacks. I decided that, no matter what, I was going to become an activist academic and, more importantly, be myself, albeit covertly. Instead of thinking of myself as a feminine lesbian who could pass for straight, I would think of myself as a fabulous femme lesbian lurking in the margins of my institution and subverting the very foundations of its conservative traditions as well as the conservative hierarchical performance and production methodologies of my own art and discipline. While I was working toward tenure, I would allow this fabulous femme alter ego to perform outrageously only in the privacy of classroom and rehearsal spaces and where together she and I would begin developing subversive ways of circulating feminist and queer gender theories.

Outside my classrooms and rehearsals, as I gradually came out to colleagues and administrators, including the chair of my department, my dean, the provost, and the president, I focused pre-tenure social chat on the children I had raised with my partner and the grandchildren they brought into our lives. I did this very consciously. I was performing a carefully crafted character, styled rather conservatively, emphasizing the fact that I had a family much like any "normal" family. I didn't bring my partner to university social events — she's a bit butch and I didn't want to scare anyone — but I did tote a cute grandchild around with me occasionally. I thought if I could create a "wholesome" public persona, I could get away with circulating feminist and queer theories in my work with students. I also got all dressed up for fancier events like opening nights at the theatre, wore dresses, panty hose, high heels, and lipstick. Later, when I began to read lesbian feminist performance theories and descriptions of performance practices that celebrated butch and femme style, I thought about creating a femme self who wore the above mentioned trappings on an everyday basis. I just couldn't bear the thought of the discomfort so I stuck with cute and wholesome and created

an imaginary femme self— a kind of Juhl in high femme drag — and fanta-
sized myself as a living, breathing, walking subversion. Inside my classrooms
and rehearsals, I circulated feminist-fueled and queer-inspired approaches
to actor training and rehearsal practices couched as and accomplished through
hierarchy-busting play and improvisation processes. I let my imaginary
femme alter-ego out to play with the students in those private spaces and
we laughed and played and cross-gendered our way into excellent performance work and highly successful productions.

I am proud of the fact that I am the first out–lesbian tenured at Southwestern University and that before I had tenure I came out to all the folks
in our administrative "big house." Coming out wasn't easy. When I came
out to the president of the university I felt like I was facing my father all
over again, and that confrontation led to an eighteen-year estrangement from
my biological family. But after those first four years of fear and self-doubt,
I discovered another way: that thinking of yourself as a character in a comedy
about subverting hierarchical institutional and disciplinary structures is a
whole lot more fun than worrying all the time. I think I'm prouder of having
subverted my own fears during the pre-tenure years than I am of anything
else, including outing myself before I had tenure. Instead of living fearfully,
I focused my attention and energy on my work with students in productive,
queer, and hilariously playful ways. My fabulous femme persona, the students
and I discovered, in secluded classroom and rehearsal spaces, that it was possible to engage multiple, complex, and progressive, even radical, subversions
of existing cultural norms and disciplinary traditions. Specifically, we were
subverting and critiquing culturally sanctioned gender norms and traditional
theatrical production procedures. Students ultimately embraced this work
and I ultimately got away with it in a conservative institution and in an even
more conservative small town where our feminist and queer theory-inspired
work was put on public display in theatre productions I directed.

I initiated the performance processes that my students and I eventually
developed in feminist, queer, and playful directions when I made audio and
video recordings of the rehearsals for a 1992 production of Georges Feydeau's
play *The Lady from Maxims*. Using a speech communication research methodology called Conversation Analysis, I transcribed and analyzed recordings of
the mania of theatre rehearsals in minute detail. Through these micro-ana-
lytic observations, I discovered that if I allowed myself to be the butt of the
joke as well as the teacher and director, and encouraged prolific goofing
around in performance processes, play episodes would spin out and enhance
the productivity of classroom performance work and rehearsals for produc-

tions I directed. I became interested in the ways that students would make jokes out of my directions and suggestions by repeating and imitating me and ultimately internalizing what I had to say. I teased them and made jokes out of their mistakes and suggestions and in this way, understood the problems they were having and could see where they wanted to take characterizations and relationships. We worked through acting and rehearsal problems in uproarious and sometimes outrageous goofing around that looked and felt like chaos. But all that mania resulted in highly productive classroom performance workshops and production rehearsals. The plays I directed — mainly comedies and farces — were popular with conservative small-town Texas audiences despite being, as one of my colleagues described it, "queered" with cross-gendered and gender-ambiguous characters that my students created with little resistance and lots of discussion about feminist and queer gender theories.

Cross-gender experimentation has allowed me to situate my work with students in contexts beyond the technicalities of performance training. It has been a vehicle for helping students understand that approaches to acting and production processes evolve within historical and cultural contexts. At the same time, cross-gendering has enhanced the technical training I can give my students. And so, our experiments with gender have evolved within a particular approach to process and pedagogy: they have been situated within evolving production and training methods that are driven by play theory and processes. I am interested in the impact of cross-gendering on audience responses to productions, but my primary interest has been in the ways feminist and queer ideas about gender can be circulated in the playfulness of classroom work and rehearsals as a toy or plaything. As such, it raises students' consciousness and encourages discussions about the political and cultural issues that surround gender. Just as importantly, it serves as a mechanism for enhancing actor-training, particularly in the areas of text analysis and the development of physical behaviors for characters.

Through facilitating a playful rehearsal protocol, I have been able to encourage the subversion of my own power and authority in acting classes and rehearsals through encouraging the students to work independently and encouraging them to take active roles in the creative process. For example, I don't always make the decisions myself about who will play what characters in plays I direct. Instead, I often cast ensembles of actors and facilitate a play-theory driven improvisation process through which students collaborate with me and with each other to cast the specific roles. For one production, I cast an ensemble with an equal number of men and women even though the play had several more male than female roles. As a result, the actors cross-gendered themselves and each other as we collaborated on casting the characters in the play. In this way, all of the actors were encouraged to work on cross-gendered performance.

My goal in workshops and rehearsals is to instigate a playful protocol. I am interested in creating a safe space where a collaborative spirit can develop freely, where actors are encouraged to explore voice and movement, and playing with gender is standard procedure. For example, one exercise my students and I invented is based on a simple follow-the leader activity. As a warm-up for class workshops or rehearsals, actors take turns leading the group around the rehearsal space, exploring their characters' walks and other physical behaviors like hand gestures and posture. These behaviors need to be distinct enough so all of the other actors can imitate them. Actors change and develop their movement patterns during a single turn as leader and over the course of a series of these warm-ups. The idea is that they develop their ideas based on observing the other actors imitating them. Everyone takes a turn at leading the group so that all of the actors "try on" the movement behaviors of the others. In this way, physical characterizations are created collaboratively as the actors carefully observe, imitate, and repeat evolving patterns of movement details. Because all the actors are imitating gender behaviors depending on the gender of the character the leader is playing, they all have an opportunity to explore gender as part of the exercise. In this way I am able to initiate playful activities into workshops and rehearsals which subtly circulate embodied explorations of gender theory.

Judith Butler suggests that gender is inherently performative, constituted in repetitions of "stylized acts" that might evolve in variations beyond the confines of mandated heterosexual binary norms "through the breaking or subversive repetition of that style" ("Performative" 27). Improvisation and play processes in theatre performance practices can provide the mechanisms through which such subversive repetitions can be explored. Through this follow-the-leader exercise, actors imitate, repeat, revise, and play on the ideas of their peers and on proliferations of physical behaviors connected to gender and to character details suggested by texts we are exploring. In this way, actors explore and exploit physical behaviors connected to gender and other factors in a complex array of combinations and configurations. The collaborations of all the actors' performing bodies lead to richly complex solutions to character and cross-gendered movement work when actors are playing cross-gendered roles. This kind of playful improvisational work with actors introduces, through embodied processes, the idea that gender is a performative construction based on coercive cultural norms. By encouraging them to subvert those norms through play and improvisation, gender signifiers become playthings, material for creating richly detailed characterizations which resist a "sedimentation" of gender norms, to use Butler's term, so actors can mix and match, combine and recombine movement, gestures, mannerisms, and embodied styles in the kind of "subversive repetition" Butler suggests. Richard Schechner says:

> Work and other daily activities continuously feed on the underlying ground of playing, using the play mood for refreshment, energy, unusual ways of turning things around, insights, breaks, openings, and especially, looseness. This looseness (pliability, bending, lability, unfocused attention, the long way around) is implied in such phrases as "play it out" or "there's some play in the rope" or "play around with that idea." Looseness encourages the discovery of new configurations and twists of ideas and experiences [42].

Once I initiate these kinds of playful group activities, there is no stopping the foolishness in my classrooms and rehearsals. Playful improvisation seems to create character details spontaneously.

While there has been occasional resistance to cross-gender work, the students have perceived these exercises as useful for creating detailed characters that have received positive responses from their peers in classes and from audiences who attend our public performances and as valuable for their actor training. Over and over, my course and production evaluations have indicated that students found cross-gender work to be the most valuable acting work they had ever done. It encouraged them to really think about creating physical and vocal details for their characters. It encouraged them to observe people around them for ideas and models of behavior they could use. It made them realize how much they tended to begin with mundane gender stereotypes when they worked on a character of their own gender. And it made the work of acting classes and rehearsals more fun. We laughed ... a lot. I sometimes think I just laughed myself through the tenure process while I was laughing my way through the classes I taught and the productions I directed. But the laughter in those pre-tenure years was never public.

Once my first tenured year began, I asked my partner what changes she had noticed in me. She said she thought I was laughing more. Out loud. And that worried me. Scared me a little. If I was laughing out loud more at home, had I been laughing out loud more at work? In public? Laughter in the classroom is my rap, my M. O., my way of doing and being with students. The most audible giggles, guffaws, and belly laughs in my repertoire had always been reserved for my interactions with them. But the laughter and the playfulness in the spaces I inhabited with students had always been a bit of a secret in my mind. A subversion ... maybe even a transgression. What if I had been laughing out loud in more dangerous spaces? What if colleagues...other than my feminist colleagues ... had noticed? Had heard me? Had done double-takes at hearing ha ha has, heh heh hehs, or hee hee hees escaping from my recently tenured body?

Yolanda Broyles-Gonzalez, through her research on El Teatro Campesino, the improvisational theatre company founded by Luis Valdez that played an integral part in the political activism of Cesar Chávez and the United Farm Workers, had taught me about the subversive nature of laughter. Broyles-Gonzalez cites "Mikhail Bakhtin's theory of the carnivalesque and of laugher and their relationship to oppression and freedom":

> Bakhtin conceptualizes laughter as a patently oppositional tool of the popular masses. He illustrates how the culture of laughter in its many forms and manifestations has traditionally opposed the authoritarianism and protective seriousness of the ruling class. Through the ages laughter has for the oppressed functioned as a rehearsal for freedom. Laughter challenges all that appears immutable, stable, and unchanging — most notably the existing social hierarchy and dominant authority [30].

When laughter, not chuckles or snorts or snickers but unstoppable, uncontrollable spasms of noisy, raucous laughter or silly irrepressible giggles, bubbles up from the human diaphragm in seemingly unstoppable, uncontrollable spasms, the body must be relaxed. Fear and its resulting physical tension must be either non-existent or temporarily repressed, and if possibilities for the subverting and resisting resistance to dominant cultural structures and systems are to must existplay out in classroom and rehearsal spaces ... and in life, and some sense of safety must be present. Before I was granted tenure, a little knot of fear or anxiety in my diaphragm kept me from subversive public performances of spontaneous laughter. I had laughed in public but not really out loudly and certainly not without a hand ready to stifle and suppress the spasms if they threatened to erupt and blow my carefully crafted performance of fairly benign, ultimately harmless, tenurable and tolerable femme lesbian and feminist academic. Had the relief I felt in achieving tenure bubbled out of my diaphragm in public academic spaces? In committee meetings, in hallways, in administrative offices? And, if this was happening, if what my partner had noticed in private was happening in public, I wondered what this meant about the subversive potential, the dangerous nature, of my laughter. I had achieved tenure as an out lesbian. I had gotten away with circulating feminist and queer theories and methodologies in my pedagogy and artistic practices. The battle had been won. I had become part of the "ruling class." I had been invited to a meeting of "senior faculty women." I no longer needed to "rehearse for freedom" with the subversive laughter Broyles-Gonzales describes. I had freedom. I had tenure. That ready hand to stifle the silly spasms was really no longer necessary. Tenure meant I no longer had to operate in institutional margins. And on some levels there was great relief in that and on other levels, sadness, and I realized that the laughter my partner had noticed at home was *not* escaping from behind my public mask. In fact, in public, in meetings, with colleagues and even students, I was laughing less and what did escape felt forced and not much fun.

As I came to this realization, I remembered a passage in the first chapter of Teresa de Lauretis' *Technologies of Gender* that had inspired the ways I developed the feminist and queer approaches to performance and rehearsal work with theatre students. De Lauretis says that besides being vigilant about not reproducing pervasive male narratives in our feminist theorizing, we must also "create new spaces of discourse, to rewrite cultural narratives, and to define the terms of another perspective — a view from 'elsewhere.'" De Lauretis describes this "elsewhere"in this way:

> not [as] some mythic distant past or some utopian future history: [but as] the elsewhere of discourse here and now, the blind spots, or the space-off, of its representations. I think of it as spaces in the margins of hegemonic discourses, social spaces carved in the interstices of institutions and in the chinks and cracks of the power-knowledge apparati [25].

The passage goes on to talk about the "elsewhere" as a site where new constructions of gender might be created, and this idea had been particularly important to the classroom and rehearsal work that I had developed with my students before I received tenure. But what initially drew me to de Lauretis' "elsewhere," was that, in a kind of romantic way, I liked the idea of working in the "margins," in the "interstices," and especially in "the chinks and cracks" of institutional power structures. I was attracted by the challenge of slipping through those chinks and cracks. And in a very unexpected way, as I slowly absorbed the fact of my tenured status, I began to feel as though through tenure I had become a part of stable, sturdy, monolithic institutional walls, and I frankly didn't like it very much. I liked the pre-tenure vision I had of myself lurking in those chinks and cracks, secretly performing my femme alter ego, wearing the SU women's studies uniform of jeans or khakis, t-shirt or turtle-neck, Birkenstocks or other comfortable shoes, and stylish vest to which some of us added very cool earrings, or substituted an occasional jumper or skirt and blazers for cooler weather and to which I added bright blue contact lenses or funky glasses, various shades of red dye on my shoulder-length hair, and best of all … mascara and a rare but ironic touch of pink…. I liked thinking about my femme self slowly closing the doors to classroom and rehearsal spaces and peaking through the chink or crack in the door, laughing inwardly and pulling the door shut, winking at my students, and letting out a deep and subversive belly laugh. I liked thinking that I was getting away with something even though my work had always been somewhat covert in the sense that, when I first introduced activities to students or talked about my methods to colleagues, I always emphasized the fact that my explorations involved play and improvisation theories and methodologies. I mentioned the cross-gender work cursorily and simply neglected to mention the feminist and queer theories that were really driving my explorations and my pedagogical and artistic passions. What they don't know won't hurt 'em. Richard Schechner's play theories, along with de Lauretis' description of the place called "elsewhere" kept me intrigued and determined to operate dangerously. Schechner talks about play as a phenomenon I imagined as the modis operandi of the "elsewhere" spaces de Lauretis proposes. Shechner states that:

> Play creates its own (permeable) boundaries and realms: multiple realities that are slippery, porous, and full of creative lying and deceit; that play is dangerous and, because it is, players need to feel secure in order to begin playing; that the perils of playing are often masked or disguised by saying that play is "fun," "voluntary," a "leisure activity," or "ephemeral"—when in fact the fun of playing, when there is fun, is in playing with fire, going in over one's head, inverting accepted procedures and hierarchies … [26–27].

Post-tenure I directed a play by a woman playwright for the first time in my years at Southwestern. Marsha Norman's *Getting Out* overtly deals with feminist issues. It is a serious drama that didn't lend itself to cross-gender work. Rehearsals were more darkly playful with less laughter and fun. Post-tenure I was elected to co-chair an important university governing body and in that role found myself able to think in structural terms, lead discussions effectively, resolve sticky issues diplomatically, stifle most of my playful urges, and spend one hour a month being productive while having absolutely no fun at all. Post-tenure I found myself less playful with students, less able to laugh off their ruses and excuses about why they couldn't turn in assignments on time and why they had missed class. My classrooms seemed less playful, less subversive. In the Feminism and Performance class I teach as part of the Women's Studies Program, I gathered together so much theoretical material and insisted on so many dense and detailed theoretical discussions,

I left little time for the play and the release and, most importantly, the embodied learning and laughter and play and improvisation and the *potential for subversion* performance processes invoke. Good grief! Even rehearsal spaces, where in the past I was more relaxed and had more fun than just about anywhere, were filled with tension.

I felt angry and outraged more often. I felt like I had lost my sense of play when I could have been laughing out loud. I tried it a few times and it felt irresponsible, silly. I suddenly realized that I was, indeed, a part of the institutional walls and that I had a responsibility to see that I was there to hold up my part of the institution and to uphold my point of view about the world within those institutional walls. At the same time, my production of Marsha Norman's *Getting Out*, which focuses on a young woman's first day out of prison and involves emotional and physical violence, a near rape, drug use, and contains strong language, was well-received by audiences. Most surprising were positive responses to the play by residents of a Sun City retirement community located on the outskirts of town. Members of that community commented that the play was difficult but that it was the best production that had seen at Southwestern. Pre-tenure I had been terrified when Sun City moved to town because I wrongly stereotyped the people who would move there as conservative folks who would not have any patience for serious drama or theatrical experimentation and innovation, and that I might be doomed to direct musicals and silly comedies for the rest of my career. Now I see possibilities for forging a relationship with members of that community and getting their support for the production of serious, challenging theatre. I also gained a lot of respect in my leadership role within university governance and was able to introduce several issues to my colleagues and to university administrators that were important for women and gay and lesbian members of the campus community. My classes seemed less playful, but students in an advanced acting class responded favorably to the post-modern analyses of acting theories and methodologies in Phillip Zarrilli's *Acting Re-Considered*. In that class, the students and I discovered playful improvisational ways of exploring differences among those theories and methods and the ways they are situated and constructed within historical and cultural contexts. We discovered embodied performative processes for exploring theory in detailed, rigorous, and productive ways. Consequently, I am confident that I can create pedagogical activities that will allow me to teach complex feminist and queer performance theories in my Feminism and Performance class through performative processes involving play, improvisation, and maybe even some laughter.

For me, receiving tenure has been a mixed blessing. I have a certain amount of nostalgia for the subversive life I constructed and romanticized for survival in the pre-tenure phase of my academic life. I loved thinking of myself leading a double-life, having a secret self, living on the edge, in the in-between, playing and improvising in de Lauretis' "elsewhere." As I look back on my first tenured year, there was a joyful moment when I allowed myself the luxury of outing my subversive self. Jill Dolan, whose feminist performance theory has so inspired my thinking and my work that she has become like a rock star of feminist theory in my mind and heart, had agreed to come to Southwestern to deliver a lecture for the Women's Studies Program lecture series, and I was to make an announcement about it in a meeting of the full faculty. When I did, I told my colleagues that Dolan is a feminist scholar in my discipline, and that she was the president of my academic professional organization, and that she is Jewish, and that she is a lesbian, and that an important part of her work involves queer theory. I announced it loudly and proudly and with such excitement in my voice I was almost laughing. I did not stifle my feelings; I let them color my voice and show on my face. My rock star, Jill Dolan, who was also the Executive Officer of the Ph.D. Program in Theatre and Executive Director of the Center for Gay and Lesbian Studies at the City University of New York, then created the Performance as Public Practice program as a theatre faculty member at the University of Texas at Austin and is now teaching at Princeton, says:

> The longer I'm engaged in these institutional structures, the more important I think it is to learn how they work so that I can open their gaps and insert contradictions. As a professor and chair, I wield institutional power, about which I can't be naïve or romantic or simplistically resistant. I hope to be oppositional within the institution but I am *within it* [9].

Having tenure means that I must now operate from a place that is visible within my institution. I can no longer lurk in secret in the gaps, peering through the chinks and cracks, doing my work behind the walls. My discipline is theatre—you can't get much more public than that. My work in the classroom and in production focuses on enhancing acting pedagogy and the construction of character in rehearsal processes through problemetizing dominant cultural constructs of gender and sexuality. Some of that work is done in private spaces but always with the goal of public presentation. Teresa de Lauretis, whose notion of the "elsewhere" was so useful to me in carving out a subversive space where my pre-tenure self could operate safely in the "chinks and cracks" of my institution's structures, says that of this "elsewhere":

that the terms of a different construction of gender can be posed — terms that do have effect and take hold at the level of subjectivity and self-representation: in the micropolitical practices of daily life and daily resistances that afford both agency and sources of power or empowering investments; and in the cultural productions of women, feminists, which inscribe that movement in and out of ideology, that crossing back and forth of the boundaries — and of the limits — of sexual difference(s) [25].

De Lauretis is not talking here about creating a movement or dialogue between two oppositional spaces, from, for example, "the symbolic space constructed by the sex-gender system to a 'reality' external to it" (25). No social reality exists outside the culturally pervasive sex-gender system. De Lauretis discusses, instead,

> a movement back and forth between the representation of gender (in its male-centered frame of reference) and what that representation leaves out, or more pointedly, makes unrepresentable.... The movement between them, therefore, is not that of a dialectic, of integration, of a combinatory, or of differance, but is the tension of contradiction, multiplicity, and heteronomy [26].

The condition of feminism in the "here and now" is living in both spaces at the same time, living the "contradiction," accepting the "tension of a twofold pull in contrary directions — the critical negativity of its theory and the affirmative posivity of its politics" (26). As a feminist lesbian academic who has been granted the luxury and the responsibility of tenure, my new way of being and doing must include opening up institutional gaps rather than hiding behind them so that I can produce what Dolan calls knowledges that will matter beyond institutional walls. My new way of being and doing must also include living the contradiction de Lauretis describes through creating blatant subversions. And to make the post-tenure journey as much fun as the pre-tenure journey, I need to discover ways to make sure that the comedy and laughter survive and to allow that fabulous femme to come out and stay out and instigate as much playful and productive foolishness on and outside the walls as she did behind them.

Only a year after I received tenure, however, my institutional position was complicated by the fact that I was made chair of the Theatre Program as a result of the rather sudden death of a very traditional man who had chaired the program for nearly twenty years. I suddenly found myself in a more prominent institutional position than I had ever wanted or imagined. The light was on me and it was bright and made me feel very vulnerable. At least part of my professional self became an administrator ... a queer administrator but an administrator all the same. And my response was to savor the privacy of classroom and rehearsal spaces where the fabulous femme still lived and helped me survive my short-lived lived life as an administrator, thriving on productive foolishness and playfulness with students. Because at that time I had a little more power and security in my new position as a tenured professor and as department chair, I also allowed the queerness of my inner femme to leak out, along with an occasionally belly laugh, in public spaces, but I was careful and thought a lot about the advantages of being a queer theatre person. I know how to inhabit multiple personae, to switch characters at a moment's notice, to play with personal stylistics in a prolif-eration of complex configurations that draw on gay, straight, lesbian, queer, butch, femme, and masculine/feminine behavioral/performance signifiers. I have come to the conclusion that the private and the public can co-exist. That I can negotiate both spaces at once because I am queer and because I live a life infused with theatrical understandings.

My theatrical way of being has kept me relatively sane through tumul-tuous recent years when I relinquished my administrative duties in theatre and chaired the Feminist Studies Program for four years. I gave up directing in our department's regular season to focus on Theatre for Social Justice to contribute to departmental productions as a voice and movement specialist. I pulled out the drama queen to survive co-editing a book and leaving my partner, and I belly laughed my way through falling in love again and being promoted to full professor. My red hair is now soft gray with what seems to me a fabulously queer and beautiful white streak that decorates my brow and that I fancy somehow gives me power, and the fabulous femme now looks and feels to me like an older and wiser though still feminine crone.

I am laughing freely and uproariously, in public and in private, planning subversions and finding subversive activities to engage with both students and colleagues in the ways I did before I was tenured but with more panache gained through experience. When I find myself laughing out loud, it some-times seems that my laughter may be too blatant. I am thinking now about slipping back into the chinks, cracks, and interstices of the institutional walls that have been my home for twenty-two years. Once again using subversive strategies to ensure the survival of feminist and queer pedagogical and schol-arly work might be important as my institution, like so many others, becomes more and more corporate and deals with economic and deeply disturbing social, political, and cultural challenges. Preserving increasingly fraught and complex relationships that feminist and queer professors of all ranks must negotiate within institutions seems to be calling for stealth tactics that can be effectively informed by the inherent subversiveness of play with healthy doses of laughter and theatre's shape-shifting strategies leaking quietly and carefully from within the private and hidden spaces of academia. I am not suggesting a retreat back into the closet, but a strategic use of private spaces where smart and careful discourse can be created with imagination and integrity to ensure that our students and our scholarship does not become watered down by the fear that has infused our culture since 2001. Belly laughs from behind the scenes must drown out fear-mongering on public stages.

Works Cited

Broyles-Gonzalez, Yolanda. *El Teatro Campesino: Theater in the Chicano Movement.* Austin: University of Texas Press, 1994.

Butler, Judith. "Performative Acts and Gender Constitution: An Essay in Phenomenology and Feminist Theory." In *Performing Feminisms.* Ed. Sue-Ellen Case. Baltimore: The Johns Hopkins University Press, 1990, pp. 270–282.

De Lauretis, Teresa. *Technologies of Gender.* Bloomington: Indiana University Press, 1987.

Dolan, Jill. "Producing Knowledges that Matter." *The Drama Review* 40:4 (1996): 9–19.

Schechner, Richard. *The Future of Ritual.* New York: Routledge, 1993.

"Mothering Language" in the Academic Workplace

ELLEN MAYOCK

> A profession's language is part of its public representation.
> — Frank and Treichler

Where is Sarah Palin now? The self-named "hockey mom" and self-deposed former governor of Alaska in a painfully visible way has taught the United States public a lesson about the dangers of transforming women laborers into mother figures. The former governor of Alaska and candidate for vice president of the United States may now be just the hockey mom whose strong, hometown, home-grown, homespun image, built largely on her reputation as mother of five, initially propelled her to political stardom and then distilled itself to its essence, "mom." Clearly, the lesson we can learn in the case of Sarah Palin is not that women laborers should not be mothers, nor even express pride if they are. It is that individuals in and out of the formal workforce still have deeply ingrained ideas about what mothers are capable of and where they belong. Once women sell themselves in the workforce as "moms," they are also inviting more widespread scrutiny based on stereotypes surrounding the abilities and potential placements of laborers who are mothers.

In this essay, I aim to examine the phenomenon of "mothering language," comment on how widespread this type of language has become in both the popular press and the workplace, and then make specific suggestions about how an organization can think more critically about its professional language and move more deliberately towards creating an environment that welcomes all employees, especially women. I wish to link the concepts of body and self through both the actual manifestation of the pregnant body

126

in the workplace and its metaphorical ramifications. In the end, my hope is that fomenting further understanding about sexist language in the workplace will serve as its own form of ongoing feminist activism.

Social psychologists (e.g. Taylor, Langer) have amply documented that actual corporal pregnancy contributes to blatant stereotyping about competence in the workplace and impedes access to high-prestige jobs (Cuddy, Fiske, Glick 714). The issue of what I have termed "compulsory motherhood"—the imposition of the ideal mother image on women in the workplace through pejorative uses of language about women and mothers in contemporary society—is rooted in language use that devalues women and their contributions in the workplace. In particular, I am interested in looking at spoken language and its ability to infiltrate the formal environment of the workplace and its institutional texts.

The actual pregnant body shifts metonymically to images of mothers and mothering. Nevertheless, a body that has never been and might never be pregnant is often blurred with this ever-present image of *woman* as *mother*. Here, I depend upon three salient points from Barbara Johnson's *Mothering Tongues*, a masterful examination of metaphors and language surrounding motherhood: (1) As human beings continue to categorize and essentialize identities, they struggle with the concepts of unity, complementarity, and individuality (19–20). These concepts appear in a different form in stereotype charts presented later in this essay; (2) many writers (Lacan is specified) "discipline the reader into sexual difference" (24). That is to say, the language used in writing forces a definition of the sex of the sender and receiver of the message sent. "So," says Barbara Johnson, "sexual difference is a problem that must be solved if equality is to work, but because it leaves a residue, it has to be legislated" (24)[1]; (3) establishing an ideal of "perfect motherhood" is damaging in particular to the mother herself, but also to all women and men (84). Johnson is saying that human beings tend to look at the world to find complementarity and, thus, that the gendered sphere stereotypes so firmly established in many cultures are difficult to undo. Highlighting sexual difference seems required, men seem preferred, and women therefore become the losers in the workplace.

In Spanish, Latin American, and Latino cultures, the motherhood ideal is encapsulated in the concept of "Marianismo," the Cult of the Mother, also known as the Cult of the Virgin.[2] The idea is that all women are destined to become mothers and, when they do, they are to be idealized in the ways that the Madonna is. The emphasis is on purity, goodness, and abnegation, and the context is the private sphere, the home, the hearth. In a fundamental way, the motherhood ideal prohibits the easy acceptance of the mother in the workforce. It is easy to grasp how a motherhood ideal limits options for women and limits the ways in which their workplace potential can be viewed. The expectation is simple: women become mothers, mothers take care of children, children are in the home; therefore, mothers (= women) do not belong, they do not "fit" in the work environment. In essence, "motherly rhetoric" keeps women (whether mothers or not) in their places. In this sense, it is logical for managers to evaluate their use of the phrase "the right fit" when they make decisions about hiring and promotion. In her piece in *The Chronicle of Higher Education*, Linda Kerber even looks at the use of the word "married" in the academic workplace as it relates to the motherhood ideal: "Nor did commentators explore the implications of the metaphor 'married.' Married, after all, does not mean only a reasonably predictable sex life. It is the short form of conveying 'mother,' someone whose work as a parent is understood to be at odds with professional competence and ambition."

McConnell-Ginet makes the point that it is now difficult for someone to use the "generic he" to refer to both female and male, that language use has changed enough so that other solutions are clearer and more accurate (46–50). The commonplace of the ideal mother image in everyday life, the press, and the workplace allows for mothering language to become a "standard" or "default" usage, whereby most women in the workplace are viewed almost automatically as wives and mothers. Contemporary society makes frequent use of the informal variations on "mother," most notably, "mom" and "mommy." Several of multitudinous examples include "soccer moms," "mortgage moms," "security moms," "working moms," "mommy tax," "mommy track," "Modern Mommy University" (reference to Princeton University's naming of a female president), "sergeant mom," and, of course, the whole, expansive "mommy blogosphere," which includes references to "Mom Central," "cool moms," and the ubiquitous, Sarah Palin-tinged "hockey mom." The cover of the Summer, 2009 issue of *Ms.* features an anxious-looking woman, baby in one arm and telephone in the other hand, with an additional six monstrous-looking arms with hands holding a pacifier, a car key, a sponge, a clock indicating the 5:00 hour, a BlackBerry, and a cooking pan. The caption reads "Mom 2.0. She Blogs, She Tweets, She Rises Up!" In the feature article, Kara Jesella states that: "The maternal impulse turns political when you mix moms, feminism and the blogosphere" (27). An article sidebar features "dot mom" (29) for further information about "moms in cyberspace."[3] Suffice it to say that the question of women in the workplace and, by the extrapolation of many, mothers in the workplace, is highly visible and polemical. The informal use of the terms "mom" and "mommy" brings to mind busy, worried, struggling, and frazzled women who, even if they are "working moms," somehow do not belong in the workplace, just as the woman depicted on the cover of *Ms.* (even if considered an ironic depiction, which I believe it to be). These terms are used in common parlance, in newspapers and magazines, in novels, and even in formal scholarly studies. In short, they are everywhere.

A standard word's informal usage can be pejorative and lead to an institutionalization, or formalization, of the pejorative phrase itself. For example, "housewife" became "hussy" (McConnell-Ginet 44–45). In addition, many other terms related to mothers and mothering are often negative: "bitch," "son of a bitch," "mamma's boy," "motherfucker." In Spanish, we can consider the juxtaposition of the words "mala" and "leche" in the term "mala leche" ("bitterness"; literally, "bad milk"), or, more aptly, "coño" ("damn" or "fuck"; literally, "cunt") with "cojonudo" ("awesome"; literally, "big-balled"). Also, "madre mía" ("oh, dear," said usually negatively; literally, "mother of mine") has its positive analog in "qué padre" ("how cool"; literally, "how father"). These last examples of the privileging of male imagery over female/"mommy" imagery relate clearly to more formal investigations about the comparative access to success of women and men in the workplace. Cuddy, Fiske, et.al. have studied stereotyping of "working moms" versus that of "working dads" and have concluded that the latter are celebrated and rewarded, while the former are not considered as frequently for hiring, training, or promotion.[4] It is appropriate to address here as well the now standard usage of the phrase "working mom," even in scholarly studies by people attuned to the nuances of gender ideology and language. If we are considering primarily laborers in the workforce who are also mothers, shouldn't the noun be "worker" or "laborer" and the modifier have to do with "parenting" or "mothering"? I personally prefer that only my children refer to me as "mom" or "mommy" and that all other professionals refer to me as a worker, or a teacher, or a professor.

The "mom"/"mommy" usage further entrenches the lack of "work credit" for the numerous undefined tasks that women often perform in the workplace. Marie C. Wilson states the following about these tasks, such as maintaining relationships with coworkers, encouraging colleagues and staff, and generally making the group run more smoothly:

> As they [a group of female design engineers] described it, these tasks were just "what needed to be done," even if they weren't part of a job description. Actions

such as these are seldom considered "work," no matter where they are per-formed—life partners and business executives don't stop to think that they take time and energy, and they're not as easy as a spreadsheet [110].

Pigeonholing a woman as a "working mom" may have two damaging effects: (1) the broad-based assumption that women will "pick up the slack" in the workplace, that they will simply see what has to be done and do it, with no articulation of the work required and no "work credit" given, and (2) for women and men in the workplace, the reinforcement of the lack of privilege and status connected to work in the home. Work in the home rightfully deserves status and privilege in social, economic, and labor realms, but we as a society have not yet resolved the question of defining and valuing skills learned in the home workplace.

In the 1989 MLA edition titled *Language, Gender, and Professional Writing*, the authors Frank and Treichler establish the need to "demonstrate the importance and value of avoiding biased language" (1). The authors are referring primarily to the avoidance of biased language in professional writing, although there is an understanding that such efforts would have a benefi-cial overall effect on the university workplace. Like the MLA scholarly volume, many studies establish the links and circles of influence between language use and societal norms. For example, Whitley and Kite state that "another way stereotypes are shared is through language itself, both from person to person and from generation to generation. As Anne Maass and Luciano Arcuri explain, stereotypes are transmitted through vocabulary" (92). Given that women's workforce attachment has increased significantly over the past four decades and that women appear to be in the workforce to stay (Rotella 385; AAUW Policy Recommendations for *A Woman's Nation*), it is essential to signal ways in which language can be used consistently and fairly in order to ensure that female and male laborers have the opportunity to be hired, to work, speak, train, and be promoted.[5] Feminist theorists such as Audre Lorde, Theodora Wells, Julia Penelope, Luce Irigary, and Hélène Cixous examine the dangers of silencing women's voices, while Marie C. Wilson recommends strategies for increasing the number of women in lead-ership roles. Workers will benefit from the active facilitation of women's "articulation of alternative models of the world" (Frank, Treichler 19). In particular, a conscious freeing of women from the four "role traps," through which privileged groups "perceive token women as mothers, seductresses, iron maidens, or pets" (Kanter in Chamallas, 97), will allow women to advance as laborers in the workforce and to have their world views finally shared and considered.

In the landmark law case of *Hopkins v. Price Waterhouse* (1989), Certified Public Accountant Ann Hopkins sued Price Waterhouse for denying her partnership on grounds of gender discrimination. Senior executives had documented that Hopkins was too masculine and that she "needed a course at charm school" (Katz, Andronici 63), although they also acknowledged that she was a key company earner and was exceptionally talented at attracting new clients. The case, won by Hopkins, establishes the "Catch-22" of women in the workplace: men in positions of power expect female peers and subordinates to exhibit traditionally "feminine" characteristics, but success in a hierarchy is firmly entrenched in the demonstration of traditionally "masculine" characteristics. Similarly, Sheila Ruth's stereotype charts establish connections between mothers and negative stereotypes, connections that become important when workers emphasize the "mom" part of "working mom." The stereotypes associated with the mothers on Ruth's charts appear in the category of "serviceable" (Virgin Mary/Mother-Wife) and "nonserviceable" (Old Ball and Chain/Wife and Kids) (133):

	Non-sexual *The Virgin Mary/* *Mother-Wife*	*Sexual* *The Playmate/Lover*
Serviceable	chaste, pure, innocent, good proper-looking, conservative, matronly, nurturing, selfless, loving, gentle, "mother of his children," submissive, pliable, receptive, compromising, tactful, loyal, fragile, needful, dependent, feeling, non-rational, aesthetic, spiritual, understanding, supportive	sensuous, sexually wise, experienced, sexy, "built," stylish, satisfying, eager, earthy, mysterious, slightly dangerous, sexually receptive, agreeable, "game" challenging, exciting, independent, carefree, "laid back," bright, fun-loving, playful, carnal, responsive, ego-building
	Old Ball and Chain/ *Wife and Kids*	*Eve/The Witch-Bitch* *Temptress*
Non-serviceable	frigid, sexually uninteresting, frumpy or slatternly, cloying, suffocating, obligating, incapable of decision, changeable, scatterbrained, dumb, passive, nagging, shrewish, harping helpless, burdensome, over-emotional, irrational, unreasonable, shrewd, manipulative, sneaky	promiscuous, bad, coarse, vulgar, trampy, tempting, leads one into sin and evil undiscriminating, she's "anybody's," bitchy, demanding, selfish, she "asks for it," immoral, makes trouble, thoughtless, sinful, evil, immodest, unladylike

*Stereotypes most relevant to the academic workplace are in bold, below.

Non-sexual *The Virgin Mary/ Mother-Wife*	*Non-sexual* *Old Ball and Chain/ Wife and Kids*
Serviceable	Non-serviceable
chaste, pure, innocent, good, proper-looking, conservative, matronly, **nurturing, selfless, loving, gentle,** "mother of his children" **submissive, pliable, receptive, compromising, tactful, loyal, fragile, needful, dependent,** feeling, non-rational, aesthetic, spiritual, **understanding, supportive**	frigid, sexually uninteresting, frumpy or slatternly, **cloying, suffocating, obligating, incapable of decision, changeable, scatterbrained, dumb, passive, nagging, shrewish, harping,** helplessness, burdensome, **overemotional, irrational, unreasonable, shrewd, manipulative, sneaky**

So, if the feminine is strongly associated with the abnegation that accompanies ideal motherhood, laborers who are mothers will continue to be viewed as "nurturing, selfless, loving, gentle" (on the "serviceable" side) or, quite possibly as "cloying, suffocating, obligating" (on the "nonserviceable" side). Neither perception of the working woman allows her to be seen as competent or worthy of training and promotion. Indeed, as soon as someone compliments me for my "nurturing role," I can assume that I have been assigned the wife/mother role and that my other contributions in the workplace will be either ignored or viewed in the same pejorative light. Nurturing faculty *is* important, but the gendered use of the term "nurturing" assigns the job task less status and value. It diminishes its importance and complexity and devalues the time that is required to maintain good relationships and encourage professional development. The other stereotypes on the chart play themselves out in the workplace in similar ways. Despite the fact that some academics in the 1989 MLA volume were already calling for avoiding "stereotyped references to nurturing, passivity, and reproductive functions" in written language (Frank, Treichler 226), such verbal references in the academic workplace are still common.

Society's acceptance and reinforcement of these stereotypes establish an infrastructure for the workplace that impedes women's success. This is especially true (1) when the female laborers occupy roles that do not fit neatly into the Mother-Wife or Old Ball and Chain paradigms and (2) when they perform tasks that are essential to the work flow but that receive no formal "work credit," much as we see in the case of the housewife. Language use in informal and formal settings serves to uncover core societal messages that are transmitted to employees and employers. Given that real and metaphorical "pregnant bodies" can encourage stereotyping tendencies about mothers and women in the workplace — the "compulsory motherhood," mentioned earlier — it must be recognized, too, that there are pressures upon some women workers to "perform" motherhood. Ramachandran cites Yoshino to elucidate this "reverse covering" phenomenon:

> Yoshino also identifies "reverse covering" demands, or demands that one somehow signal one's identity — a demand that he believes is frequently placed on women. For example, women are sometimes penalized in the workplace for not acting "feminine" enough, such as by not dressing femininely. Others have described these "covering' and "reverse-covering" demands as regulation of "identity performance," or "identity work," or "assimilationist bias." One could even simply call them role-playing demands [Ramachandran 306].

The stereotyping in the workplace, therefore, can have the unwitting effect of having laborers who are mothers perform their motherhood in the workplace. For example, an administrator whose superiors initiate every conversation with her by talking first about her children might find herself complying with the performance of motherhood by starting the conversations herself in exactly this way. This performance provides relief to the superiors, who might be more comfortable with the administrator's role as mother than with her role as administrator.[6] This phenomenon is easily reinforced by stereotyping that takes place outside of the work environment, such as assumptions by child care workers about which parent is the primary caregiver, relegation of wives to secondary positions on federal forms, and assumptions in restaurants about who "should" get the check. These examples of workplace harassment are reinforced through non-work assumptions and interactions that are often equally subtle and pernicious.

Colleges and universities have still not addressed these issues in a wholesale way. While *quid pro quo* sexual harassment was the basis for many sexual discrimination and harassment training sessions that were executed throughout the 1990s, it is now safe to say that most employers recognize the impropriety and legal risk of this form of sexual harassment. Hostile environment sexual harassment is still less well defined for most employers and employees and therefore requires that we study spoken language to see what effects it has on fairness in the workplace. For example, in 1999, one institution was providing training on its policy on sexual discrimination and harassment. When an employee asked the session leader what constituted "pervasive" harassing behavior, the joking response was, "you can only get in one good grope." In 2006, when the same institution provided the same type of training, the initial segment provided information on both *quid pro quo* and hostile environment harassment, but the case studies focused entirely on the former. On this particular occasion, session leaders cited the gendered-spheres argument from *Men are from Mars and Women are from Venus* as a way to explain the occurrence of sexual harassment in the workplace, thus reinforcing any preconceived gendered-sphere notions that supervisors and employees in the room might have had. In addition, they used legal terminology regarding the strategy of "removing the thin-skinned plaintiff" (in all cases referred to as a woman) from the harassing situation. "Thin-skinned" relates clearly to the "overemotional, irrational, unreasonable" section on Ruth's gender stereotype charts and, therefore, its use in training sessions (and, of course, in legal cases) should be carefully considered.

It is clear that University counsel, supervisors, and employees still have not embarked upon the difficult project of sorting through complex issues of language use and its real and metaphorical implications. Of course, the language of Title VII ("because of such individual's race, color, religion, sex, or national origin") does not help because it does not differentiate between sex and gender, and, as Kirshenbaum has stated, Title VII legal history has not gone much further to clarify these issues (163). "Mothering" language has its origins in sex (male versus female) but becomes significantly more complex because of the gendered performance demands involved in the equation woman=mother=homemaker=inferior laborer. Perhaps we can bring to spoken language in the workplace what scholarly work from 1989 brought to written language — the awareness that metaphor matters.

With all of this information before us, what can we do? How can we encourage gender equity in the language used in the workplace? Joan C. Williams, Director of the Center for WorkLife Law at the University of California Hastings College of the Law, has used an NSF grant to create an interactive "game" titled "Gender Bias Bingo" (http://www.genderbiasbingo.com/games.html). The game allows visitors to submit stories that apply to patterns of gender bias, such as the Maternal Wall, Double Jeopardy, and Prove It Again! Williams' project goes a long way in allowing individuals and institutions to learn and use a fixed set of terms surrounding gender bias in the Academy. We must use strategies such as Williams' to continue to raise consciousness about patriarchal language — in training sessions, meetings, job interviews, performance evaluations, conferences, and around campus. Although recent research (e.g. Nosek et.al.) reveals that implicit stereotyping is difficult to eradicate, it is certainly possible to train people in the simple "think before you speak" model.[7] This type of consciousness about language needs to start at the top. University administrations need careful training about language use. The training should be well based in studies from law, social psychology, sociology, and women's studies, as well as from other disciplines that focus on language meaning and use in informal and formal contexts. Administrators must consider how human beings tend to stereotype and then encourage language that "is compatible with the goal of social justice" (Frank, Treichler 107). They must assess the ways in which they articulate university missions, goals, and community ethos through "family" and "mothering" metaphors and the patriarchal essence that community members might glean from the discourse. Furthermore, both women and men should hold significant administrative posts. If women continue to be "rarities" in administration (Chamallas 100), they will lose voice through the same stereotyping tendencies and loss of status that their female employees face.

We must also insist upon the public correction of wrongdoing. Individuals, and especially those in positions of authority, must speak out when they hear stereotyping language and need to suggest corrective language that would better serve the purpose. Two years ago I was at a meeting of the NCAA. As the director of this huge organization gave a speech to a large crowd, he made a reference to "the great work of the men in the front office." Before I could even register what was wrong with the statement, the director had quickly and effectively corrected himself by saying, "that is, the great work of the accomplished women and men in the front office." The director was well-versed in Title IX law, well aware of equity issues, and comfortable enough in his position to correct himself publicly. Modeling language of social justice and correcting ill-used language, especially from the top down, will go a long way to establish a work environment that is more consistently and appropriately set up for the success of all the laborers who constitute its work force. This simple quote by Susan Fiske summarizes this notion:

> People's tendency to stereotype is intentional in that, first, they demonstrably have alternative ways of thinking about people, as members of a category or as unique individuals; everyone can do this (Fiske & Neuberg, 1990). Second, people can implement their alternative ways of thinking about other people according to how much attention they pay to those other people [626].

Although we as human beings might be slow to eliminate implicit stereotyping, an effort to eliminate the explicit form is certainly possible. An appropriate training program might even begin with this Fiske quote in order to establish that most individuals are capable of paying more attention to others and to learn from the attention they are paying.

In her essay titled "Language Planning, Language Reform, and Language Change," Francine Wattman Frank addresses the question of language use and stereotyping in this way:

> Few would suggest that sexual or racial inequality exists because of language use. Nor would many argue that banishing sexist and racist labeling would in itself result in a just society. At the same time, it is clear that language not only reflects social structures but, more important, sometimes serves to perpetuate existing differences in power; thus a serious concern with linguistic usage is fully warranted [109].

She goes on to provide useful, specific guidelines for nonsexist language use. These guidelines can be applied to both oral and written language and can help individuals and institutions to avoid "mothering language." I make the following recommendations to build upon Franks's work in order to help institutions to create a more welcoming work environment for all employees:

- Hire women at all levels and in all areas; be attuned to retention issues and address problems as soon as they arise.
- Ensure that physical surroundings support women and men equally (e.g.: office space; locker rooms).
- Encourage women to apply for posts that enhance their careers; encourage women to negotiate for better salary and benefits packages in these positions.
- Examine and address equity issues in the allocation of types and amounts of work assigned.
- Recognize difference and value it at all levels; seek out ways to encourage all individuals to participate in workplace discussions; be particularly attentive to sex, race, class, sexual orientation; be vigilant about the "silencing" phenomenon.
- Encourage all to speak; encourage dissent; encourage working together towards articulating problems and finding solutions.
- Support a community (or communities) of women (e.g. mentoring groups; research groups; status of women committee).
- Conduct surveys and gather pertinent data in order to analyze women's experiences empirically.
- Examine committee composition to ensure that women's voices are being heard throughout the workplace.

- Recognize women's successes informally and formally (campus media).
- Support internal and external programming related to gender issues.
- Examine core values and their cultural import vis-à-vis gender (e.g. honor; civility).
- Write clear, fair policies that establish workplace equity (healthcare; leaves; hiring, training, promotion; salary; discrimination, harassment, and retaliation) and have the policies vetted by a variety of groups on and off campus.
- Train employers and employees with clear, "local" examples of policy violations and relevant case studies. Ensure ongoing and increasingly sophisticated training.
- Adhere to policy; be careful with idealistic (and therefore possibly hypocritical) rhetoric about zero-tolerance on discrimination, harassment, retaliation. Use the rhetoric if it fits the environment. Do not allow scapegoating.

These suggestions are at once practical and lofty — they can be practiced every day, and they contain an ethos of equity and equality.[8] In this sense, academic institutions, most of which have mission statements that demonstrate their desire for a multicultural community and their wish to prepare students for an increasingly diverse society, can use this list as a simple way both to fulfill mission and to take practical measures to create an improved work environment for all.

Notes

1. Martha Chamallas speaks to this point in two ways: (1) "The comparative standards asks us to perform the mental feat of taking away (or changing) the gender of a person and then determining what would have happened" (104) and (2) "The question of difference becomes more complicated, however, if we start from an assumption that differences can be socially constructed and that dominant culture is marked by a profound gender imbalance in power, numbers, and ability to affect the working environment" (109).

2. See Alicia del Campo for an examination of "Marianismo" in women's movements in Chile.

3. Find additional "mom/mommy" references at the end of this essay.

4. These are the terms that the authors use in the formal context of the scholarly article.

5. The 2008 Department of Labor statistics confirm that women comprise 46.5 percent of the workforce. A February 2009 *New York Times* article cites the Bureau of Labor Statistics' figure of women comprising 49.1 percent. More recently, a *Ms.* article titled "Paycheck Feminism" (October 23, 2009) states: "In a subtle shift with momentous implications, women are on the verge of becoming more than 50 percent of U.S. paid workers."

6. In a work in progress, I examine the links between this performance phenomenon and the acceleration of the cycle of violence referred to in the literature on domestic violence.

7. See Linder and Nosek's "Alienable Speech: Ideological Variations in the Application of Free-Speech Principles" for information on how and why groups of people are less willing to protect speech they dislike than speech they like. See also Nosek, Banaji, and Jost's "The Politics of Intergroup Attitudes" for an examination of how ideologies surrounding ethnocentrism, authoritarianism, system justification, social dominance, and morality inform the formation of implicit and explicit preferences.

8. See also Mary Ann Mason's "Title IX Includes Maternal Discrimination," published in November 2009 in *The Chronicle of Higher Education*.

Works Cited

American Association of University Women Policy Recommendations for *A Woman's Nation*. http://www.aauw.org/advocacy/issue_advocacy/womansnation.cfm, Accessed October 20, 2009.

Chamallas, Martha. "Listening to Dr. Fiske: The Easy Case of *Price Waterhouse v. Hopkins*." *Vermont Law Review* 15:89 (1990–91): 89–124.

Cuddy, Amy J.C., Susan T. Fiske, and Peter Glick. "When Professionals Become Mothers, Warmth Doesn't Cut the Ice." *Journal of Social Issues* 60:4 (2004): 701–18.

Del Campo, Alicia. "Resignificación del Marianismo por los movimientos de mujeres de oposición en Chile." *Poética de la población marginal: Sensibilidades determinantes*. Ed. James V. Romano. Minneapolis: Prima, 1987, pp. 429–65.

Fiske, Susan T. "Controlling Other People: The Impact of Power on Stereotyping." *American Psychologist* 48:6 (June 1993): 621–28.

Frank, Francine Wattman. "Language Planning, Language Reform, and Language Change: A Review of Guidelines for Nonsexist Usage." In *Language, Gender, and Professional Writing*. Eds. Francine Wattman Frank and Paula A. Treichler. New York: MLA Commission on the Status of Women in the Profession, 1989.

_____ and Paula A. Treichler. *Language, Gender, and Professional Writing*. New York: MLA Commission on the Status of Women in the Profession, 1989.

Jesella, Kara. "Cyberhood is Powerful." *Ms*. Summer (2009): 27–29.

Johnson, Barbara. *Mother Tongues. Sexuality, Trials, Motherhood, Translation*. Cambridge, MA: Harvard University Press, 2003.

Katz, Debra S., and Justine F. Andronici. "No More Excuses! It's Time to Abolish the 'She-Didn't-Ask' Defense for Wage Discrimination." *Ms*. 16:4 (Fall 2006): 63–64.

Kerber, Linda K. "We Must Make the Academic Workplace More Humane and Equitable." *The Chronicle of Higher Education*, March 18, 2005. http://chronicle.com/weekly/v51/i28/28b00601.htm, accessed September 15, 2006.

Kirshenbaum, Andrea Meryl. "'Because of ... Sex': Rethinking the Protections Afforded under Title VII in the Post-*Oncale* World." *Albany Law Review* 69:1 (2005). 139–77.

Kornbluh, Karen, and Rachel Homer. "Paycheck Feminism." *Ms*. Fall (2009). http://ms magazine.com/Fall2009/paycheckfeminism.asp#, accessed October 24, 2009.

Lindner, Nicole M., and Brian A. Nosek. "Alienable Speech: Ideological Variations in the Applications of Free-Speech Principles." *Political Psychology* 30:1 (2009): 67–92.

Mason, Mary Ann. "Title IX Includes Maternal Discrimination." *The Chronicle of Higher Education*, November 19, 2009, accessed November 19, 2009.

McConnell-Ginet, Sally. "The Sexual (Re)Production of Meaning: A Discourse-Based Theory." In *Language, Gender, and Professional Writing: Theoretical Approaches and*

Guidelines for Nonsexist Usage. Eds. Francine Wattman Frank and Paula A. Treichler. New York: MLA, 1989, pp. 35–50.

Nosek, Brian A., Mahzarin R. Banaji, and John T. Jost. "The Politics of Intergroup Attitudes." In *The Social and Psychological Bases of Ideology and System Justification*. Eds. J.T. Jost, A.C. Kay, and H. Thorisdottir. Oxford: Oxford University Press, 2009.

Ramachandran, Gowri. "Intersectionality as 'Catch 22': Why Identity Performance Demands are Neither Harmless nor Reasonable." *Albany Law Review* 69:1 (2005): 299–342.

Rampell, Catherine. "As Layoffs Surge, Women May Pass Men in Job Force." *The New York Times*. February 6, 2009. Accessed online February 6, 2009.

Rotella, Elyce J. "Women and the American Economy." In *Issues in Feminism: An Introduction to Women's Studies*. Ed. Sheila Ruth. Mountain View, CA: Mayfield, 2001, pp. 383–97.

Ruth, Sheila. *Issues in Feminism. An Introduction to Women's Studies*. Fifth Edition. Mountain View, CA: Mayfield, 2001.

Samarrai, Fariss. "Gender Gap: Implicit Stereotypes May Contribute to Underachievement and Under-participation Among Girls and Women in Science." *University of Virginia A&S Online*. http://aands.virginia.edu/x15919.xml, posted July 23, 2009, accessed August 3, 2009.

Taylor, S.E., and E.J. Langer. "Pregnancy: A Social Stigma?" *Sex Roles* 3 (1977): 27–35.

Title VII of the Civil Rights Act of 1964. The U.S. Equal Employment Opportunity Commission. http://www.eeoc.gov/policy/vii.html, accessed October 9, 2006.

United States Department of Labor Women's Bureaus. Statistics and Data. http://www.dol.gov/wb/stats/main.htm, accessed August 13, 2009.

Williams, Joan C. "Gender Bias Bingo of the Gender Bias Learning Project." http://www.genderbiasbingo.com/games.html, accessed on October 29, 2009.

Wilson, Marie C. *Closing the Leadership Gap: Why Women Can and Must Help Run the World*. New York: Penguin, 2004.

Wilson, Robin. "New Game Plays on Women's Experiences of Gender Bias in Academe." *The Chronicle of Higher Education*, October 29, 2009. http://chronicle.com/article/New-Game-Plays-on-Womens/48966/, accessed on 10/29/09.

Whitley, Bernard E., and Mary E. Kite. *The Psychology of Prejudice and Discrimination*. Belmont, CA: Thomson Wadsworth, 2006.

Yoshino, Kenji. "The Pressure to Cover." *The New York Times Magazine*, January 15, 2006, pp. 32–37.

"Mom" and "Mommy" References in the Popular Press

Birnbaum, Jeffrey H., and Chris Cillizza. "'Mortgage Moms' May Star in Midterm Vote." *Washington Post*, September 5, 2006, p. A01.

Foderaro, Lisa W. "Working Mothers Find Some Peace on the Road." *The New York Times*, November 1, 2006, accessed online November 1, 2006.

Hall, Katy. "Placement of Women in Senior Posts Stirs Debate at Princeton." *The New York Times*, January 21, 2004. (Reference to "The Modern Mommy University.")

Jones, Del. "Do Moms Make Better Managers?" *U.S.A. Today*, May 11, 2006.

Lu, Stacy. "Cosmopolitan Moms." *The New York Times*, November 9, 2006, accessed online November 13, 2005.

Selvin, Molly. "This Mommy Track May Go Somewhere." *Los Angeles Times*, September 5, 2006.

Sheehan, Cindy. "Me, Hugo, and George." *Common Dreams News Center*, July 16, 2006, accessed online July 18, 2006. Sheehan states about Hugo Chávez: "He never called me 'Mom' once the entire time I was with him — unlike George (Bush)."

Tierney, John. "The Immoral Majority." *The New York Times*, October 31, 2006, accessed online October 31, 2006.

Additional References

Adams, Amy. "Barres Examines Gender, Science Debate and Offers a Novel Critique." *Stanford Report*, July 26, 2006, accessed online September 3, 2006.

American Association of University Professors Policy Documents and Reports. Ninth Edition. Washington, DC: AAUP, 2001.

Angier, Natalie. "One Thing They Aren't: Maternal." *The New York Times*, May 9, 2006, p. D1.

Claes, Marie-Therese. "Women, Men, and Management Styles." In *Workplace/Women's Place: An Anthology*. Third Ed. Eds. Paula J. Dubeck and Dana Dunn. Los Angeles: Roxbury, 2006, pp. 83–87.

Dean, Cornelia. "Dismissing 'Sexist Opinions' About Women's Place in Science." *The New York Times*, July 18, 2006, p. D4.

_____. "Women in Science: The Battle Moves to the Trenches." *The New York Times*, December 19, 2006, accessed online December 19, 2006.

Deutsch, B. "The Male Privilege Checklist: An Unabashed Imitation of an Article by Peggy McIntosh." http://colours.mahost.org/org/maleprivilege.html, accessed December 20, 2006.

Katz, Debra S., and Justine F. Andronici. "No More Excuses! It's Time to Abolish the 'She-Didn't-Ask' Defense for Wage Discrimination." *Ms.* (Fall 2006): 63–64.

Labi, Nadya. "The Baby Gamble." *Yale Alumni Magazine* (March/April 2006): 36–43.

Merkin, Daphne. "Gender Trouble." *The New York Times*, March 12, 2006, accessed online March 12, 2006.

MLA Committee on the Status of Women in the Profession. "Women in the Profession, 2000." *Profession* (2000): 191–217.

Nielsen, Laura Beth. *License to Harass: Law, Hierarchy, and Offensive Public Speech*. Princeton: Princeton University Press, 2004.

O'Brien Timothy L. "Why Do So Few Women Reach the Top of Big Law Firms?" *The New York Times*, March 19, 2006, accessed online March 21, 2006.

Pear, Robert. "Married and Single Parents Spending More Time with Children, Study Finds." *The New York Times*, October 17, 2006, p. A12.

Pérez-Reverte, Arturo. "La osadía de la ignorancia." *XL Semanal* no. 960 (March 19–25, 2006), accessed online March 22, 2006. Pérez-Reverte, member of the Spanish Royal Academy, says that "someone ought to tell certain bullheaded feminists, including those from the National Government or the Regional Andalucía Government, that they just need to get used to it [lack of distinction in the use of the masculine to represent the universal]."

Ragins, Belle Rose, Bickley Townsend, and Mary Mattis. "Gender Gap in the Executive Suite: CEOs and Female Executives Report on Breaking the Glass Ceiling. In *Workplace/Women's Place: An Anthology*. Third Ed. Eds. Paula J. Dubeck and Dana Dunn. Los Angeles: Roxbury, 2006, pp. 95–109.

St. John, Warren. "The Politics of Good Touch, Bad Touch." *The New York Times*, July 23, 2006, Section 9.

Scully, Malcolm G. "Challenging the Status Quo." *The Chronicle of Higher Education*, February 9, 1970, accessed online September 15, 2006.

Tyre, Peg, and Julie Scelfo. "Why Girls Will Be Girls." *Newsweek*, July 31, 2006, pp. 46–47.

Valian, Virginia. *Why So Slow? The Advancement of Women*. Cambridge, MA: MIT Press, 1999.

Wilson, Robin. "Where the Elite Teach, It's Still a Man's World." *The Chronicle of Higher Education*, December 3, 2004, accessed online September 15, 2006.

Woyshner, Christine A., and Holly S. Gelfond, eds. *Minding Women: Reshaping the Educational Realm*. Cambridge, MA: Harvard Educational Review, 1998.

On the Front Lines

Feminist Activism
in a Catholic University

CATE SIEJK AND JANE A. RINEHART

When our Women's Studies Program began in 1991, we recognized that our institutional support was fragile, and the overall local climate inhospitable. We are located in a highly conservative part of our geographical region, and our university's affiliation with the Catholic Church meant there was a minefield of potential conflicts around issues affecting women. Still, we had been developing the foundation for the program over seventeen years, sponsoring different kinds of activities for faculty and students, and developing a solid core of courses focused on the impact of gender and the hidden contributions of women. Our proposal for the program highlighted the ways in which women's studies expressed key elements of our university's mission statement and its traditions. We had earned support from faculty members across the disciplines and schools of the university, and many students were eager for the official status of cross-listed courses and a concentration in women's studies. So, while we began with some trepidation, we were also excited about making a strong start.

We now have many years of experience as a distinct academic program, and our history is typical in many ways. We have struggled to maintain commitment to women's studies in an academic environment that ties most rewards for faculty to their home departments. There have been moments of discouragement regarding our ability to influence decisions about hiring and to improve our financial resources. We have also repeatedly had to answer criticisms of the program by students and faculty writing in the campus newspaper. To some degree, these struggles have been offset by the many awards for excellent teaching received by many of the program's faculty, and consistent evidence that our students are enthusiastic about women's studies courses. However, the bigger and more troublesome change at our university has been the emergence during the last ten years of a vehement and organized opposition to women's studies and feminism that explicitly invokes the authority of Catholic leaders and traditions as its foundation. Both of us have served as directors of our university's Women's Studies Program during this recent period of intense criticism.

Since Pope Paul VI's 1968 statement on birth control, *Humanae Vitae*, church authorities have been increasingly intransigent around issues of sexuality. As levels of dissent regarding official church teachings on matters of contraception, abortion, and the moral status of homosexuality have increased, church authorities have intensified their efforts to regain control. As the long history of the Catholic Church shows, maintaining a healthy tension between authority and theological inquiry has never been easy. Those who value tradition and papal authority often regard impulses toward theological exploration as dangerous. Those who value freedom in theological inquiry see the emphasis on maintaining tradition as authoritarianism. Often, theological disagreement within the church, in particular around issues of women's sexuality and ministry, has evoked overt opposition by church authorities to the perspectives and arguments of feminist scholars who value theological openness and imagination. According to theologian Timothy Luke Johnson, theology depends on the delicate negotiation of fidelity to tradition and receptivity to new understandings. When theological values that should be held in balance are instead thought by many to be opposed, the integrity of theology and the church's intellectual life of the church are endangered.

Some aspects of the discourse at our Catholic university can be described as highly "polarized" around feminist issues and activism, but this word does not capture what has been going on. "Polarization" refers to a situation in which there are two sides at great distance from one another, but still in the same debate — opposites whose views are shaped by their contrasts and contestations. Our situation has evolved over the past eight years into something different, beyond opposition and into a struggle for survival. We are in a debate over heresy, rather than an argument over opposing intellectual perspectives. In Roman Catholic Canon Law, heresy refers to "a sin of one who, having been baptized and retaining the name of Christian ... denies or doubts any of the truths that one is under obligation of divine and Catholic faith to believe" (Buckley 1069). The idea of heresy emerged during the first three centuries over issues of church unity and expansion throughout the Roman Empire. Bitter battles waged in the church resulted in a series of councils and formulations of what is considered Christian orthodoxy versus false doctrines or heresy. The dynamic of orthodoxy and heresy continues today within the Roman Catholic Church configured, as Appleby notes, "within a larger struggle over the control of knowledge, meaning, and religious authority" (20).

In the Roman Catholic Church, heresy and orthodoxy operate as dual aspects of a social process within which systems of belief are defined and expressed. This social process also influences social arrangements within the faith community. According to Kurtz, heresy is understood as an affront to the authority and the order of the church. As a result, heretics are viewed, as "deviant insiders" — the common enemies within the church (1085). The institutional elites (in the case of Catholic Church, the *magisterium*) challenge their commitment to the church, and suppress them in their effort to preserve the sacred institution and traditions of Catholicism. Defining certain beliefs as heresy shapes the organization of an institution. As Kurtz writes, "The identification of heretics shores up the ranks, enables institutional elites to make demands of their subordinates, and reinforces systems of dominance" (1085–86). The administrators, faculty, students, and benefactors who criticize women's studies do not seek to correct our project, but to eliminate it — to excommunicate feminist scholarship and activism from our university in order to restore its clear and uncompromised fidelity to the official teachings of the Catholic Church.

This is a move against what Berger has called the "heretical imperative" within modernity. In Berger's view, the crisis of religion in modern societies is rooted in pluralism that undermines the authority of religious traditions and plunges individuals into the necessity of choice. As individuals encounter a range of possibilities, religious authorities confront their own choices: defy challenges and affirm tradition, secularize tradition, or retrieve the experiences embodied in the tradition (xi). We have been struggling with individuals at our university who choose the first response to pluralism's challenges. In their construction, feminist teachers and students are dangerous dissenters who threaten the certitude that their version of faith requires. Berger favors the third option — an acceptance of reflection on both tradition and experience that rejects any imposition of authority that would close off thinking and discussion. This embrace of reflection would seem to be necessary within a university.

We believe that political and theological conversations can and should occur among people who identify with the same tradition and community, even as they may not share the same interpretations of all the beliefs and values they hold in common. When some members of the community characterize these differences as unacceptable and appear to welcome an eventual reconstitution of the community that depends upon the termination of disputes and assertion of uniformity, perhaps necessitating the forced exile of dissenters, this ignores the complicated and creative work of many years that has sustained connection despite strong contrasts.

It seems important to analyze this, to probe possibilities for conversation in the midst of differences, in order to understand that retreats into dichotomous categories are not inevitable or closed off from transformation. In this essay, we will explore what has happened in our university, where the anti-women's studies side has positioned itself as unwilling to accommodate any disagreements with authoritative pronouncements, and often refuses to engage with those opposed to their views. We will present a case study of some contests around feminism at a Catholic university, and propose that the construction of such disputes in terms of a defense of sacred traditions against the erosions of secularism and feminism ignores a crucial dimension that has both important theoretical and practical implications.

Dillon identifies this dimension in her study of the tensions between diversity and community within the Catholic Church. She takes the position that this community is not destroyed by differences, and that its tradition is not undermined by dissent, including dissent about the definitions of gender and their consequences. She offers a more positive assessment — that differences "are an essential ingredient in the process of communal change, vibrancy and adaptability" (5). These views are illustrated by specific debates within Catholic universities about interpretive authority, and these debates enrich our knowledge of the social construction of institutions and individual identities, while also providing insight into the dynamics of agency, resistance, and change.

Attention to disagreements inside communities and traditions directs us past dichotomous labels and abstractions (e.g. church versus world, in or out, faith or doubt) that are false depictions of actual choices within an increasingly more complex and differentiated social environment. Unsworth presents the stories of "Catholics on the edge" as examples of what it means to challenge the concept of religion as establishing a moral framework of indisputable parameters in favor of a view that defines what Jesus said and did as expanding and deepening freedom. Gillis recommends the disputes among people who are both connected and separated as enabling us to think and act more creatively because these differences remind us to practice continuous negotiation.

Margaret Steinfels suggests re-naming the struggles of Catholics over the meaning of their identity in order to call attention to how both sides are "deeply committed to the church and the Catholic tradition" (13). She calls the two sides the "resisters" (those who oppose contemporary culture's fixation on consumerism and the new, wanting the church to preserve and defend its traditional ethos) and the "engagers" (those who regard current cultural ideals and practices as challenges that the church can meet in dialogue). This reformulation contains the reminder that the arguments are between people who claim and celebrate many of the same ideals and resources. Examining both a specific university's debates and more general contests over the meanings of feminism for Catholic education links these struggles to broader questions about inclusion and development, to an examination of the choice between openness to multiplicity and closed absolutism and what this means for the intellectual life of any university. It also helps to delineate what feminist activism requires within a context where feminists are routinely characterized as threatening to the common good.

Feminism challenges the patriarchal gender paradigm that associates men with human characteristics defined as superior and dominant (power, judgment, discipline, and reason) and females with those defined as inferior and auxiliary (weakness, mercy, lust, and unreason) (Bynum 277). Feminists reject this configuration of gender embedded in the Western tradition, and reconstruct the gender paradigm in order to include women in full and equal humanity. As Ross notes, "The denigration of the female body has been evident in ritual proscription against female contact with the holy, in the classification of women as ontologically different from (and consequently, inferior to) men, and in a negatively obsessive concern with sexual matters in a tradition where women symbolize the sexual to celibate men" (118). Feminist theologians regard human embodiment as the place where humans encounter God. This is a clear critique of the church's long tradition of contempt for the flesh (and, consequently, special contempt for women, who were identified with the flesh), and its enduring belief that women's humanity is so flawed that it requires the protective boundaries of the cloister and patriarchal control.

The Catholic Marian tradition, developed in the medieval period, has reinforced an androcentric image of women. It praised a woman who had surrendered to a male God, and valued her because of her abstinence from a human sexual life. It did not seem fitting that Mary, the New Eve and

Virgin Mother of God, should be identified in any way with the realm of the body. Warner writes of Mary that "the very conditions that make the Virgin sublime are beyond the powers of women to fulfill unless they deny their sex" (77). Daly notes that the identification of Mary as Virgin Mother of God has had "devastating effects" on women (61). As far as Daly is concerned, veneration for Mary has not changed the way Catholic leaders have defined women.

No feminist theologian has done more to reconnect Mary to the lived realities and goals of women's lives than Elizabeth Johnson. She criticizes the conventional symbolism of Mary that simultaneously glorifies her and subordinates all other women. The ideal of womanhood symbolized by Mary is characterized as passively obedient, asexual, and consumed by domestic responsibilities. That many women reject this plastic image of Mary is no surprise, and Johnson creates an alternative "Marian theology rooted in scripture read through women's eyes with feminist hermeneutical methods" (xvi). She develops a spiritually empowering and socially liberating interpretation of Mary as a concrete and graced individual, rooted in history. Mary emerges from Johnson's historical quest as a passionate, self-affirming, and prophetic woman in partnership with God, whose memory has the power to create "liberating energies for justice, especially given her low estate as poor and female" (112). Remembering and emulating Johnson's Mary as "our sister" can provide contemporary women with support in the struggle against all forms of demeaning injustice.

Schneiders provides a definition of feminism that explicitly connects efforts to reinterpret the lives of women with activism: "a comprehensive ideology which is rooted in women's experience of sexual oppression, engages in a critique of patriarchy as an essentially dysfunctional system, embraces an alternative vision for humanity and the earth, and actively seeks to bring this vision to realization" (15). The several components of this definition remind us that feminism is more than a theoretical system for analyzing, criticizing, and evaluating. It is also a worldwide movement committed to re-visioning and transforming our conventional understanding of reality. Schneiders is clear that one cannot be a "closet" feminist. Self-identifying as a feminist means incarnating the feminist vision in the social and political orders in which we live. Feminism calls us to actively fight against injustice, a call that is fully consistent with our university's description of its desire to prepare all of its students (Christian and non–Christian) "for an enlightened dedication to the Christian ideals of justice and peace" by helping them to develop qualities of "self-knowledge, self-acceptance, a restless curiosity, a desire for truth, a mature concern for others, and a thirst for justice" (our University Mission Statement).

It is difficult to deny the consistency between Schneiders' definition of feminism and our Mission Statement's vision of the ideal university education. Both challenge ignorance, encourage empowerment, and embrace diversity. Most importantly, they recognize the inextricable connection and mutual interdependence of theorizing and acting. It is not enough to intellectually understand the forces that contribute to inequality, oppression and discrimination. Nor have we done our job if we only develop theoretical strategies for resistance. We must actively employ strategies for social change both inside and outside of the academy. With the Mission Statement supporting and affirming us, efforts by women's studies professors and students to work passionately against the oppression of women might be expected to have enthusiastic institutional support. Instead, our work to give voice to women and to be a resource for women has been routinely sanctioned, silenced, and punished by the University's administrators for being, at least in their judgment, anti–Catholic and inconsistent with the ideals of a Jesuit university.

There have been three highly public and intense struggles at Gonzaga University that illustrate the tensions around Catholic identity and feminism: the university president's decision to refuse permission for a speaker from Planned Parenthood to address a meeting of the Women's Studies Club on the topic of "abortion politics," his insistence that two student productions of *The Vagina Monologues* had to be performed "off campus," and university administrators' efforts to control student-initiated and student-led celebrations of "Take Back the Night." It is not a coincidence that each of these controversies turned on matters of sexual behavior and expression, and in all of them the controversy itself was constructed as detrimental to the university's Catholic identity. Anyone even slightly familiar with struggles within the Catholic church over the past forty years is aware that reproduction, sex, and sexuality are key areas of contestation between Catholics who assert the absolute authority of papal teachings, and those who press for continuing conversation and respect for points of view that question these positions.

In the spring of 2000, the Women's Studies Club invited a staff member from the local Planned Parenthood office to give a presentation on the politics of abortion. When he was informed about her visit, the university president ordered a member of the Student Life staff to cancel it. The members of the club were astonished and upset. In their view, they had scheduled the presentation in response to a previous anti-abortion speaker and exhibit sponsored by another student club, Gonzaga Organized to Affirm Life. The women's studies students asserted that the university should support the presentation of diverse viewpoints, even when church authorities have clearly taken a position. The president claimed that such diversity contradicts the university's Catholic identity, and confuses its stakeholders and public. It is not obvious that this event had a high enough profile to produce such confusion since the speaker's appearance was not publicized beyond the campus, although it might have been reported after the fact in the student newspaper. It seems clear that the president's action gave the event considerable publicity, and inspired a great deal of conversation among students and faculty.

Toward the end of that semester, a faculty panel addressed the question of whether it is possible to address reproductive issues at Gonzaga University in a manner that includes perspectives that disagree with views expressed by leaders of the Catholic Church. This panel addressed the differences between what happens in Gonzaga classrooms and what happens in public venues, agreeing that thus far there had not been efforts to close off consideration of dissenting views within classrooms, but disagreeing about whether the cancellation of co-curricular events such as the speaker from Planned Parenthood constitutes an infringement on the obligations of a university to present a variety of perspectives. Some panelists argued that this obligation is particularly important when the issues focus on sexual ethics and gender equality because these topics have produced widespread dissent with the church, especially in the United States.

Two years later, with campus struggles now having moved on to student productions of *The Vagina Monologues*, the president took the position that the play could not be presented "on campus," and rationalized his opposition with an argument claiming that "non-sponsorship" is different than censorship, and that the university has a right not to associate itself with an event that he deemed supportive of attitudes and behaviors condemned by the church. This led to their performance in locations close to campus at two different hotels, including one that includes a wing that served as a temporary dormitory for Gonzaga undergraduates. When the second year's performances took place farther from campus, buses were provided to transport people from the campus. In both instances, then, the university's decision to withhold permission to use an on-campus facility seems to have been more a matter of maintaining the appearance of dissociating itself from *The Vagina Monologues*, than of actually preventing its students from attending.

Each production of *The Vagina Monologues* created lively conversations on the faculty e-mail list serve, as well as in the student newspaper. Those opposing the *Monologues* argued that everything the university offers must uphold the teachings of the church and promulgate the "Truth" as defined by the pope and bishops (capitalized here to reflect the commitment of the opposition to an absolute and objective formulation), while students and faculty supporting the production maintained that the university has an obligation to present students with a variety of views. A few members of the faculty pointed out that the Catholic Church does not have an official stance on the play, and that an appeal to Church authority on this matter is unjustifiable. Some student critics who supported the president's view of the play organized an alternative program, called "Women of Dignity," that was held in the university chapel and featured music, readings, and prayer celebrating the "special gifts of womanhood." *The Vagina Monologues* generated just the sort of lively conversation typically associated with a university.

One might think that "Take Back the Night"—an event dedicated to ending all forms of sexual violence — would not be controversial. But at our university it has been and continues to be contentious, mostly because of concerns about "controlling" it: preventing injury to the university's image, silencing speech that might be critical of university responses to instances of rape and sexual assault, and limiting the possibility that male students might find the talks and the speak out "alienating." The larger disagreement that underlies all of these points is whether silence or speech about sex is most compatible with the definition of a Catholic university. Such speech inevitably points toward sexual experiences that fall outside church-approved forms of sexual expression — loving heterosexual intercourse between married partners. Opening up a conversation about sexual violence — without condemning non-violent, consensual, mutual, and respectful sex between individuals who are not identified as married heterosexuals — is regarded as contradicting Church teachings about sexual morals, even in the absence of direct and explicit declaration of an alternative view that accepts widespread sexual activity outside of marital relationships as a feature of contemporary life in the United States. "Take Back the Night" is regarded as dangerous because it tacitly recognizes a sexual landscape that differs from the one affirmed within Catholic Church teaching.

The controversies at our university concerning the compatibility of Catholicism and feminism have been sharpened by continuing efforts within the Catholic Church to define its teachings and rules in opposition to contemporary trends and challenges. There are national organizations (e.g., the Catholic League and the Cardinal Newman Society) that define their mission in terms of "saving" Catholic identity, and their statements and activities often focus on opposition to feminism. Their view is reflected in the defensiveness and righteousness often expressed by critics of women's studies at our university, especially those who declare that anyone who cannot accept all of the doctrines in the official Church Catechism should find another place to teach or learn. The national and local expressions of opposition are the result of fundamentalism: "At present the Catholic Church's official stances on sexual morality and on the role of women constitute a form of Catholic fundamentalism ... a defensive reaction to threatening change" (Peter Steinfels 305). Carroll, writing about the recent uproar over Notre Dame's decision to confer an honorary degree on President Obama (considered unacceptable because of his pro-choice position on abortion), describes the critics of the university as warriors against modernity. The editors of *America,* a national Jesuit magazine, use the label "sectarian" to describe those who target Catholic universities that "defend the richer, subtly nuanced, broad-tent Catholic tradition."

Our campus conversations have become urgent and intense. The Women's Studies Program, and particularly the student activism associated with it, has been a focus for these battles. Perhaps this would have been less likely if feminist perspectives had not been institutionalized into a specific academic unit of the university, remaining more individualized, unorganized, and marginal. Their official location in both an academic concentration and a student club has offered the opportunity to have a more visible role in the university, and thus become a target for opposition. No other academic program or club at Gonzaga has been attacked as vehemently and forced to defend its right to exist. Women's studies club members who are strongly committed to claiming their own voice in conversations about what it means to be Catholic and how a Catholic university should understand its mission have often engaged in pointed exchanges with students who regard women's studies courses and co-curricular projects as both wrong and likely to cause harm. Their tenacity and courage live up to the demands of Schneiders' definition of feminism, and their resistance to attempts to silence differences has enlivened and enriched our university community. As Dillon has argued, their refusal to give up on community has been a source of continuing transformation on our campus.

After much conversation with colleagues and reflection on this matter we have come to recognize that the dissonance between what we say we value in our Mission Statement and the way in which women's studies professors and students are actually treated is rooted in a number of interconnected factors. Among them is an epistemological problem that one confronts when dealing with a hierarchically structured and patriarchal system. Feminist

activists at our university are experiencing the clash between a classicist consciousness that prizes stability, absolutes, and hierarchical structures, and the
postmodern sensibility that there is no "master story" that accounts for all
reality according to some unitary scheme that puts everything and everyone
is some pre-assigned place.

Some of our university leaders read and interpret the Mission Statement
through a lens that requires control over students' "free intellectual inquiry"
because they believe that the unchanging "Truth" that grounds all knowledge
has already been established. They uncritically accept the patriarchal master
story that maleness is normative for humanity, and that powerful males have
the right and obligation to determine what is true and who and what should
be valued. Any claims to new visions of truth are viewed as a turn toward
nihilistic relativism and are, therefore, considered dangerous. Anything that
threatens the fixity, certainty and hierarchical structure of classical consciousness, and therefore the authority of our administrators, deserves punishment.

On the other hand, the Women's Studies Program faculty and students
resist the notion of false absolutes and the imposition of abstract, universal
norms on diverse people and situations. Shaped by postmodern thinking,
they believe that the path to truth is free-flowing inquiry that is open to a
variety of opinions and experiences, especially to the voices of those who
have been marginalized, unnoticed, and silenced. They recognize that truth
is relative to the community of knowers, and that all knowledge is incom-
plete. As a result, all systems of meaning and truth are open to new interpretations. Our women's studies faculty and students are interested in the
issues that touch the daily lives of contemporary women of all social classes,
races, ethnicities, sexual orientations, and abilities. We are committed to
speaking the truth about oppression and to working for its elimination.
Faithful to our commitment to feminism, especially as it is articulated by
Schneiders, we regard activism as central to our lives as both students and
scholars. Also, agreeing with Dillon, we are convinced that this activism on
behalf of new voices and perspectives builds a better community.

While we cannot claim to know the motives driving the efforts of some
individuals to forbid discussion of the political issues surrounding abortion,
to keep *The Vagina Monologues* off campus, to denounce the Women's Studies
Club as contributing to the objectification of women, and/or to criticize
"Take Back the Night" as harmful to the university community, we suggest
that these actions are based on an inaccurate understanding of the meaning
of feminism. Those who are committed to feminist projects have been demo-

nized as enemies of the church, of Truth, of genuine education, and of good women and men everywhere. This is happening in a university, which should be a place where ideas are examined and contested, not one in which caricatures and slogans are substituted for careful inquiry and conversation.

Another important factor is the emergent fragility of "Catholic identity." There is a wide and often contentious discussion within the Catholic Church and Catholic universities about what it means to say that a particular university is "Catholic." Catholic universities within the United States are dealing with the struggle to define their identities as leadership is shifting away from religious communities and is being assumed by lay administrators and faculty, many of whom are not Catholic by background or current affiliation. One position identifies "Catholic" with certain teachings or doctrines that are currently emphasized by the Vatican, and is supported by a small, but highly organized and vocal, segment of the American Catholic laity. Primary among these are teachings about sexual behavior, sexual orientation, and gender, as well as some of the so-called "culture of life" issues, particularly abortion.

Within this definition of fidelity to the pope, the exclusion of feminism becomes a major theme in the story of our university as Catholic because it acts as a bulwark against vulgarity, sexual license, abortion, and the normalization of homosexuality. This version says that the Catholic university is a place that stands up for official Catholic teaching, and the appeal of this definition is that it seems both simple and unassailable. It also makes implicit claims that this is how we will prosper, that the university has the right to defend its identity, and that this protects the university's meaning from relativism and confusion.

Attitudes toward "authority" and "control" are a significant element in the arguments about identity. On one side of the debate, people claim that fidelity to official church teachings is what makes a university Catholic, and the university leader has the responsibility to ensure that its public activities and messages conform to those teachings. On the other side, people claim that participation in a continuing conversation about those teachings, including criticizing and changing them, is what makes a university Catholic: the place where the church does its thinking. For this side, Catholic values require relinquishing the desire to control other people's interpretations, recognizing that good people differ.

Critics of the "non-sponsorship" vs. "censorship" frame chosen by the administration have pointed out that in hosting speakers who may present views that dissent from current church positions, the university is not sponsoring their ideas, but the conversation about ideas that their contribution helps to further. They point out that public universities allow various religious groups and activities on campus without seeming to confuse the public about their identity. Inviting difference onto the college campus, then, is understood as the opposite of threatening to the university's identity or image; it is, rather, its essential mark: the freedom to engage in the discovery and examination of contesting interpretations and arguments.

It is not accurate, however, to attribute support for academic freedom to only one side of this struggle. At Gonzaga, at least, those who wish to protect the Catholic nature of the university would not see their actions as incompatible with this fundamental aspect of higher education. They are not insisting that everyone at the university espouse the same beliefs, or refrain under all circumstances from criticizing church positions; at least some of them have acknowledged that this may and does occur in university classrooms. Instead, their position is that the beliefs for which the university must stand if it is to be considered "Catholic" delineate the guidelines for what can be done under its public banner.

There is some disagreement about the meaning of "public" in this context. Some students and faculty have asserted that the women's studies program is inappropriate in itself—separate from its particular curricular and co-curricular contents—because its existence wrongly identifies the university with support of feminist positions that contradict church doctrines and papal writings. More generally, proponents of a clearly and distinctively Catholic identity for Gonzaga University have confined themselves to attacking specific activities sponsored by women's studies and strongly advocated by its students, rather than arguing that the program itself defiles the university's Catholic tradition. The battles we have described here have focused on the activist side of women's studies at our university — co-curricular projects led by women's studies students who have taken seriously Schneiders' view that feminism is the *practice* of resistance, not only the theory of why it is necessary.

Those who argue for an understanding of academic freedom that includes publicized campus events, and therefore extends beyond the thresholds of classrooms, are urging the university to tell a different kind of story — a less authoritative and controlled one, filled with ambiguities. For them academic freedom is not in tension with Catholic identity, and does not preclude upholding Catholic principles. It asserts openness to the responsible expression of ideas, understood as both respectful of individuals' beliefs and values, and as challenging to them. It is relational and complex. It is worth noting that one of the most prominent faculty critics of the administration's actions regarding *The Vagina Monologues* is a Jesuit philosophy professor who published an opinion in the student newspaper arguing that the performance of the monologues "embodies precisely what it means for us to be a Catholic university." He connects the raw language and crude stories of *The Vagina Monologues* to Jesus' criticism of cultic purity and welcome for the outcasts.

Economic pressures and the general adoption of vocabularies of business by universities further complicate the argument between church authority/ Catholic identity and academic freedom. Although one aspect of the debates over Catholic identity is exceptionalism, in the sense of resisting absorption into aspects of American culture that are viewed as threatening fundamental Catholic principles, another side reflects submission to the dominance of consumerism in this society. Since the university is defined as a business selling a product, it must protect its image and brand from association with ideas and perspectives that disturb or threaten some customers. "Branding" has spread from the marketing of consumer goods such as jeans and soap to encompass all sorts of efforts to develop and market a distinctive identity: 'Branding has always been an exercise of power ... a brand name differentiates a product from its competitors; it controls the meaning of a product, designer, or company; and, most important of all, in the current age of rapid image circulation, it tells a product's story — a story that compels us to believe" (Zukin 208–209).

The audience for the brand of a university includes students, parents, benefactors, and members of the wider audience who have the potential to become members of these groups. Catholic institutions are often dependent upon the generosity of benefactors who are politically and religiously conservative, wary of or outright disapproving of feminism. As divisions within the American Catholic Church have become more visible and boldly marked, these have contributed to the creation of marketing niches that further reinforce the business model. Specific issues may trigger contests between those who seek to protect different values and articulate contrasting versions of faithfulness.

So, these factors of contrasting epistemologies, a fragile and contested "Catholic identity," different understandings of academic freedom, and investment in a business model of the university are the context for arguments about feminism. A Catholic university is hard ground for planting the seeds of feminism. Catholic traditions and current official church stands are at odds with many feminist positions. But at the same time, there are many feminist resources within the stories and teachings. No less than other parts of academe, a Catholic university such as ours can be characterized as having a mixed pattern of "opportunity, constraint, and possibility" (Laslett and Thorne 17). Thoughtful inquiry depends upon thoughtful conversation. Such conversation always contains the potential for conflict. Building and sustaining an academic community cannot mean repressing conflict, because pretending to agree simply makes disagreement covert and unproductive. A university requires hospitality to differences and a commitment to working with conflicting perspectives that is grounded in the hope of achieving enough agreement to keep the conversation going and make it productive. Our university is best understood as a community dedicated to thoughtful inquiry that aims to create better individuals and societies. Its excellence depends upon everyone's investment in the continual creation of this kind of community.

What can we draw from the characterizations we have offered of the current struggles within Catholic institutions, especially universities, over the compatibility of Catholicism and feminism when feminism is translated into forms of activism that question the non-negotiable positions of those who regard themselves as custodians and protectors of Church principles? We suggest some points that have both specific relevance to these particular contests within Catholicism, and also broader significance for understanding disagreement in positive terms.

The university is both a particular form of community and an exemplar of the conditions that generally make serious conversations about ideas possible and productive among people with different starting points, including religious ones. Schwehn claims that spirited academic inquiry depends upon reviving the ideal of the academy as a community of friends. The friendship he has in mind is Aristotle's *philia*, which embraced a broad range of human relationships. Schwehn carefully insists that academic friendship is not cliquishness or intimate self-disclosure. Its common project is the search for truth. Its respectful affections are those found in rigorous conversation between thoughtful and virtuous individuals. At its best, such academic friendship enables individuals to be most fully themselves when thinking together.

This kind of friendship prevents the university from becoming a "mere technological project." It is founded on a commitment to maintaining the tie of community. Of course, it can be destroyed by the view that conversations about issues regarded as "settled" by church authorities are forbidden, aversion to a change of minds, and the refusal to attribute good motives and integrity to those who differ. It is difficult to imagine either a university or a church under those terms. If we imagine instead that Schwehn's conditions for a vital academy require the expression of a multiplicity of perspectives and positions within a framework of the practice of intellectual virtues that make friendship possible, then feminism within Catholic institutions becomes what Dillon posits: a resource for change. Feminist activism nourishes this image of a changing, developing understanding of a Catholic university.

This is reinforced by the dimension of historical consciousness that reveals evidence of past changes in the church and its teachings, which introduces a necessary form of relativism. The histories of the Catholic Church and the United States are filled with examples of previously ostracized groups and discredited ideas becoming included and accepted. Catholic universities have a vital role to play in developing this consciousness, and nurturing the contemporary contestations that may offer resources for future transformations. Universities are an important location for questioning what is taken-for-granted and imagining possibilities not yet realized. Historical consciousness also reminds us that the church is a story — a narrative — rather than a fixed set of propositions.

Feminist perspectives can be a provocation for active education: intellectual questioning that leads us to the boundaries of our current knowledge, community, and commitments. In her history of the American Catholic feminist movement, Henold argues that "Catholic feminists not only outlined a new vision for the church, they also claimed that this vision was legitimately Catholic.... This is a liberated Catholicism in which Catholic women understand that the unjust institutional power structure does not have the power to define them" (243). This is a not a denial of a shared tradition and identity, but the expression of a commitment to examine what we know and who we claim to be. It means employing tradition as a shared horizon within which arguments are expected and welcomed, and defining "church" as the people of God and not just the officials at the top of the hierarchy.

At Gonzaga, there are key decisions to be made. Women's studies cannot be sustained here without a strong institutional commitment. This will require a transformation in our understanding — away from the patriarchal model and toward a vision of gender justice — and the courage to make our institutional commitment known to all of the university's constituencies. It requires, as well, the courage to embrace serious conversations about differences as necessary for both the university and the greater community. These requirements are the necessary conditions for vigorous feminist teaching and activism everywhere. In the United States, organized feminism has been profoundly shaped by its criticisms of right wing politics (Burack and Josephson). The disputes at Gonzaga University have sharpened our thinking, affirmed our commitment to education for justice, and deepened our gratitude for students who take the requirements for feminist praxis seriously.

Hertzberg has suggested that the controversy over Notre Dame's invitation to Obama revealed a "real division between social conservatives, on the one hand, and social moderates and liberals, on the other, not between Catholics and non–Catholics. But that doesn't make it any less deep" (22). We can attest to the deep division at Gonzaga, and we appreciate some of its effects on our students and faculty: we have been pushed to develop better arguments and strategies, and we have gained many allies. The persistent struggle to resist efforts to cast us out as enemies of our university's Catholic identity and to continue a conversation about feminism's contributions to our university's mission has often been demoralizing, but not deadly. It helps to place our local efforts on a broader landscape, and to recognize that we are doing our small part in shifting the meanings of knowledge, justice, and community.

Works Cited

Appleby, R. Scott. "American Idol: Rome vs. the 'Modernists.'" *Commonweal: A Review of Religion, Politics, and Culture,* September 14, 2007, pp. 12–20.

Buckley, G.A. "Sin of Heresy." *The New Catholic Encyclopedia.* New York: McGraw Hill, 1967, p. 1069.

Burack, Cynthia, and Jyl J. Josephson, eds. *Fundamental Differences: Feminists Talk Back to Social Conservatives.* Lanham, MD: Rowman and Littlefield, 2003.

Bynum, Caroline Walker. "'… And Woman His Humanity': Female Imagery in the Religious Writing of the Later Middle Ages." In *Gender and Religion: On the Complexity of Symbols.* Ed. Caroline Walker Bynum, Stevan Harrell, and Paula Richman. Boston: Beacon, 1986.

Carroll, James. "Inside the Obama–Notre Dame Debate." *Nation,* May 14, 2009, <http://thenation.com/doc/20090601>.

Daly, Mary. *The Church and the Second Sex.* New York: Harper and Row, 1974.

Dillon, Michele. *Catholic Identity: Balancing Reason, Faith, and Power.* New York: Cambridge University Press, 1999.

Gillis, Chester. *Roman Catholicism in America.* New York: Columbia University Press, 1999.

Henold, Mary J. *Catholic and Feminist: The Surprising History of the American Catholic Feminist Movement.* Chapel Hill: University of North Carolina Press, 2008.

Hertzberg, Hendrik. "College Try." *The New Yorker,* May 18, 2009, pp. 21–22.

Johnson, Elizabeth A. *Truly Our Sister: A Theology of Mary in the Communion of Saints.* New York: Continuum, 2003.

Johnson, Luke Timothy. "After the Big Chill: Intellectual Freedom and Catholic Theologians." *Commonweal: A Review of Religion, Politics, and Culture,* January 27, 2006, pp. 10–14.

Kurtz, Lester R. "The Politics of Heresy." *The American Journal of Sociology* 88 (1983): 1085–1115.

Laslett, Barbara, and Barrie Thorne. *Feminist Sociology: Life Histories of a Movement*. New Brunswick, NJ: Rutgers University Press, 1997.

Ross, Susan. "Feminist and Sacramental Theology and the Body." In *Horizons on Catholic Feminist Theology*. Ed. Joann Wolski Conn and Walter E. Conn. Washington, DC: Georgetown University Press, 1992.

Schneiders, Sandra. *Beyond Patching: Faith and Feminism in the Catholic Church*. New York: Paulist, 2004.

Schwehn, Mark. *Exiles from Eden: Religion and the Academic Vocation in America*. New York: Oxford University Press, 1993.

"Sectarian Catholicism." Editorial. *America: The National Catholic Weekly,* May 11, 2009, <http://americamagazine.org/content/article11636>.

Steinfels, Margaret O'Brien. "The Church and Benedict XVI: What Can We Hope For?" *Commonweal: A Review of Religion, Politics, and Culture,* May 6, 2005, pp. 12–14.

Steinfels, Peter. *A People Adrift: The Crisis of the Roman Catholic Church in America*. New York: Simon and Schuster, 2003.

Unsworth, Tim. *Catholics on the Edge*. New York: Crossroad, 1995.

Warner, Marina. *Alone of All Her Sex: The Myth and the Cult of the Virgin Mary*. New York: Alfred A. Knopf, 1976.

Zukin, Sharon. *Point of Purchase: How Shopping Changed American Culture*. New York: Routledge, 2005.

Motherhood Status and the Limits of Flexibility

Recognition and Invisibility among Women Faculty at a Public Liberal Arts University

KARIN E. PETERSON AND
ALICE A. WELDON

Flexibility and control of one's time are perceived benefits of working in a liberal arts university environment. Our essay explores the costs of flexibility and control as they play out in the lives of women faculty at a southeastern public university. We use a critical methodology that focuses on the dual tasks of giving space for women to name their experiences and then have the opportunity to respond to our interpretation, and identifying the underlying systems that shape their experiences (Smith). In so doing, we identify some of the hidden costs of flexibility in academic work environments. We also specify how the strains vary by motherhood status (women with children and women with no children) and are complicated further according to faculty rank (lecturer, tenure-track and tenured women). We conclude by describing the need for both collective support among faculty and institutional changes that recognize these costs and their impacts on work load, reward structures and job security. In the words of Inez Shaw, "The issues that affect women faculty at all stages of their academic career confirm the need for changes in higher education" (13).

A Study of Mothers and Non-mothers in the Academy

In the 2006–2007 academic year, we initiated a study on the conditions of women faculty at our institution, focusing on the question of how being a parent or not being a parent impacted their experiences of their careers. Our university, designated as a public liberal arts institution, employs 202 full-time faculty members, including lecturers, instructors, and tenure-track or tenured professors, forty percent of whom are women (2006 statistics). The university operates on a semester system and faculty teach seven or eight courses per year. The university does not offer childcare on campus, but does offer, since 2000, a one-semester paid family leave to those who have a "medically verifiable sickness or injury which prevents the faculty member from performing usual duties, including temporary disability connected with childbearing and recovery" (UNCA *Faculty Handbook*). In addition, those who take family leave may choose to delay the tenure clock. Because individual departments determine class schedules, the amount of flexibility faculty have in managing their time varies across campus.

We conducted a series of focus groups during the summer and fall, followed by individual interviews with most of the participants, and two follow-up meetings at which we presented our initial findings and sought additional input and responses from participants.[1] We provided focus questions on four themes: the idea of motherhood in general, strategies for balancing home and professional life, navigation of one's career in light of the status of mother/"non-mother" and perceptions of expectations held by colleagues and students of women faculty. Our procedure allowed for participants to consider questions silently and then share their first responses individually prior to a general discussion of the topic. We tape-recorded and transcribed oral material from the focus groups and disguised information that might reveal the identity of any individual participant.

At the conclusion of each focus group, participants were asked to complete an open-ended reflection piece about the group experience and to indicate whether they would participate in a follow-up interview with one or both of the investigators. Follow-up interviews were conducted as face-to-face interactions between one of the researchers and a participant. In these interviews we asked our colleagues what was most significant for them about the focus group conversation. We also asked them to share anything else that they wanted us to know about their experiences as women academics. In

May 2007, we held two reporting sessions, each of which included both mothers and non-mothers. Of the 26 women faculty who participated in one of the six focus groups, 12 were able to attend a full-group reporting session. After an initial presentation by each of the researchers/authors, individuals were invited to share any questions, comments, concerns, or suggestions they might have about the whole project.

In an effort to create scholarship inspired by feminist methodology, we intentionally created these multiple formats, opportunities for participants to refine our interpretations and to determine how the research might be used to advocate for change within our institution and beyond. This paper discusses some of the experiences of our respondents and some of the ways in which we as researchers began to see our institution in a different light as a result of this work. The question of motherhood status leads us in unexpected directions in our analysis — away from viewing the statuses as creating very different experiences and towards viewing the experiences of women in general as revealing more subtle negotiations of time, visibility and rewards among faculty.

In designing our study, we wished to examine the way a particular institutional environment (small, public liberal arts university) shapes and is shaped by the experiences of its women faculty concerning the idea of motherhood. We believed that all women experience the dominant cultural expectations of motherhood — whether or not they fulfill them or try to — and therefore it was important to us to include women who are not mothers, in order to hear the voices that are seldom heard on this issue. We were also eager to use a focus group methodology that would give participants a chance to hear from others and to articulate their experiences collectively. We believed this methodology would reveal some of the dynamics of the institutional experience more clearly than individual interviews.

Dominant and Quiet Voices

A focus group methodology allowed women the opportunity to have a voice and a shared experience. Both groups find that significant parts of "who they are" are not visible in a work context that still privileges a particular image of the ascetic male scholar. We think this experience is important and indicative of why women on campuses need spaces to affirm their identities and their commonalities. The six focus groups created a space for conversation in which women academics could express thoughts and share some hope of addressing issues that were surfacing through these conversations. In each of the focus groups and in follow-up interviews, all but one or two participants indicated that they liked having the opportunity to share, express their feelings, hear about others and know they were not alone. In this sense, there was an atmosphere of egalitarianism and support.

In groups of mothers, we heard expressions of appreciation for the opportunity to discuss the experience of being mothers. But the focus groups were not always an easy experience; one participant said that it "threw me off" because it brought to the surface issues of juggling identity, priorities and loyalty. Discussions of motherhood identity and roles may not generally win "points" for women in academia. Studies of women in the academy point to the ways in which the subject of having children is ignored in the hiring process (Philipsen) and to the fact that in general people's family commitments are routinely rendered invisible. Indeed, Joan Williams suggests the following:

> Even today, universities continue to operate on the basis of a set of expectations about the role of the Scholar (generically male) that have hardly altered over several centuries and are thus clearly out of step with the massive social changes that have occurred over the past 40 years or more in the world beyond the portals of academia. The particular problem this presents for women is that the Scholar, traditionally remote from the everyday world in his ivory tower and thereby removed from its trivial distractions, is still expected to be free to commit himself totally to his field of study — irrespective of any other commitments he might have [182].

Women faculty with children may avoid discussing their roles as mothers in an effort to avoid the impression of not conforming to this image (termed "bias avoidance" in Drago and Williams) by attempting to "conform to ideal norms of what it means to be a productive, successful, and good worker" (Austin 151).

The sessions provided a forum where participants felt invited to discuss something absent or at least underemphasized in collegial small-talk as well as in formal institutional settings. One participant stated that hearing some of the other mothers tell their stories was "very eye-opening" because she felt "usually so lonely" and powerless. To her, despite some uneasiness it unearthed, it was "powerful to share." Some women identify being a mother as the most important aspect of their identity; one participant said that being a mother is "one hundred percent of my identity." Mothers shared stories of how their motherhood identities sometimes have to be underplayed in academic settings. They shared stories about the joys of mothering, as well as

the struggles of managing work and family schedules. They spoke of returning to campus to complete work after the children were put to bed in the
evening. A dominant voice in these discussions was celebratory of motherhood, emphasizing the rewards and pleasures of having children. One mother,
for example, spoke about raising a son: "that thrill you mentioned is always
there, and pride.... I love him in a very different way and I don't think you
can explain that to people; it's something you have to feel. You can intellec-
tualize it all you want ... but until you feel it, you don't know what that can
mean, and how many chillbones that can give you to think about it." The
discussion of the rewards of mothering was paired sometimes with concern
that other women who were not mothers were missing "the most important"
experience women could have; one participant said, for example, "I think
about all these great things about motherhood, and I really feel sorry for
women and children who don't feel these thoughts about motherhood."

Women without children, too, were pleased to have a space to discuss
what their lives were like. This group of women found in focus groups a
space only rarely available in academic settings as well as in most cultural
settings. Many participants indicated that non-motherhood was a choice
they were glad to have made. They discussed the freedom that came with
not having parenting obligations and the flexibility available to them in
arranging schedules and professional commitments. They also expressed frustration that others sometimes were not able to see their lives as fulfilled.
Some indicated that they were "motherly" in other ways, either in terms of
caring for children in their lives or in other realms such as keeping social
connections alive among family members or colleagues in their work environments, or in terms of supporting students during and beyond office hours.
Women faculty may experience this nurturing either as an expectation
imposed on them by others or as something that they themselves understand
as important. A dominant voice in these discussions was as celebratory of
non-motherhood as were the mothers' voices of motherhood in other focus
groups.

While all focus groups found common ground and appreciation for the
opportunity to hear from one another, there is a deeper level, which leaves
us less than content with the claim that focus groups are inevitably feminist
or able to meet the burden of providing voice for all. This observation comes
from both the parental status groups. It suggests that focus groups may tend
to produce a kind of dominant voice rather than readily allowing for difference. We are committed to attempting to interpret our findings using strategies that support the valorization of women's voices. However, we want to

emphasize that the critical interpretation we offer here operates from the assumption that we have some responsibility for recognizing and bringing forth the most marginalized voices in our project. It is our purpose not to devalue the experience of having voice reported by many participants, but to underline that even in such a "safe" setting, there were voices that were quieter or even silent. One respondent in a mother group, when asked about how she understood motherhood in her own life, spoke, almost under her breath, of feeling ambivalent about becoming a mother. Having lived into her late thirties before having a child, she spoke of what she considered her long career as a childfree woman. Others in the group, however, did not echo this notion of ambivalence, nor did the participant elaborate on it again during the session. In another group of mothers, a woman who is dealing in the current moment with children in emotional and social crisis also described parenting as much more exhausting and difficult than did women who were mostly talking about their struggles as things more or less manageable or outweighed by the joys of watching children grow up. While this participant's voice was heard, the context was not one in which others knew exactly how to respond to it or support what was different about it.

A similar incident occurred among those without children. Because a number of respondents declined our invitation to participate, indicating that they had too much grief around not having children to speak about it, we believe that our sample of non-mothers tended to include primarily women who had made deliberate choices not to have children. A few women who did participate in the childless groups, however, either had lacked a partner with whom to have children or had been physically unable to have children. One such person indicated that she wanted children and that she felt sadness around what she experienced as a loss. In her particular group, the language of choice coming from others in the room outweighed her voice expressing regret.

We conclude then, that our focus groups provided an atmosphere that was affirmative for many participants. We are also cognizant that this affirmation occurred among women academics, people who have generally cultivated the tools to present themselves as competent, rational beings. The talk that occurred in the focus groups represents in this sense a kind of discursive agency — a site where women were able to use language and the ears of others to fashion a representation of themselves that appeared coherent and purposeful, and that reaffirmed their ability to talk about themselves in an academic manner. This discursive agency is also a voice of power among a group of sensitive, intelligent academic women, and such power can erase marginalized experiences quite readily. This concerns us. We also believe that this finding reflects other things we discovered in our study about the links between institutional vitality and women in the academy.

Institutional Culture and the Benefits of Flexibility

One of the prevailing responses we heard from mothers was that our institution is largely compatible with the project of raising children and having a career; this was particularly true for tenure-track and tenured women, especially those already tenured at the time of our study. Some who had worked at other educational institutions or other work environments reinforced this idea. Participants who have had children since 2000 discussed ways in which the family leave policy had benefited them personally; women with older children, in contrast, described the machinations they underwent to miss as little time as possible if they gave birth during a semester, and to time pregnancy to coincide with the longer summer break. Respondents mentioned supportive department chairs and colleagues who allow them to plan their teaching schedules around their children's needs.

Some mothers who reported a positive experience with institutional support of their childrearing endeavors also talked about the ways in which having the dual responsibilities of parenting and working allowed them to become better time managers. Many indicated that after having children they became more efficient in completing work tasks and worried less over minor details of work than before they had children. The compatibility of having incorporated time management as a conscious strategy along with the flexibility of both daily schedules and career/family life lead women to speak of our institution as quite suitable for their life needs.[2]

Institutional Culture and the Hidden Costs of Flexibility

A second look at our focus group interviews suggests an intriguing parallel between institutional structure and the voices in our focus groups. The dominant voices of women faculty expressed high satisfaction with their work environment and with their motherhood status. But just as our focus groups tended to privilege some voices over others, some voices of the non-mother participants and younger or non-tenure track faculty suggest that the perception of the institution's support varies with the status of the faculty member across all academic divisions represented in our study.[3]

A less than glowing report of institutional support came from non-mothers and some mothers with young children, who, while also valuing the institution for the kinds of careers they wish to pursue (the teacher-scholar model), were less than enthusiastic about their work loads and sense of fair-play among colleagues. A few tenured women with young children observed that male colleagues who have taken family leave when their children were born have taken advantage of the additional time to further their careers (finishing a book or article). Women commented that these young fathers appear to "get credit" when they show up on campus with one of their children or indicate their need to be home at a certain time of day because of their parenting duties. Women also reported that there seems to be a double standard in this regard, in that very rarely did they experience approval for having to reschedule a meeting or for showing up on campus with a sick child. Research on gendered faculty workloads suggest that men still benefit from the traditional image of the male Scholar in real terms because their lives still tend to be arranged so that domestic obligations do not hinder their professional careers (Phillipsen 198). Moreover, for women academics, conforming to the traditional scholar model runs against the dominant cultural understanding of women's roles as nurturers. Carole Munn Giddings argues, for example that "expectations based on sexist stereotypes of women's caring skills have been capitalized on by expecting women to take on a large part of pastoral care of students either formally or by default" (58). This is further complicated for women who are committed to changing academic culture and who are sometimes therefore invested in creating a more supportive and less stodgy classroom environment. Rebecca Mark, for example, quoted in Spore et al.'s *Stories of the Academy: Learning from the Good Mother*, discusses her work with gay and lesbian students and her efforts to help create a safer and more open environment for them as part of her activist faculty identity (7). This experience of conflicting expectations regarding nurturing roles was shared by many of the childfree women in our study.

Similar to findings by Ramsay and Letherby, women in our study who do not have children reported feeling that colleagues assumed that they would take on any number of "extra" obligations to help keep programs running, because they are seen as "lacking" family or other personal commitments. These extras included things such as planning social events, taking on additional advising, holding extended advising sessions, and other kinds of institutional service that does not have a big payback in terms of financial or status awards. This phenomenon was coupled with an experience reported by non-tenured women, with or without children, of sometimes creating more of this kind of work for themselves. These women reported feeling as if they never knew if or when they had done enough to assure their job security. They also said they got the impression from higher-ups that taking on additional responsibilities was expected; some of these included investing significant time planning programs that serve the community at large and/or evening and weekend time.

We suggest that the flexibility experienced by tenure-track mothers is a product of their own survival strategies. The institutional culture is to some degree compatible with parenting, not so much because the institution recognizes the role of raising children as legitimate but rather because informal practices of flexible scheduling and negotiating of duties are permitted. Those who benefit less from this informal culture are those with the least power. The care-giving role written into the mission statement of many liberal arts institutions demands time of faculty well beyond the classroom. This kind of "mothering" falls to mothers but also especially to others who do not have "legitimate" reasons to take advantage of the available flexibility in scheduling and commitments. Those who are the most marginalized in terms of gender and marriage status (non-mothers, singles, gays and lesbians) as well as those in the least secure faculty positions (lecturers on renewable contracts and untenured faculty), pay a great deal in terms of making up for the work not done by others.[4]

We are not suggesting, however, that mothers intentionally place this burden on non-mothers or others. Many participants without children expressed a great sense of compassion for the challenges academic mothers face in balancing home and career, and some of the non-mothers were quite articulate in identifying the issue as an institutional one. Policies that aid parents with young children, they suggest, should be fully supported by the institution. In a context where financial resources and political pressures do not favor granting universities more faculty positions and better compensation, however, our findings show that women without children and faculty of lower ranks shoulder more of the burden of the labor deficit of our institutions.

Our focus group analysis suggests an interesting parallel between the kind of discourse carried out in the focus groups and the way participants described the division of labor at our institution. This parallel involves the distribution of privilege and marginalization. The marginalization of women vis-à-vis men continues to put some pressure on all to see the role of an academic as an ascetic male scholar who devotes himself solely to the pursuit of knowledge. It marginalizes women who are mothers because important parts of their lives are still perceived as detriments to a devotion to their careers. It marginalizes those without children because they live with the cultural definition of their status as "unfulfilled women" and because, although they may be able to conform more readily to the image of the devoted academic, they share a disproportionate load of the necessary but non-status generating service work of the institution.

The image of motherhood and academics as a "lethal cocktail" seems inaccurate to us. In arguing for the viability of that image, Carole Munn Giddings suggests that the university "more than most, creates a culture in which the expression of the tensions and emotions raised at times by role conflict of parenting and working, is deemed more unacceptable than in other settings. This can be particularly powerful when coupled with the pervasive assumption that being an academic requires staff to be permanently and therefore exclusively engaged and interested in academic pursuits" (59). While we agree with the author's analysis of how the academic culture imposes expectations on faculty commitment, most of the mothers in our focus groups felt that there were tangible benefits in having a flexible work environment. The costs we identify are not so much lethal as unrecognized and therefore underaddressed in policy and practice. Our finding suggest that mothers have more agency in making their lives work in a liberal arts context than the term "lethal" would imply. At the same time, administrative policies and practices do not generally acknowledge the amount of work it takes to make an academic life work for mothers. This has a cost for all of us. The amount of work that gets shifted onto those perceived as "free from other obligations" is also generally not recognized. The fact that this work is largely regulated informally, with vaguely stated expectations of what constitutes "enough" service, further complicates the issue. What appears less than complicated, however, is that this creates enough uncertainty in the minds of those on the margins that they are most likely to say "yes" to yet one more task.

Fine-Tuning Through Ongoing Conversations

When we began our study, we committed ourselves to the process of giving our participants, our colleagues, the opportunity to respond. Here, we share some of their responses to our analysis, collected at two sessions where mothers and non-mothers came together for the first time to learn about our initial findings.

Many of the same themes from the initial focus groups were reiterated, but there was very little identity-based discussion. By that we mean that people devoted little talk to issues affecting either only mothers or only those without children. Indeed, the participants seemed almost reluctant to elaborate on the topic, perhaps out of fear of offending others. Overall, the non-mother individuals wanted the mothers to recognize that non-mothers, too, struggle with identity, caretaking, and time management. Mothers reiterated the difficulty of trying to do it all and wondering if it "ever gets better."

In addition, the participants appeared particularly disinvested in elaborating on our institutional analysis. As one participant told us after the meeting, admitting that there are structural impacts on our jobs and that flexibility is all or partly an illusion is not something most people want to do in a casual way. It calls too much into question.

Women participating in our findings sessions were eager to elaborate on several themes, including the need to share experiences with one another; the ambiguity of the faculty rewards system especially concerning tenure, promotion, and contract renewals; the perceived risks of saying "no" especially among untenured and non-tenure-track faculty; and the invisibility of much of the work of being an academic in our setting. What the group members emphasized most was the importance of sharing their experiences with others and the need for action and change in the institution.

Ambiguity of Rewards Systems and Perceived Risks of Saying "No"

Both women without children and mothers expressed concerns about the need for greater clarity and transparency concerning requisites for tenure, promotion or renewed contracts. Perhaps the trump was the issue of rank and how difficult it is for untenured and, especially, non-tenure-track women to know what is enough and when they can say no to what all agreed was our "greedy institution." Participants of all ranks shared frustration over a lack of communication about what constitutes "good" work, and how the work of faculty "counts" in evaluative processes. A lecturer who appreciates that she contributes a higher quality of instruction compared to when she was an adjunct, exclaimed that "At the same time I get no feedback as to whether I am doing enough or not. I just do what I think I want to do, I do a good job in my classroom, I do things I'm interested in, and I don't know until the end of the year when I get my little letter if I'm doing enough or not." A tenured associate professor picked up on that saying that she too is frustrated by the lack of direct feedback, particularly critical. "I would like to be criticized openly. I've never been told what I can do better." Her explanation for that lack has to do with our institution's discourse about our being a family, about wanting to "bridge the divide between the personal and the professional — we want to be friends with each other, we talk about [the university] family." Because of legal concerns both here and at other universities, chairs and deans believe the less said, or written, the better. Even though there are ways to elicit and give more detailed feedback, it does not happen because we are a "dysfunctional family," according to a full professor with experience on the tenure and promotion committee. We therefore must look at our issues on the institutional level. Indeed, when we do we find that there have been instances of faculty members going to ask for specific tangible feedback, certain administrators "have laughed in those faculty members' faces, directly." According to this participant, this is a "great example of the way that institutions can take advantage of the lack of clarity about expectations. It is in the institution's best interest not to tell us what we need to do."

When evaluative criteria are ambiguous and feedback is less than concrete, respondents indicate they feel a high level of uncertainty about how to make choices in the activities they undertake. Because "saying no" is never rewarded (except perhaps by lip service), even when some faculty are less than effective because they have taken on too heavy a work load, the institution has no mechanism for preventing people from taking on more than is fair, good, or effective. The area of service was a particularly important issue to the respondents, who noted that institutions like ours do not function without people who give time to activities that receive little recognition.

Invisible Work

After listening to the tapes of our reporting sessions, we are particularly concerned about invisibility. The invisibility issue relates directly to rank and to both mothers and those who are not mothers. It is as if the non-tenure-track and not-yet-tenured faculty members are constantly trying to make themselves more visible, believing that is the only way to survive. The focus groups allowed higher rank faculty members to see and hear clearly the difficulty of those without tenure. In the words of a full professor mother with grown children, the "tenuousness of those positions — how it would be really impossible if I were an adjunct to say no, if someone like me asked will you do x, even though I would try to make it so clear that no is okay. I wouldn't trust it. Even pre-tenure ... I worried until the very moment when the letter was in hand." She went on to explain that she cannot legitimately ask instructors to attend meetings, yet if they don't, then they miss out on both information and the chance to voice their concerns. The question of how institutions work this out is very complicated.

Lecturers in the groups helped make visible "all the stuff" adjuncts and lecturers do. One spoke of her worry about her department's plan to hire another tenure-track person to replace a lecturer, because, "huh, another tenured person; that means fewer lecturers to do all this stuff that lecturers do. In a big department you need a balance of people who do this stuff." A full professor talked about the "pressure [for instructors and lecturers], both internal and external, to volunteer for everything that moves." Another lecturer from a different department added that she never hears any discussion about the benefit to student learning of hiring lecturers rather than more adjuncts, because lecturers can do a better job when they don't have to travel to three different institutions to teach. Yet she, too, echoed the reality that this same advantage meant "how much more I can give."

A number of mothers believe that many of their colleagues equate less than eight-hour days spent on campus with minimal or insufficient "work." A majority of women without children perceive a shared assumption among colleagues that, because of a lack of childcare responsibilities, they have few non-work responsibilities and thus more "work" can be and is expected of them. Even for the one of us who is a mother, but of children in their thirties, it can be hard to identify with mothers of young children. Recognizing that their work may occur at odd hours (grading papers until 2:00 A.M. because the kids had to be in bed first, or going into the office or lab in early hours of the morning to prepare for the next day). As Juliann Allison states,

> The flexibility academic mothers share with their counterparts in creative professions and nontraditionally organized businesses allows them to append more than average amounts of this time hugging, holding, transporting, feeding, assisting, playing with, listening to, and otherwise caring for their children. Consequently, it is not unusual for academic mothers to attempt fulfilling full-time professional obligations on campus and the expectations of full-time motherhood simultaneously [27].

One mother stated very clearly her belief that the flexibility idea is a myth at our university and that unless we recognize the jargon connected with it, we just keep looking inward as an institution. Her example was about why we keep scheduling things on weekends. "I think that is for mothers and non-mothers. I would like my weekends, baby or no baby, for myself. I give you all my five days. Isn't that enough? Why do we keep doing things on the weekend, on Saturdays, on Fridays, on Sundays? Many other universities don't do it, and they function — they're fine actually."

Despite the popular press hype of the "mommy wars" and other ways non-mothers and mothers appear to fare differently in the work place, we believe the real issue we are looking at is the cost of flexibility for women (in particular) in terms of their capacity to manage work loads and visibility. The question of how much is enough is a function of flexibility, which we recognize through this study as being an illusion. The higher one's rank, the lower this cost — an accrued privilege of rank is the privilege of saying "no" and the ability to trust that that decision will not harm one's status or rewards. This is complicated further by a culture that relies on the discretion of administrative leaders; supportive department chairs make choices easier. If a department chair or department culture is less supportive or less cognizant of the dynamics of flexibility and rewards, their members receive fewer assurances and live with greater uncertainty. The fact that administrative offices shift over time heightens uncertainty at an institutional level.

Enacting Change

Our study is a useful first step for our institution in that it has provided a context for a group of women faculty to begin recognizing the dynamics of flexibility and invisibility in our institution. We also heard from our respondents that we need action.

Indeed, one of the last questions raised at our group reporting meetings was, "How will you communicate your results to the administration?" The groups emphasized their desire for the administration to see what we write about our research, or to hear a presentation of our argument along with concrete recommendations. There was a sense that something important had been articulated and the message needed to be conveyed to those with power to shape institutional practices and culture. In addition, the groups indicated the need to be together, to know at this level what is going on in each other's lives, to have a setting to gather that moves beyond the cocktail party chatter of many official university settings. Foremost in their minds were the unique opportunities our research had provided for women faculty to share and recognize common experiences. Many in our study reported a sense of isolation around issues of managing careers and institutional demands. They suggested that having a forum such as the one we created in and of itself lessened the impact of that sense. Rank unites and intersects all of these concerns, as does the one strongest expression shared across the two groupings: the need for more chances to share and compare stories, to meet, greet, and eat together, and thus to recognize that our own individual experience, worry, confusion, frustration, disappointment, and ambivalence about commitment to our chosen profession are not ours alone.

Cheryl Geisler, Debbie Kaminski and Robyn Berkley accentuate the importance of women faculty monitoring data and coming together to share their stories to counter ignorance of institutional workings. With this kind of understanding, women academics can feel called and equipped to act upon the issues we together discover as either barriers or facilitators for our continuing growth as teachers, scholars, campus and community citizens and activists and change agents.

Notes

1. During the summer of 2006, we mailed post and electronic invitations to all full-time women faculty in our institution, regardless of rank, to participate in a focus group interview on women, motherhood and the academy. Those who responded by signing consent and participant response forms were invited to a session based on their self-identification as mother (whether by birth, adoption or by formation of a stepfamily) or non-mother. Of the 81 women faculty members who were sent invitations, 39 returned response forms and an additional five responded informally; of the combined formal and informal response groups, four non-mothers and two mothers declined. We were able to match schedules with 26. Each of the six focus groups — two of non-mothers (eight) and three of mothers (18)—consisted of the two investigators and three to six women and lasted for two hours and 15 minutes.

2. We note for our readers that, although the participants did not mention the lack of childcare in the focus groups, some individuals did raise the issue in their one-on-one interviews. Over the past decade it has been a recurring subject of conversation in campus forums.

3. As some of our respondents pointed out, our analysis is limited to faculty experiences. We suspect the situation of university personnel echoes some of what we discuss here and is also subject a range a variations less common among faculty (such as no flexibility for some). A full institutional study would need to engage both faculty and staff to fill out the picture of work life in a university setting.

4. Anecdotal evidence suggests that the burden is also shared by other faculty identified as single, child-free, as well as GLBT-identified individuals. This group, of course, consists of both women and men. Intersections with rank also shape this burden; those in non-tenure track positions in particular may find themselves handed less desirable service assignments.

Works Cited

Allison, Juliann. "Composing a Life in Twenty-first Century Academe: Reflections on a Mother's Challenge. *NWSA Journal* vol. 19, no. 3 (Fall 2007): 23–46.

Austin, A. E. "Conclusion." In Bracken et al., pp. 147–157.

Bassett, Rachel Hile, ed. *Parenting and Professing: Balancing Family Work with an Academic Career.* Vanderbilt: Vanderbilt University Press, 2005.

Bracken, Susan J., J.K. Allen, and D.R. Dean, eds. *The Balancing Act: Gendered Perspectives in Faculty Roles and Work Lives.* Sterling, VA: Stylus, 2006.

Drago, R., and Williams, J. "A Half-Time Tenure Track Proposal." *Change* vol. 32, no. 6 (2000): 46–51.

Faculty Handbook. (UNCA). 4.2.1.2. III, accessed September 14, 2008.

Geisler, Cheryl, Debbie Kaminski, and Robyn Berkley. " The 13+ Club: An Index for Understanding, Documenting, and Resisting Patterns of Non-Promotion to Full Professor." *NWSA Journal* vol. 19, no. 3 (Fall 2007): 145–162.

Munn Giddings, Carole. "Mixing Motherhood and Academia — a Lethal Cocktail." In *Surviving the Academy: Feminist Perspectives.* D. Malina and S. Maslin-Prothero, eds. London: Routledge, 1998, pp. 56–68.

Philipsen, Maike Ingrid. *Challenges of the Faculty Career for Women: Success and Sacrifice.* San Francisco: Jossey-Bass, 2008. Ramsay, Karen, and G. Letherby. "The Experience of Academic Non-Mothers in the Gendered University." *Gender, Work and Organization* vol. 13, no.1 (January 2006): 25–41.

Shaw, Inez. "Issues after Tenure." *NWSA Journal* vol. 19, no. 3 (Fall 2007): 7–14.

Smith, Dorothy. *Conceptual Practices of Power: A Feminist Sociology of Knowledge.* Boston: Northeastern University Press, 1990.

Spore, M.B., M.D. Harrison and N.L. Haggerson, Jr. *Stories of the Academy: Learning from the Good Mother.* New York: Peter Lang, 2002.

Williams, Joan. *Unbending Gender: Why Family and Work Conflict and What to Do About It.* New York: Oxford University Press, 2000.

The Tender Track

SARA WARNER

Women have made significant progress in higher education in the years since the passage of Title IX. Females enter colleges and universities in unprecedented numbers, and we reflect, in varying degrees, the diversity of race, ethnicity, religious affiliation, sexual orientation, and age that comprises the American body politic.[1] Women earn more undergraduate degrees than men, and we account for roughly half of the students accepted to medical and law schools. In 2006, women received 45 percent of all doctorate degrees, up from 23 percent in 1976 (Touchton 15). A report titled "A Measure of Equity: Women's Progress in Higher Education," published by the Association of American Colleges and Universities (AAC&U) in 2008, shows that while women have made great strides in the academy, disparity still exists, especially along class lines. The authors of this study find that progress has not been consistent across all demographics of women, and they conclude that "economic status at birth determines more than our national mythology likes to admit" (Touchton 31). Women born into working-class and working-poor families are less likely to attend college, and those who do are less likely to pursue graduate school and to secure full-time employment in the academy than their middle-class and upper-middle-class peers.

I am the first person in my blue-collar family to graduate from high school and am, to-date, the only one to earn a college degree. I completed a doctorate and hold the position of assistant professor at Cornell University. While a college degree helps many people, like myself, break the cycle of poverty, a career in higher education creates for most women new class divisions. Multiple reports confirm that women in academia have advanced at a much slower pace than our peers in comparable professions. Though the number of female faculty and administrators has risen over the last thirty years, women are much less likely than men to occupy positions of leadership and influence, especially at research institutions. We earn substantially less than our male colleagues, and we are much less likely to secure and keep a full-time tenure track position, or as my mother calls it a job on the tender track.

"Tender track" is what linguists Geoffrey Pullum and Mark Liberman refer to as an eggcorn, an idiosyncratic substitution of a word or phrase for one(s) that sound similar or identical to the "correct" usage. The eponymous "eggcorn" is what a colleague of theirs heard used in place of "acorn." Ostensibly, the substitution stems from the fact that acorns are oval-shaped (egg) and contain seeds (corns). The use of "old-timer's disease" for the condition known as Alzheimer's is an example of one of the most common occurrences of an eggcorn. "Old-timer's" replaces an obscure medical term with a more common turn of phrase. It has a slightly different meaning than Alzheimer's, but it is still plausible in the same context. My mother is one of the thousands of Americans who believe that "old-timer's" is the actual name of the disorder. She is, to my knowledge, the first person to coin the eggcorn "tender track," a phrase that has spread throughout my extended family.

Eggcorns are linguistic blunders, errors more likely to be made by members of the working-class and working-poor than members of the educated elite. They differ from malapropisms in three important ways. First, the latter involves a substitution that gives rise to an inappropriate and nonsensical phrase, one that often creates an unintended comic effect. "Sure if I reprehend anything in this world it is the use of my oracular tongue and a nice derangement of epitaphs!" exclaims Mrs. Malaprop in Sheridan's Restoration comedy *The Rivals* (46). The substitution of *reprehend* for *apprehend*, *oracular* for *vernacular*, *derangement* for *arrangement*, and *epitaphs* for *epithets* elicits squeals from theatrical audiences and shows how these sonic slips can be accidental or staged for laughs by authors wielding a rapier wit. Second, malapropisms are errors committed by individuals whereas eggcorns are more common mistakes made by multiple people. Of the 400 million native speakers of English worldwide, linguists deduce that approximately 400,000 are likely to believe that oaks grow from egg corns. This is a small minority, one not likely to affect the development of our written language, but sizeable enough to influence the spoken word. Third, while malapropisms are typically associated with ignorance, eggcorns exhibit both logic and artistry. Liberman refers to them as "tiny little poems, a symptom of human intelligence and creativity" (Peters 18).

Eggcorns are one of the ways we continuously reinvent language. They are quite common in the oral traditions of the deep South, including the part of rural Louisiana where I grew up. As a form of folk wisdom, these solecisms can teach us a great deal about the world and the beings that inhabit it. In this essay I explore what my working-class mother's eggcorn, "tender track" has to teach us about the gender and class politics of the contemporary academy. It is delivered in the form of an autoethnography, a mode of performative storytelling and cultural accounting endemic to Southern life. Parsing "tender track," I chart an affective etymology of the phrase, one that situates my journey from a trailer park to the ivory tower in a conceptual framework that sheds light on specific forms of institutionalized disparity in higher education. My story is one of upward mobility but this trajectory does not constitute a progress narrative, as the rarefied atmosphere of academia is not necessarily more enlightened, more civilized, or more humane than the ambient environs of my humble roots.

Tender *(noun): one who attends or has charge of another*

My mother is legendary for her verbal snafus, which range from mondegreens (a mishearing of song lyrics) to mispronunciations of common words (e.g., *crandle* for *candle*). Many of these mistakes stem from the fact that my mom did not receive much formal education. She dropped out of high school after her sophomore year. What this woman lacks in verbal acumen, she makes up for in mother wit, sound practical judgment based upon common sense. Mom developed her street smarts at a young age; her survival depended upon it. She was the eldest of four children reared by an abusive mother (herself a high school dropout) and an extremely violent alcoholic father (whose education stopped at age nine when he was forced to quit school and get a job). Mom's family lived well below the poverty line, so securing basic provisions, food and shelter, took precedence over everything else.

Having never been to college, my mother possesses a very general idea of what it is that academics do. As a blue-collar worker who uses her hands to make a living, she does not understand many of the tasks that occupy my day, in part because intellectual labor does not seem like work to her. She knows that I am a professor, which in her mind is a teacher. As far as she is concerned, teachers (be they elementary school instructors or college professors) take charge of the educational and personal needs of pupils. In other words, they are the tenders of students. I think most people, at least most non-academics, would agree with the definition of professor as student tender. It is easy to see how my mother applied this concept to the process of tenure to come up with the term tender track. Approached from this vantage point, my mom's eggcorn makes perfect sense, so it is no wonder the phrase caught on with the rest of my family. To dismiss tender track as a simple error born out of ignorance would be to miss the inventiveness of the term. I will show how parsing the eggcorn tender track defamiliarizes tenure, making a well-established process seem strange by opening it up to new possibilities of signification.

Tender *(noun): an offer of money or services; currency that may be legally issued in payment*

What my mom does not understand is that the tending of students is not my primary occupation, nor is it for most tenure track professors I know. Research and publication account for the bulk of my labor and will be the factors weighed most heavily in my bid for tenure. Teaching is important — and at many schools, including my own, it is given considerable attention — but mediocre student evaluations are not likely to get you denied tenure if your book garners favorable reviews or wins a prestigious prize. It is increasingly the case that professors whose primary occupation is teaching are not on a tenure track. In recent years we have seen the development of a dual tiered structure in many schools across the nation, a kind of academic caste system in which faculty are tracked into distinct classes. In this model "top tier" faculty are tenure track scholars who are evaluated on the quality of their research. They continue to teach, but typically only one or two classes per term (depending upon their status within this tier), dedicating the lion's share of their time to research and publishing. "Second tier" faculty are non-tenure track lecturers and teaching associates who offer four or more classes per semester. They are not expected to publish, but they are required to do service work. They typically earn considerably less than their "top tier" colleagues, though many work far more hours per week than researchers. What this tiered caste system does, in essence, is create two paths: a tenure track and a tender track. The key factor in the proliferation of this model is the economic advantage it holds for institutions that pay teaching associates substantially less than the prorated equivalent for comparable work by tenured faculty.

Tender *(adj.): fragile; easily broken*

"Nearly three-quarters of people who teach at colleges are poorly paid instructors who lack job security and health benefits," according to Randi Weingarten, President of the American Federation of Teachers (June 1). A detailed study entitled, *The State of the Higher Education Workforce (1997–2007)* conducted by the AFT, reveals that the number of tenure-track positions has declined steadily in recent years. In 1997, one-third of instructional staff held tenured lines, compared to one-quarter in 2007 (7). During this time period, the overall number of faculty positions increased to keep pace with surging student enrollments, but nearly two-thirds of this growth was in contingent labor, which now accounts for almost three-quarters of all instructional staff across the nation (7). This trend is reflected in all sectors of higher education, but varies significantly by institutional type. Community colleges employ the greatest number of contingent faculty, with more than 80 percent of the workforce on non-tenure track lines and nearly 70 percent teaching on a part-time basis (7). At public research institutions, the proportion of faculty teaching part-time increased significantly, from 34 percent to 44 percent while full-time non-tenured faculty increased from 9 percent to 11 percent (7).

The demise of tenure coincides with the rise of a corporate model of academic administration, with the adoption of governance structures and asset management strategies from the capitalist sector. This is evidenced by the staggering increase in non-instructional staff. The number of full-time administrative positions at academic institutions rose 41 percent between 1997 and 2007 (8). The job of this increasingly large managerial class is to protect the bottom line. One way this is being done is by employing a disproportionate number of low-paid, part-time instructors who do not qualify for vacation pay, sick leave, or health care benefits. Corporate models have been taken up by all types of institutions, by public and private schools, and by four year programs and two year community colleges.

The phasing out of tenure also parallels a dramatic rise in the number of women receiving doctoral degrees. Since 2002, women have received more than half of the Ph.D.'s awarded in the United States, and many of these scholars go onto to a career in higher education. A recent A.A.U.P. fact sheet on the status of women in the academy shows that we account for 31 percent of the faculty at doctoral-granting institutions, 40 percent of the faculty at baccalaureate institutions, and 50 percent of the faculty at institutions without ranks (Davis 1). These statistics show women fare well at junior colleges and associate degree granting programs and have made significant inroads at master's degree granting institutions. At universities with doctoral programs, however, women continue to face serious obstacles, accounting for only 25 percent of full professors (Touchton 19; see also Weingarten 22–23).

In the past decade enrollment has increased by over three million students, resulting in the creation of thousands of new faculty positions, but the overwhelming majority of these jobs (63 percent) are being staffed by contingent labor, by adjunct lecturers and graduate students (Weingarten 13). As the number of tenure-track faculty appointments in this country decreases and the number of part-time positions increase, this trend impacts men and women disproportionately. Women are much less likely than their male colleagues to hold a full-time tenure track position. We are 15 percent more likely to be employed as contingent labor, and we earn, on the average, 27 percent less per course (Touchton 19–21). Due to increased demands upon our emotional labor (caregiving responsibilities, child birth, household management, etc.) and the geographical limitations faced by dual-career couples, many women find themselves in part-time positions, providing the bulk of the low-paid labor for corporate-modeled institutions.

The problem is not simply that we are hitting our heads against a glass ceiling. The problem is that as more and more women are entering the profession, the profession is becoming increasingly factionalized. This is not an uncommon occurrence. The same fate befell the position of secretary. The title originally referred to learned men charged with the high-level administrative functions of powerful individuals and/or the state, but it became increasingly associated with women after the invention of the typewriter in the 1880s. As the post became more feminized, it became increasingly less prestigious, to such an extent that a new lexicon was invented to delimit it from the more exalted positions occupied by men. For example, administrative assistant, personal assistant, and secretary with a lowercase "s" refer to clerical jobs typically held by women (whose job often involves providing support for powerful men), whereas Secretary with a capital "S" denotes an (elected) officer, a position typically held by males.[2]

Tender *(adj): considerate; protective*

We can expect these discriminatory trends in academic hiring to continue as women enter graduate programs in greater numbers, especially in the humanities and social sciences. Though there will be fewer and fewer full-time academic jobs, most institutions will continue to admit large pools of graduate students. The majority of these students will not find stable employment in their field, but institutions have become dependent upon their cheap labor to staff the majority of their classes. A disproportionate amount of teaching now falls on the shoulders of graduate students. Across the country, they teach almost half of all classes offered by institutions of higher learning (Weingarten 7). In fact, the largest growth in contingent faculty from 1997 to 2007 was in graduate student labor (16). The more teaching graduate students do, the longer it takes them to complete their degree. As fellowships and funding packages dry up, students are forced to accept more teaching assignments to survive, which means they are available to teach even more classes. Predictably, schools that rely upon graduate student labor for the majority of their instruction have lower graduation rates.

As institutions become more and more corporatized, it becomes almost impossible for them to claim that graduate assistants are students who receive financial aid rather than employees to whom they pay paltry wages. With increasing frequency graduate students and adjunct laborers, at both public and private institutions, are unionizing to demand better wages and benefits. As institutions become more preoccupied with corporatized models and the business of education, they become less considerate and less protective of graduate students, which is to say a lot less tender.

Tender *(adj): bruised; painfully sore*

My mom's eggcorn tender track sheds light on the gender and class dynamics of the tenure system, and it provides a conceptual framework for thinking about how these issue influence who becomes an academic in the first place. There is a glaring disparity in college attendance among higher and lower income students. According to a recent report by The Education Trust, 75 percent of students from the top income quartile complete a bachelor's degree by the age of 24, compared to only 9 percent of students from low-income families (Haycock 2). The statistics are even more staggering when we consider race. Black students from poor families earn bachelor's degrees at one-half the rate of poor white students and Latinos at one-third the rate (2). Most alarming is the fact that these gaps are wider today than they were three decades ago (5). Rather than a vehicle for fostering social and economic mobility, higher education has become a mechanism for reinforcing class divisions.

Financial constraints keep many students from pursuing and completing college degrees, but other factors also play a role, including inadequate preparation, Byzantine application processes for both admissions and financial aid, and institutional indifference. When students fail to qualify for college or drop out before they earn their degree, we often put the blame on the individuals, telling ourselves that they are simply not motivated enough, not smart enough, or not willing to make short term sacrifices for long term gains. To come to any other conclusion would be an affront to our national myth, which holds that America is a country where merit, not privilege, determines an individual's success. I know because I am one of the 9 percent, and I am painfully aware of the obstacles that keep the working-poor and the working-class from getting an education. It is a tender subject indeed.

Tender *(adj): young; inexperienced; a rookie*

I grew up in a sleepy Southern town on the shores of Lake Pontchartrain, about thirty minutes northeast of New Orleans. Originally home to the Choctaw, the area became a Creole settlement around 1699 when Pierre le Moyne d'Iberville camped there en route to the mouth of the Mississippi River on his expedition to colonize the territory for the French. I can see why he and his troops stopped there. It is an idyllic place, framed by majestic cypress trees and miles of bayous teeming with alligators, crawfish, and blue herons. While rich in natural beauty, it is incredibly poor by economic standards and plagued by high levels of unemployment, teen pregnancy, addiction, and illiteracy.

Reading is not highly valued in this part of the rural South. The culture is based upon oral traditions and highly ritualized modes of performance. In fact, reading is often used as a form of punishment. When parents catch their children misbehaving, they ground them from watching television and playing with their friends and send them to their bedroom with a book. A child can also be reprimanded for reading too much. If my parents caught me with my nose in a book when they thought I should be outside playing or joining the family in some communal activity, I would be charged with laziness and accused of being uppity. Whatever punishment I received would be accompanied by a lecture from my mother about how books were ruining my future. "You will never find a husband," she warned. "Boys do not like girls who are smarter than they are." Mom associated books with teachers and teachers with spinsters and depressed divorcees. I think she knew even then that I was a lesbian. Afraid that I was destined for a life of hardship and heartache, she took it upon herself to try to change my course of development by making sure I was not too smart for my own good. When mom wasn't looking, I read anything I could get my hands on, from cereal boxes to Harlequin Romance novels that the lady I babysat for saved for me. I think I read every book in my junior high school's tiny library, twice.

Hurricane Katrina ravaged that school library, as it did much of the Gulf Coast. After several years of rebuilding, the town looks much the same as it did before the storm. There is still no red light, no major businesses, and no high school. After the eighth grade, children from my hometown are bussed to a wealthy and primarily white suburban area twenty minutes to the west. I hated that high school and the snotty preppies who made fun of our accents and less than fashionable clothes. They taunted the Creole and Black students with racial slurs and ostracized anyone who associated with them. I begged my parents to transfer me to another school, threatening to run away if they did not. Catholic school was not an option because we were not members of the church, and we could not afford it anyway. My parents enrolled me in a different high school in a larger town to the east by claiming that I was a problem child temporarily residing with family friends who lived in that district. My problem was that I wanted an education. This school was thirty minutes away, and since I was not on the bus route I had to drive there. My dad traded our riding lawn mower for a tangerine 1972 VW bug with holes in the floorboard. I had to cut our many acres with a push mower, but I did not care. Though I missed my friends, I fit in much better with the students at my new school, most of whom were also from working-class families. I did well in all subjects without really trying and graduated 8th in my class. My GPA could have been higher had I actually studied, something I had little time for because I was working at a restaurant and babysitting (up to 20 hours per week). I had to pay for gas, car insurance, and repairs, and I was trying to save as much money as I could for college.

I knew I wanted to continue my education, but I had absolutely no idea how to go about this so I made an appointment with my guidance counselor. I told her I wanted to go to Tulane, a private university in New Orleans. Mind you, I knew almost nothing about Tulane except that it was considered a "good" school and it was located near the French Quarter, where I wanted to live. Despite my good grades, high test scores, and obvious enthusiasm, the guidance counselor said she did not feel Tulane was a "realistic" goal. She suggested I enroll at the local community college, which was "a much better fit for a student like me." She gave me an application for Delgado

Community College and whisked me out of her office. What did she mean "a student like me"? I told my mother what the counselor said. While mom was not particularly keen on me going to college at all, she took umbrage at anyone telling her child what she should and should not do. Mom told me not to bother with that woman and just to phone up the university and request an application myself, which I did.

Completely ignorant about the college application process, and with no one to assist me, I mishandled the paperwork for Tulane. Though I was accepted, I was not eligible for financial aid because I had not correctly filled out the required forms. I knew there was no way I could afford the tuition without a scholarship or grant. Tulane was the only school to which I had applied. It never dawned on me to have a contingency plan. Devastated but determined to go to college directly after high school graduation, I called the LSU admissions office. The counselor said I could submit a late application, but I would not be eligible for financial aid my first year. I knew my savings would cover my living expenses and tuition, which in the mid 1980s was only a few hundred dollars a semester.

When the acceptance letter came, my father was elated. He told everyone at work that his daughter was going to college, and he put an LSU sticker on his truck's bumper. My mother was much more reserved. I assumed she was simply sad that her eldest child was leaving the nest, and to go away to school instead of getting married and settling down. I soon discovered the real reason for her measured response. She had spent the majority of the money I was saving for college, over three thousand dollars, on bills and other household expenses. As the signatory on my savings account, mom had been withdrawing money quite regularly to make ends meet. My dad had no idea that this was going on. She did not want him to know that he was not earning enough money to provide for his family.

My father grew up in even more abject conditions than my mom. His family, which consisted of my grandmother, a brood of children, and whichever no account man she happened to be attached to at the time, were squatters. They would move into abandoned houses — with no running water, heat or lights (no wonder dad became an electrician) — and stay until someone kicked them out. One winter they lived in a shack with dirt floors and cardboard walls. The family's diet consisted primarily of pancakes with lard and sugar, and some days they were lucky to have to anything to eat at all. Like many young men in this kind of environment, dad turned to truancy. My mom helped him clean up his act, and they got married when she was seven months pregnant with me. Life was very hard for them. They eked out a living toiling at factory jobs to support a growing family. In the beginning, the only jobs they could find, with their limited education and experience, were at a dog food factory, where maggots crawled all over the floors and walls. The plant smelled so bad with the stench of rotting horsemeat that it made mom sick the entire time she was pregnant with my little sister. My dad earned his G.E.D. and got a job in the maintenance department of a national hotel chain, which proved to be his ticket out. The company transferred him from Michigan to Georgia and then Louisiana, where we settled permanently.

Mom and I agreed not to tell dad about my nearly depleted college savings fund. I went to LSU as planned, but I had to get a job to cover tuition, room and board. Working thirty hours per week as a waitress, I had little time for anything but class and homework. This was just as well because I was too self-conscious to take part in any extracurricular activities. While I loved my classes and was earning good grades, I felt really out of place at school. I spoke in class only when spoken to, and I went to professors' office hours only when forced to do so. I fit in much better with the waiters and bartenders at work. I did not apply for a scholarship my sophomore year because I thought if I got one, I would have no reason to keep my job, and the restaurant was the one place I felt comfortable. I was so afraid to take part in clubs and organizations that I even declined an invitation to join Phi Beta Kappa. When the envelope came, I heard my high school guidance counselor's voice in my head saying "a college honor society is not for students like you."

I double majored in philosophy and English. Most of my literature classes were in women's studies, a subject that was just beginning to be taught at LSU. These courses helped me understand the difficulties I encountered, as a female and as person from a lower-class background, trying to navigate the world. They also helped me see what made women like my high school guidance counselor work to keep other women down instead of lifting them up. What I did not understand, however, was why the critical theory we read depicted women as victims, as always already oppressed. The women I knew were survivors. My mother was a fighter, and she taught her daughters how to invent solutions when none presented themselves.

I managed to graduate, with honors, but it would be years before I actually believed I deserved an education. It would take moving to California, becoming an activist, and discovering queer theory at San Francisco State University, where I attended school part-time in the M.A. program in comparative literature, before I would feel education was a right to which I was entitled. I have no regrets about attending LSU instead of Tulane, but sometimes I wonder what my life might have been had the high school guidance counselor shown me any tenderness. Had she helped me, would I have attended a private school with smaller classes, a more rigorous academic program of study, and more personalized attention instead of a large public institution where I disappeared into a sea of students in an overcrowded lecture hall? Would I have flourished in a more privileged environment and taken full advantage of the resources at my disposal, or would I have floundered under the pressure and scrutiny, dropping out of school, perhaps never to complete a degree at all?

Tendered *(ppl. a.): making tender; becoming gentle; treating others with compassion*

After graduating from SFSU, I began work on a doctorate in comparative literature at Rutgers, the State University of New Jersey. I wrote my dissertation on a prison theater troupe in San Francisco called the Medea Project. Upon the completion of my degree in 2003, I accepted an adjunct assignment as a one-semester replacement in the Department of Theatre, Film, and Dance at Cornell University. This turned into a longer temporary arrangement, a two-year visiting assistant professor position. At the end of my contract, a tenure-track line in the department opened. I applied and was awarded the job. It is humbling to work at a university that would not have accepted me as an undergraduate or a graduate student (after serving on the admissions committee several times, I know this to be the case). Admittedly, I sometimes feel like a fish out of water working at an ivy league school, an elite institution where the majority of my colleagues have been trained by peer universities and have never worked outside the academy, and where most (but not all) of the students come from a privileged socio-economic background. I confess to raising a ruckus when I hear one of my colleagues complain about the "lack of culture" in upstate New York or lampoon "the rednecks" who live in the townships surrounding Ithaca. These classist attitudes are not only personally offensive, they reinforce the structures that discriminate against the working-class and working-poor, barring them from their right to an education.

It is even more humbling to have the security of a tenure track position when many talented minds and gifted professors across this country work as contingent laborers, including the majority of faculty in my department at

Cornell (most of whom are artists without a Ph.D.). The vote on my third year review, in spring 2009, coincided with the announcement of unprecedented budget cuts and layoffs. In response to the global economic crisis, Cornell laid off 15 percent of all lecturers, and the top brass have warned that there will be additional cuts in 2009–2010. The university also reduced the number of teaching assistantships and offered early retirement packages to tenured professors. Like many educational institutions across the nation, Cornell is compensating for this substantial loss by decreasing course offerings, increasing class size, and raising tuition. The administration refused an offer by the faculty to take a voluntary reduction in pay to forestall layoffs of lecturers. They cited many reasons why the Board of Trustees would find this an unacceptable resolution to the university's financial woes, including what they believed was the likelihood that lowering base salaries would decrease the quality of tenure track faculty Cornell could attract once the hiring freeze is lifted, making the institution less competitive in the academic marketplace. When, in the midst of all this, I received word that I had passed my review and my contract would be renewed for an additional three years, I felt both relieved and guilty.

I phoned my mother to share the news. She asked, "Does this mean you are tendered now?" Answering one eggcorn with another, I replied, "No, I'm still on tenderhooks" ("tenderhooks" is commonly (mis)used in place of "tenterhooks," which means to be as tense with anticipation as a canvas stretched on a tenter). I cannot predict the future to know whether I will be tenured or whether the system originally designed to protect intellectual freedom will survive, in any form, in an increasingly corporatized culture of education. I can, however, assay the past and state unequivocally that my academic journey has tendered me. It has made me a lot more delicate and fragile than my hearty parents. It has pained and bruised me, making me more acutely sensitive to discrimination and oppression of all kinds. While education has made me more careful and considerate of the world around me, it has not empowered me in the ways I (rather naively) thought it would, and often I am distressed by my inability to effect change and to combat institutionalized forms of disparity.

I have been disabused of the notion that being a humanities professor is a vocation tending toward intellectual and emotional growth. Academia is a business, one with clearly delineated career tracks. The gender and class politics of this increasingly rigid academic caste system is revealed through an exploration of my mother's acorn, tender track. An affective etymology of this phrase enables us to see that the tenure process serves as the contingent foundation for the knowledge industry, where production (of books, articles, patents, etc.) is valued above and beyond teaching and service. This system places the overwhelming majority of working faculty at the tender mercies of number-crunching bureaucrats who are more concerned with tendering contracts than in tending students. The increasing reliance upon contingent labor threatens the quality of higher education, and the relegation of disproportionate numbers of women into contingent faculty positions threatens the progress we have made since the implementation of Title IX.

Notes

1. While great strides have been made in terms of racial parity, there is much work to be done in this area, especially at the doctorate level. Of all the professional degrees awarded to women in 2006, white females earned 27 percent, Asian Americans 10 percent, African Americans 3 percent, Hispanics 2 percent, and people identifying as mixed-race/other 4 percent (Touchton 15).

2. There have been noted exceptions in the realm of American politics in recent years, including Secretary of State Madeline Albright, Secretary of State Hillary Clinton, Secretary of Labor Hilda Solis, Secretary of Homeland Security Janet Napolitano, and Secretary of Health and Human Services Kathleen Sebelius, to name only a few.

Work Cited

Davis, Sara. "Women and the Tenure Track." *The Chronicle of Higher Education*, July 13, 2001. *http://chronicle.com*, accessed October 9, 2009.

Haycock, Kati. "Promise Abandoned: How Policy Choices and Institutional Practices Restrict College Opportunities." The Educational Trust, August 2006. http://www 2.edtrust.org/NR/rdonlyres/B6772F1A-116D-4827-A326-F8CFAD33975A/0/Promise AbandonedHigherEd.pdf, accessed October 9, 2009.

June, Audrey Williams. "Labor Leaders Call for Collective Efforts to Reduce Reliance on Adjuncts." *The Chronicle of Higher Education,* April 21, 2009. http://chronicle.com, accessed 09 October 09.

Liberman, Mark, and Geoffrey K. Pullum. "The Language Log" [weblog], September 2003. http://itrc.cis.upenn.edu/~myl/languagelog/, October 9, 2009.

Peters, Mark "Word Watch: The Eggcorn — Lend Me Your Ear." *Psychology Today* 39.2 (March/April 2006): 18. http://psychologytoday.com/articles/pto-20060214–000002. html, accessed October 9, 2009.

Sheridan, Richard Brinsley. *The Rivals*: *The School for Scandal and Other Plays*. Oxford: Oxford University Press, 1998, pp. 1–86.

Touchton, Judy, with Caryn McTighe Musil and Kathryn Peltier Campbell. *A Measure of Equity: Women's Progress in Higher Education*. Washington, D.C.: AAC&U, 2008.

Weingartner, Randi, et al. "The State of the Higher Education Workforce (1997–2007)." Washington, D.C.: American Federation of Teachers, 2009. http://www.aft.org/pubs-reports/higher_ed/AmerAcad_report_97–07.pdf, accessed October 9, 2009.

About the Contributors

Jennifer A. Boisvert is a clinical psychologist and mediator in Alberta and California. She engages in feminist psychological teaching, research and practice. Her interests in these areas include women's psychological and physical health, particularly eating disorder symptomatology; sexual objectification; sex differences/roles; diversity issues (ethnicity, culture, sexual orientation, age); ethics and feminism. She has published and presented her work at professional meetings and has received awards and research grants in support of her scholarship on women's experiences.

Norma Bowles is the founder and artistic director of Fringe Benefits Theatre. She has conducted "Theatre for Social Justice," acting, *commedia dell'arte* and new play development residencies at theatres and universities in the United States, Australia, Canada, Spain and England. Bowles completed a B.A. in masked performance at Princeton and an M.F.A. in directing at the California Institute of the Arts. She edited *Cootie Shots: Theatrical Inoculations Against Bigotry* and *Friendly Fire*, anthologies of works by Fringe Benefits. Bowles is a recipient of PFLAG/LA's Oscar Wilde Award, Cornerstone Theater Company's Bridge Award for "building bridges within and between communities," and, in 2009, the Association for Theatre in Higher Education's first Award for Leadership in Community-Based Theatre and Civic Engagement.

Kathleen Juhl is a professor of theatre at Southwestern University, where she has been teaching voice and movement, acting, performance studies, theatre for social change, and feminist studies since 1987. She has also directed many student productions. She holds an M.A. in performance studies from the University of Illinois–Urbana, an M.F.A. in acting and directing from the University of North Carolina at Greensboro and a Ph.D. from the University of Texas at Austin in performance studies. She has published several articles on teaching acting and co-edited a book titled *Radical Acts: Theatre and Feminist Pedagogies of Change*.

Robin M. LeBlanc, a professor of politics at Washington and Lee University has also served as interim head of the Women's and Gender Studies Program. Her teaching interests include comparative politics, political theory, and gender and politics. She is the author of *Bicycle Citizenship: The Political World of the Japanese Housewife* (University of California Press, 1999) and *The Art of the Gut: Manhood, Power, and Ethics in Japanese Politics* (University of California Press, 2009).

Ellen Mayock, a professor of Spanish and core faculty in women's and gender studies and Latin American and Caribbean studies at Washington and Lee University, specializes in the twentieth-century novel of Spain and Latin America, U.S.–Latina/o studies, and women's studies. She has published broadly on the contemporary novel, literary naturalism, and feminist and gender theory. She is the author of *The Strange Girl in Twentieth-Century Spanish Novels Written by Women.*

Karin E. Peterson is an associate professor of sociology at the University of North Carolina at Asheville. As a sociologist of culture, she specializes in theory, qualitative methods, the politics of cultural recognition, feminist and queer theory, and the scholarship of teaching and learning.

Domnica Radulescu is professor of French and Italian and Head of the Women's and Gender Studies Program at Washington and Lee University. Winner of a 2007–2008 Fulbright to Romania, she has taught and published extensively on French, Italian, and Romanian literature and on the theory, pedagogy, and practice of theater. Radulescu's first novel, *Train to Trieste* (Knopf, 2008), won the 2008 Library of Virginia Award for Best Fiction.

Jane A. Rinehart, a professor of sociology and women's studies, is one of the founders of the Women's Studies Program at Gonzaga University and is its director. She has published articles on teaching feminist theory and the introductory course in women's studies. She has also written about integrating feminist activism into the work of university women's studies programs.

Cate Siejk is an associate professor of religious studies and women's studies at Gonzaga University in Spokane, Washington. Her primary interests in teaching and scholarship include issues in feminist theologies and religious education. She was director of the women's studies program from 2000 to 2003.

Jeanine Silveira Stewart is vice president for academic affairs and professor of psychology at Hollins University. She was trained in sensory and systems neuroscience, and her research examines the factors that contribute to healthy workplace dynamics. Other interests include applications of positive psychology, the development and use of positively framed metrics in scorecard-style management systems, and strategic planning for educational institutions and other nonprofit organizations.

Beverly Yuen Thompson is an assistant professor of women's studies at Texas Woman's University. Her teaching interests include critical race, gender, and sexuality studies, Asian/American mixed race theory, ethnographic methodology, social movements, urban studies, marginalized cultures, visual anthropology, digital video, photography, and deviance. She has published widely in these areas.

Sara Warner is an assistant professor of theater at Cornell University, where she is a core faculty member in the Feminist, Gender and Sexuality Studies Program and the LGBT Studies Program. Her research interests include dramatic literature and performance studies, theater and social change, theories of gender and sexuality, and affect theory. Her work has appeared in *Theatre Journal, Journal of Dramatic Theory and Criticism, Feminist Studies, Dialectical Anthropology,* and *Nineteenth Century Prose.* She is secretary of the Association for Theater in Higher Education, where she chairs the Electronic Technology Committee, and is a member of the board of directors of the Center for Lesbian and Gay Studies (CLAGS).

Alice A. Weldon is a professor of Spanish and interim director of women's studies at the University of North Carolina at Asheville. Her research focuses on women writers in Latin America, translation, trauma and story especially related to dictatorships, and the scholarship of teaching and learning.

Index